contents

Peaches preserved at their seasonal peak served on homemade shortcake is like a taste of summer any time of year. Recipe for this easy-to-make dessert is on the inside back cover.

Fresh Preserving Help Line: 1-800-240-3340 • FreshPreserving.com

just one step beyond cooking

Row after row of empty Ball® pint, quart and jelly jars stand at the ready. What will you fill them with? The possibilities are endless. When gardens overflow with the harvest, it's time to capture the abundance of the summer season.

Whether you are a first-timer or you have been canning for decades, you want to give your family the tastiest, healthiest, most nutritious foods possible. In the pages of this book, you will find everything you need to know about canning and preserving, as well as a host of sweet and savory recipes that will bring nature's goodness to your table—right through the winter months.

This section of the book contains detailed information about food classification, canning equipment, and methods for preserving—everything from pre-canning planning basics to post-processing storage. No one offers an easier-to-follow, more complete reference than the *Ball Blue Book® Guide to Preserving*. We'll walk you through every step, complete with tested recipes and time-saving tips.

The irresistible appeal of canning and preserving is timeless. Let the whole family join in the fun of harvesting, preparing, simmering and preserving homemade goodness. Seal the freshness of the season in Ball jars; you will be amazed at the sense of accomplishment you feel when you place your trophies on the pantry shelf.

The *Ball Blue Book Guide To Preserving* has been the unrivaled guide to home canning for more than 100 years. We hope this collection of recipes will inspire you to create flavorful, healthy dishes that come from the best place of all—your kitchen.

Home Canning Principles

Understanding how to prevent food spoilage and deterioration is the key to canning safety and success. In the air and all around us are invisible microorganisms, such as molds, yeasts and bacteria. Many of these microorganisms are beneficial to us, while others can be harmful under certain conditions. These "spoilers" live and multiply on the surface of fruits, vegetables, meats and all other types of food. Foods affected by bruising, insect damage and disease are more likely to have greater levels of microorganisms associated with spoilage. Enzymes change the color, texture and flavor of food and are found throughout the tissue of each food type. If enzyme activity goes unchecked, food quality will deteriorate. Molds, yeasts, bacteria and enzymes are the major causes of food spoilage and loss of quality.

Controlling the conditions which encourage the growth of molds, yeasts, bacteria and enzymes is an important factor in controlling spoilage and decaying. Washing foods is helpful in removing some of the spoilage microorganisms. Peeling and blanching reduces even greater numbers of spoilage microorganisms. Blanching is also a good way to minimize the effects of enzyme activity.

Canning interrupts the normal spoilage and decaying cycle of food by heating the food contained in a home canning jar that has been closed with a two-piece vacuum sealing cap. When heat is applied at the correct temperature and held there for the time designated by a specific tested home canning recipe, it destroys potentially harmful microorganisms; at the same time, it drives air from the jar. Upon cooling, the lid seals onto the jar. The vacuum that has formed prevents other microorganisms from entering and contaminating the food. This procedure is also known as processing. Correct processing methods and times adequately destroy normal levels of heat-resistant microorganisms. Proper storage and handling of sealed jars also helps ensure that home canned foods will be free of spoilage.

Ensuring Quality Foods

Controlling microorganisms, enzymes, oxygen and moisture loss in food helps ensure a quality canned product. To achieve a top-quality finished product, start with top-quality fresh produce. Select produce at its peak of freshness and flavor, and choose varieties best suited for canning. Remember, preserving food does not improve its quality. It is best to can fruits and vegetables immediately after harvesting or purchasing. Any foods you are unable to can within a couple hours must be properly stored to minimize further deterioration. When you are ready to can, carefully remove small diseased areas or bruised spots. Discard heavily diseased, moldy, insect-damaged and overripe food. Microorganisms multiply rapidly on damaged or diseased areas and may be at such high levels that the processing times, developed for quality foods, will not destroy all the microorganisms present in lesser-quality foods.

It is helpful to understand how acid and temperature affect molds, yeasts, bacteria and enzymes.

Molds And Yeasts

Molds are fungi that grow as silken threads and appear as fuzz on food. Some molds can produce mycotoxins which are harmful to eat. Molds thrive on the acids that are a protection against bacteria. Yeasts, which are also fungi, cause food to ferment, making it unfit to eat. Fortunately, the acid in foods protects against the growth of bacteria; however, molds and yeasts are ever-present. Molds and yeasts are easily destroyed at temperatures between 140° and 190°F. Boiling-water processing heats foods to 212°F, more than enough to destroy the molds and yeasts without destroying the quality of the product (*see figure 1*).

Bacteria

Bacteria are not easily destroyed. Certain bacteria actually thrive at temperatures that destroy molds and yeasts. Salmonella is destroyed when held at 140°F. Staphylococcus aureus, or "staph," is destroyed if food is kept above 140°F. Staph bacteria produce a toxin that must be destroyed by heating the product to 240°F for the time specified by a tested home canning recipe (*see figure 1*).

Botulism is a food poisoning caused by the bacterium Clostridium botulinum. This bacteria is also readily destroyed by boiling; however, the toxin producing spores cannot readily be destroyed at 212°F. Furthermore, the botulism-causing bacteria thrives on low acids in the absence of air in moist environments—exactly the conditions inside a jar of canned vegetables, meats and other low-acid foods.

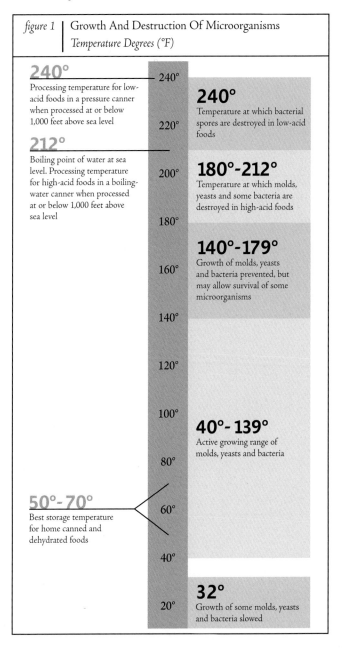

figure 1 | Growth And Destruction Of Microorganisms
Temperature Degrees (°F)

240°
Processing temperature for low-acid foods in a pressure canner when processed at or below 1,000 feet above sea level

212°
Boiling point of water at sea level. Processing temperature for high-acid foods in a boiling-water canner when processed at or below 1,000 feet above sea level

50°-70°
Best storage temperature for home canned and dehydrated foods

240°
Temperature at which bacterial spores are destroyed in low-acid foods

180°-212°
Temperature at which molds, yeasts and some bacteria are destroyed in high-acid foods

140°-179°
Growth of molds, yeasts and bacteria prevented, but may allow survival of some microorganisms

40°-139°
Active growing range of molds, yeasts and bacteria

32°
Growth of some molds, yeasts and bacteria slowed

Because of bacterial spores and the toxins they produce, low-acid foods must be processed at 240°F, which is hotter than the boiling point of water. This can be accomplished only with a pressure canner.

Enzymes

Enzymes are present in all living things. They promote the normal organic changes necessary to the life cycle. Their action can cause food to change flavor, texture and color, making it unappetizing. Enzymes, like molds and yeasts, are easily inactivated by heat at temperatures beginning at 140°F. Enzymes are inactivated by the boiling-water process.

Classification Of Foods

The importance of the pH, or acidity of foods, is that it determines the method of heat processing necessary for a safe canned product. Figure 2 lists common foods and gives their relative acidity.

For the purpose of canning, all foods are divided into two classifications determined by the amount of natural acid present in the food or the acidification of the food to a specific pH level. The two classifications are:

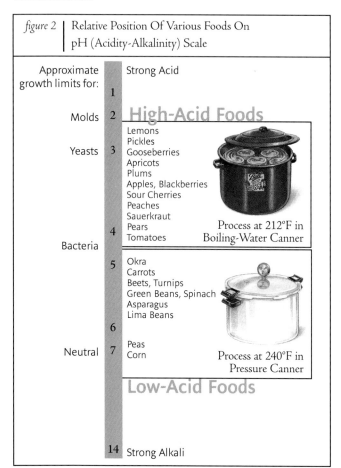

| *figure 2* | Relative Position Of Various Foods On pH (Acidity-Alkalinity) Scale |

Approximate growth limits for:		Strong Acid
	1	High-Acid Foods
Molds	2	
Yeasts	3	Lemons Pickles Gooseberries Apricots Plums Apples, Blackberries Sour Cherries Peaches Sauerkraut
Bacteria	4	Pears Tomatoes — Process at 212°F in Boiling-Water Canner
	5	Okra Carrots Beets, Turnips Green Beans, Spinach Asparagus Lima Beans
	6	
Neutral	7	Peas Corn — Process at 240°F in Pressure Canner
		Low-Acid Foods
	14	Strong Alkali

High-Acid Foods And Acidified Foods

These foods have naturally high levels of acid or have a sufficient amount of acid added to increase the pH level. Bottled lemon juice, citric acid or vinegar labeled 5 percent acidity are sometimes added to recipes to increase acidity. Foods in this category must have a pH of 4.6 or less. The boiling-water method of processing is adequate for high-acid foods. Generally, all fruits and soft spreads are classified as high-acid foods. Figs and tomatoes require the addition of an acid so they may be safely canned using the boiling-water method. Fermented foods, such as sauerkraut and brined pickles, and foods to which a sufficient amount of vinegar is added are also treated as high-acid foods. Some recipes may call for high-acid and low-acid ingredients but still be classified as a high-acid product; these recipes must have a pH level of 4.6 or less.

Low-Acid Foods

These foods have very little natural acid. Vegetables, meats, poultry and seafoods are in the low-acid group. Soups, stews, meat sauces and other recipes which contain a combination of high-acid and low-acid ingredients, yet remain with a pH level greater than 4.6, must be processed as a low-acid product.

Proper Processing Methods

Instructions in this book apply only to two proven processing methods—boiling-water canning and pressure canning. As discussed earlier, the processing method required for foods is determined by the pH of the specific food being canned. The processing method and processing time given for each recipe in this book must be followed exactly as stated. Processing methods and times are not interchangeable.

Periodically, old methods of preserving food are revived. These methods are not reliable and not recommended. Conversely, the advancements in technology bring new methods and equipment to the forefront. Unless proven to be safe and reliable by appropriate authorities, they must be avoided.

The tested processing times in this book are only for use with boiling-water processing and pressure processing. These times have not been tested for use with any other methods or recipes for home canning.

Boiling-Water Method

High-acid foods are processed in a boiling-water canner. The heat is transferred to the product by the boiling-water which completely surrounds the jar and two-piece cap. A temperature of 212°F is reached and must be maintained for the time specified by the recipe. This method is adequate to destroy molds, yeasts and some bacteria, as well as to inactivate enzymes.

A boiling-water canner must not be used for processing low-acid foods. The boiling-water method never reaches the high temperatures needed to destroy certain bacterial spores and their toxins, which can produce botulism.

All of the boiling-water processing times given for the high-acid recipes in this book are for processing at or below 1,000 feet above sea level. If you are located at an elevation greater than 1,000 feet, you must increase the processing time to compensate for the lower boiling point of water (*see figure 3*).

Pressure Method

Low-acid foods must be processed in a pressure canner. In order to destroy all bacteria, their spores and the toxins they produce, low-acid foods must be heated to a temperature of 240°F and held there for the

time specified by the recipe. Because the steam inside the canner is pressurized, its temperature exceeds the boiling point of water. At 10 pounds pressure, using a weighted-gauge canner, the temperature will reach 240°F (at or below 1,000 feet above sea level), which is hot enough to destroy the bacterial spores that emit toxins.

The pounds of pressure given for low-acid recipes in this book are based on the use of a weighted-gauge canner and for processing at or below 1,000 feet above sea level, for the time indicated by the recipe. If you are located at an elevation greater than 1,000 feet above sea level, you must increase the processing temperature by adjusting the pounds of pressure used; the processing time remains the same. Adjustments for using a dial-gauge canner or processing at higher altitude areas are listed in the Altitude Chart (see figure 3).

Altitude Adjustments

Barometric pressure is reduced at high altitudes, affecting the temperature at which water boils. This means boiling-water and pressure canning methods must be adjusted to ensure safe processing. When using the boiling-water method, additional processing time must be allowed. With the pressure method, additional pounds pressure is required. The Altitude Chart gives the requirements for both methods at various altitudes (see figure 3).

---

figure 3 | Altitude Chart

Boiling-Water Method

The processing times given in this book for high-acid foods are based on canning at or below 1,000 feet above sea level using the boiling-water method. When processing at altitudes higher than 1,000 feet above sea level, adjust the processing time according to this Boiling-Water Canner chart.

Boiling-Water Canner Altitude Adjustments

Altitude In Feet	Increase Processing Time
1,001 to 3,000	5 Minutes
3,001 to 6,000	10 Minutes
6,001 to 8,000	15 Minutes
8,001 to 10,000	20 Minutes

Pressure Method

The pressure method is used for low-acid foods. The pounds pressure given for low-acid foods in this book are based on using a weighted-gauge canner and processing at or below 1,000 feet above sea level. When using a dial-gauge canner or processing at altitudes higher than 1,000 feet above sea level, adjust pounds pressure according to this Pressure Canner chart.

Pressure Canner Altitude Adjustments

Altitude In Feet	Weighted Gauge	Dial Gauge
0 to 1,000	10	11
1,001 to 2,000	15	11
2,001 to 4,000	15	12
4,001 to 6,000	15	13
6,001 to 8,000	15	14
8,001 to 10,000	15	15

General cooking and baking times and temperatures are based on altitudes at or below 1,000 feet above sea level. Follow standard cooking and baking guidelines for your elevation.

If you do not know the altitude for your location, contact your county Cooperative Extension Service. Alternative sources of information are your local Soil Conservation Service and your Public Library Service.

Equipment

Improvements in canning equipment, kitchen utensils and small appliances make canning a simple, safe and efficient method of food preservation. Most equipment used for home canning is readily available in a well-equipped kitchen. A little pre-planning to check that all equipment and ingredients are on hand in advance of the intended day of canning will allow you time to acquire any items you may need (see page 8).

Jars

Glass home canning jars, sometimes called Mason jars, are the only glass jars recommended for home canning. They come in a wide variety of sizes and styles (see page 8). These jars are carefully made to fit home canning lids, ensuring a good seal is achieved when tested recipes and processing methods are followed correctly. The glass in the jars is manufactured to withstand the heat of the pressure canner or the sub-zero temperature of the freezer. However, standard home canning jars, those with rounded shoulders, are not suitable for freezing and must only be used for canning. Jars designed for canning and freezing have tapered sides without the rounded shoulders.

Other features designed into home canning jars may include fruit embossed or quilted glass patterns, space for labels, regular or wide mouth openings, and sizes ranging from four ounces to one-half gallon.

Use only the jar size indicated by a specific, tested home canning recipe and follow the processing method and time exactly as stated.

Older style canning jars once suitable for home canning should no longer be used for this purpose. Many of these jars cannot be properly fitted with two-piece vacuum caps, and new closures of original design are not available. Commercial jars like coffee, spaghetti sauce, fruit and baby food jars are designed for a single commercial application; therefore, they are not recommended for home canning. Commercial jars may not withstand the temperatures required for home canning. In addition, commercial jars vary in size which may prevent the lid from sealing and possibly leave the food underprocessed.

Lids and Bands

Home canning two-piece vacuum caps (lid and band) come in regular and wide mouth sizes (see page 8). The set consists of a flat metal lid with a flanged edge, the underside of which is filled with a sealing compound, and a threaded metal screw band that fits over the rim of the jar to hold the lid in place during processing. Lids are not reusable; however bands can be reused if they are in good condition.

Incidence of seal failure is very high when older style closures and commercial caps are used. Zinc caps and glass lids that seal with a jar rubber should not be used for canning. These closures are not recommended since there is no way to determine if the closure is sealed. Commercial caps are only intended for one-time commercial application, making them inadequate to use for home canning.

Note: The processing methods and times given in this book apply only to Ball brand and Kerr brand home canning jars, lids and bands marketed by Jarden Home Brands.

Boiling-Water Canner

Foods naturally high in acid and acidified foods having a pH of 4.6 or less may be processed in a boiling-water canner (*see figure 4*). The boiling-water method is essential for safely canning fruits, soft-spreads, tomatoes, pickles and other acidified foods. Filled jars sealed with two-piece caps are submerged in water to cover by 1 to 2 inches. Water in the canner must maintain a boil, 212° F, during the entire processing time as specified by a recipe tested for canning. Heat is transferred through the food by convection. High-acid and acidified foods must achieve an internal temperature of 212° F when processed at or below 1,000 feet above sea level (*see figure 3*).

Boiling-water canners are commonly made of stainless steel, enamel on steel or aluminum. They have a wire rack and tight fitting lid. Boiling-water canners can be purchased commercially or easily made of equipment readily available at home.

Pressure Canner

Low-acid foods or a combination of low-acid and high-acid foods that have a pH greater than 4.6 must be processed using a pressure canner (*see figure 5*). The pressure method is necessary to safely can vegetables, meat, poultry, seafood and recipes containing a combination of low-acid and high-acid foods. Filled jars sealed with two-piece caps are placed in

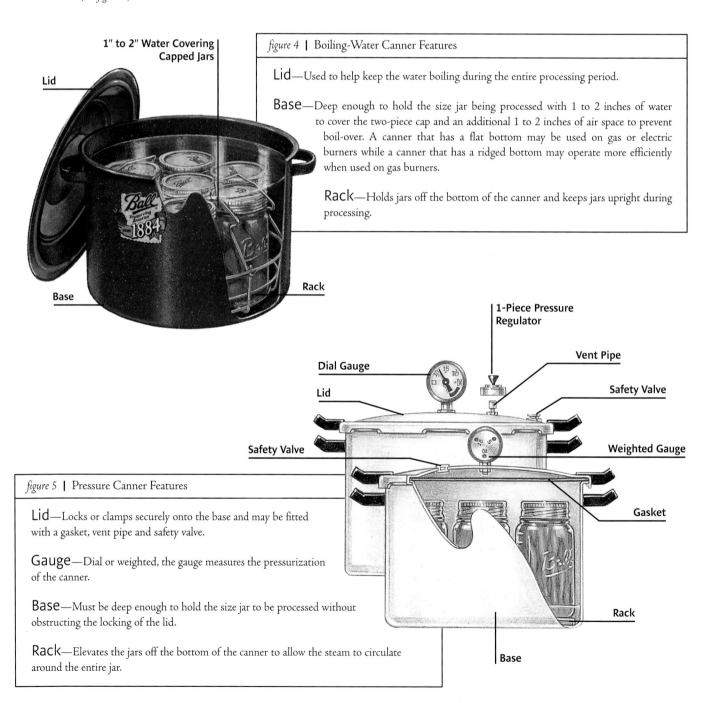

1" to 2" Water Covering Capped Jars

Lid

Base

Rack

figure 4 | Boiling-Water Canner Features

Lid—Used to help keep the water boiling during the entire processing period.

Base—Deep enough to hold the size jar being processed with 1 to 2 inches of water to cover the two-piece cap and an additional 1 to 2 inches of air space to prevent boil-over. A canner that has a flat bottom may be used on gas or electric burners while a canner that has a ridged bottom may operate more efficiently when used on gas burners.

Rack—Holds jars off the bottom of the canner and keeps jars upright during processing.

1-Piece Pressure Regulator

Vent Pipe

Dial Gauge

Lid

Safety Valve

Safety Valve

Weighted Gauge

Gasket

Rack

Base

figure 5 | Pressure Canner Features

Lid—Locks or clamps securely onto the base and may be fitted with a gasket, vent pipe and safety valve.

Gauge—Dial or weighted, the gauge measures the pressurization of the canner.

Base—Must be deep enough to hold the size jar to be processed without obstructing the locking of the lid.

Rack—Elevates the jars off the bottom of the canner to allow the steam to circulate around the entire jar.

the canner containing approximately 2 inches of water, or follow canner instructions for adding water. When the gauge indicates the pressurized canner has reached 10 psi, steam circulating within the canner has reached 240° F. The canner must maintain 240° F during the entire processing time as specified by a recipe tested for canning. Contents of the jars are being heated by conduction. Low-acid foods must reach an internal temperature of 240° F when processing at or below 1,000 feet above sea level (see figure 3).

Pressure canners are made of heavy-gauge stainless steel. The lid locks onto the base and has a vent pipe and safety valve. Pressure canners are either fitted with a weighted-gauge or dial gauge.

Dial Gauge—must be tested once a year for accuracy. It is preferable the dial gauge is tested prior to the beginning of canning season. If the gauge registers high by 1 pound (psi) or more at 5, 10 or 15 pounds pressure, it must be replaced. Should the gauge be inaccurate, all of the bacterial spores that emit toxins may not be destroyed during processing. Your county Cooperative Extension Service or the manufacturer of the canner will be able to tell you where the gauge can be tested for accuracy. Dial gauge canners are fitted with a one-piece pressure regulator to help maintain the correct pounds of pressure. Small amounts of steam exhaust from the regulator during the entire processing period. The dial gauge must be visually monitored during the entire processing period to ensure accurate temperature is maintained.

When processing recipes in this book using a dial gauge canner, process at 11 pounds pressure at or below 1,000 feet above sea level (see figure 3).

Weighted Gauge—exhausts small amounts of steam during the entire processing period. The movement of the weighted gauge during processing indicates pressure is being maintained at the selected pounds of pressure. The weighted gauge does not require testing for accuracy. But, if the weighted gauge is damaged in any way, it must be replaced.

Some pressure canners are fitted with a weighted gauge that adjusts for 5, 10 and 15 pounds pressure while some canners only operate at 15 pounds pressure. When using a weighted gauge canner that only operates at 15 pounds pressure, follow the same recipe processing times as those for 10 pounds pressure. Do not reduce processing time.

Low-acid recipe processing times in the Ball Blue Book are tested for processing with a weighted gauge canner at 10 pounds pressure at or below 1,000 feet above sea level. To make adjustments for high altitude processing or when using a dial gauge canner refer to the altitude chart (see figure 3).

Pressure processing is essential for canning meats, poultry, seafoods, vegetables and low-acid combination recipes.

Canning Utensils

Specially designed utensils for home canning, while not essential, help make the canning process easier and safer. Most pieces are available where home canning supplies are sold. You will find these canning utensils to be most helpful (see page 9).

- *Jar Lifter*
- *Jar Funnel*
- *Bubble Remover & Headspace Tool*
- *Lid Wand*

Specialty Equipment

With the exception of home canning jars, lids and bands, canners and canning utensils, most kitchens will already have most of the equipment needed for canning. Some recipes call for specialized equipment; therefore, recipes should be checked before the day of canning to determine if all equipment is available and to allow time to have it on hand if it is not. Through careful planning, you can avoid searching for a necessary piece of equipment during the critical time of preparing and processing the product. Some additional specialty items needed may include:

- *Food Scale*
- *Food Mill or Electric Puréer*
- *Food Processor or Grinder*
- *Electric Juice Extractor or Juice Strainer*
- *Ceramic, Stone or Glass Jar or Crock*
- *Candy/Jelly Thermometer*
- *Spice Bag or Cheesecloth*
- *Cooking Timer*

Precanning Planning

For some people the canning season begins with planting a garden. For others it begins with a visit to a farmers market. Whichever source for fresh produce you choose, plan well in advance to determine your family's needs.

Based on your family's needs: decide the type of food and recipes to be canned; assemble the jars, lids and bands designated for the food type and recipes selected; be certain the canner needed to process the foods and recipes you choose is in proper working condition. Shop for any supplies needed before your scheduled canning day. This will allow adequate time to locate the supplies you want, and you will be prepared to can when fruits and vegetables are at their peak of ripeness. Doing this helps prevent inconvenient breaks in the preparation and canning process as well as last minute shortages when canning supplies are in demand.

Plan to can produce immediately after harvesting or purchasing to ensure the quality and safety of home canned products. If it becomes necessary to hold produce for more than a couple hours, store produce properly to minimize the effects of deterioration from enzymes and microorganisms. Also, follow the recipe guidelines as stated. Do not make substitutions or changes to the recipe. The canning method and processing time designated by the recipe must be followed exactly. If you have questions about a recipe or proper processing, get additional assistance before proceeding.

Set aside enough time to prepare and process the recipes to be preserved. Plan to complete only those recipes which can be easily prepared within the time you have available to finish the project. Once the processing of a recipe is started, it must not be interrupted. Shorter canning sessions are easily scheduled and less overwhelming. Making small batches over a few days will actually be easier and more enjoyable. Refer to the Home Canning Planning Guide (see page 116) for jar estimating and seasonal planning.

equipment...all the right stuff

Many of the tools for home canning are found in any well-stocked kitchen. Here is a list of kitchen basics and home canning supplies you will find helpful for easy preparation and processing of recipes in this book.

Ball® Mixed Pickling Spice

This blend of herbs and spices ensures your pickle recipes have the right balance of flavors. Use it in any recipe that calls for mixed pickling spice.

Ball® Mason Jars

There is a wide variety of jar sizes and styles to meet every day needs and gift-giving occasions. Because they're specifically designed for preserving foods at home, these quality jars stand up to repeated use whether in the boiling-water canner or pressure canner. Tapered styles are suitable for freezer storage.

- *Regular Mouth* – Standard home canning jars are available in half-pint, pint and quart sizes. They're perfect for everything from pickle relish, to whole tomatoes, to green beans.

- *Wide Mouth* – Standard wide mouth jars offer pint, quart and half gallon sizes. Select the right size for the right job: pint for sliced beets, quart for peach halves and half-gallon for fruit juice.

- *Quilted Crystal*® *Jelly Jars* – Specially crafted with a delicate cut diamond design, these jelly jars add sparkle to any jam, jelly or preserve. They are available in popular 4-ounce, 8-ounce and 12-ounce sizes and come with decorative caps.

- *Collection Elite*® *Wide Mouth* – A new look for home preserving lends itself to one-of-a-kind gift-giving, crafting and home décor. Both 8-ounce and 16-ounce sizes have the popular wide mouth opening for easy filling. Silver colored two-piece vacuum caps complete the contemporary look.

Ball® Lids And Bands

Two-piece vacuum caps, consisting of a lid with sealing compound and a screw-on band, are the only closures recommended for home canning jars. They are carefully designed and manufactured to fit properly and seal when following the instructions in this book. Replacement lids and bands are offered in regular and wide mouth sizes.

Ball® Pickle Crisp® Granules

Make delicious crunchy pickles and relishes at home using Pickle Crisp® Granules. The same ingredient found in commercial pickles is easy to use – just add granules into prepared jars and process as usual. It's that simple!

Ball® Boiling-Water Canner

Contemporary and traditional boiling-water canners provide the quality, features and safety needed to make each canning experience enjoyable and successful. Twenty-one quart capacity holds up to 7 quart jars. boiling-water canning is recommended for high-acid and acidified foods such as fruits, soft-spreads, pickles and tomatoes.

- *Stainless-Steel Waterbath Canner* – Brings a new level of convenience, performance and versatility to preserving. Features include: aluminum core base for even heat distribution, stay cool silicone handles on lid and pot, a chrome-plated rack that resists corrosion and a glass lid that lets you see the boiling water throughout the canning process.

- *Enamel-Coated Steel Waterbath Canner* – This durable canner heats quickly and has a non-porous finish for easy cleaning. Designed with a flat bottom and straight sides to accommodate nearly every cooking surface. It comes equipped with a tight-fitting lid and chrome-plated, corrosion resistant rack.

Pressure Canner

A pressure canner is made of heavy gauge stainless steel. It is equipped with a lid that locks onto the base, jar rack and either a weighted gauge or dial gauge. Pressure canning is the only processing method recommended for low-acid foods such as vegetables, meat, poultry, seafood and combination recipes containing low-acid and high-acid foods.

Ball Citric Acid

Ensure tomato recipes have the correct acidity level by adding citric acid to each jar according to recipe guidelines.

Ball Salt for Pickling & Preserving

Use this pure salt – free of iodine and non-caking additives – when making pickles to ensure they retain their appetizing color and flavor. Pure salt may be used in any recipe for canning and cooking.

Ball RealFruit™ Pectin

Four key ingredients used in the correct balance allow soft spreads to gel: fruit, sugar, acid and pectin. Additional pectin is needed only when listed as an ingredient in the recipe. Three types of pectin are available for cooked recipes. However, they are not interchangeable, so use only the type of pectin as stated in the recipe.

- *Classic* – Natural powdered pectin derived from fruit aids in gelling soft spreads. Use only the amount of pectin listed in the recipe.

- *Liquid* – Comes in a box with two 3-ounce foil pouches. Each recipe will state the number of pouches to use: one or two. Use just the amount indicated in the recipe.

- *Low or No-Sugar Needed* – Is specially formulated for select recipes found in this book or those in the pectin package. This type of pectin may be prepared with less sugar than classic powdered pectin. Choose from no sugar or up to three cups of sugar, depending on dietary need and personal preference.

Ball Home Canning Utensils

Specialized utensils help make each step of preserving food at home a little easier.

- *Bubble Remover & Headspace Tool* – A flexible tool with gradations on one end to accurately measure headspace and tapered on the other end to remove trapped air from inside filled jars. Made of plastic to prevent damage to the jars.

- *Jar Funnel* – A plastic jar funnel having a wide opening that fits regular and wide mouth canning jars makes filling jars easy and quick. The translucent plastic lets you see the fill level so there are no mishaps to clean.

- *Jar Lifter* – Hot jars can be safely removed from the canner with large sure-grip tongs. These tongs handle any size regular and wide mouth jars with ease.

- *Lid Wand* – This handy utensil has a magnetic tip for removing lids from hot water.

Ball Plastic Freezer Jars

Plastic freezer jars with twist-on lids come in three convenient sizes: 8-ounce, 16-ounce and 32-ounce. Stack and lock feature helps keep freezer organized. These jars are perfect for freezer jam, delicate berries and keeping vegetables crisp as well as refrigerating leftovers.

Ball Fruit-Fresh® Produce Protector

Protect the color and flavor of fruits and vegetables that darken when peeled or cut with Fresh-Fruit®. Use in a presoak when preparing produce for canning, freezing, dehydrating or serving fresh. Or, add to syrups for canning and freezing.

Ball RealFruit™ Instant Pectin

This unique pectin is simple to use. Combine crushed fruit, pectin and sugar – no cooking – refrigerate for immediate use or freeze for use later. Instant jam pectin is not interchangeable with other types of pectin.

Ball Plastic Storage Caps

Plastic storage caps in regular or wide mouth sizes fit any style Ball home canning jars. Once canned products are opened, the two-piece caps can be replaced with a plastic storage cap for convenient refrigerator storage. They also help extend the use of home canning jars to store shelf-stable foods like pasta, herbs, dried fruit and nuts. Or, everyday items around the home: cotton balls, potpourri, soap, and thread.

Ball Dissolvable Labels

Dissolvable labels adhere securely on jars or lids during storage and use, but dissolves easily in water during clean-up. The oval shape allows ample room to write on.

Recipe Preparation

Preparing recipes for canning does not require special or involved skills, but a working knowledge of basic cooking is helpful.

Many of the fruit and vegetable recipes in this book allow flexibility in canning the exact amount of food that meets the needs of your family. These guidelines let you adjust the quantity you can from one jar to as many jars as your canner will hold at one time. These recipes give an approximate weight measurement of produce needed for one quart jar. Divide the weight measure in half when using pint jars. Other recipes in this book have set measurements that determine the yield and must not be changed.

Prior to starting, read the recipe completely, making certain you have a clear understanding of the instructions before beginning. Gather all ingredients and equipment needed before proceeding. Do not start preparation until you have all the necessary items on hand to complete the recipe. Prepare only enough food for one canner load or work with only one recipe at a time. Spreading your canning projects over a reasonable period of time will help you achieve successful results and satisfaction.

Follow recipe measurements exactly. Measure ingredients carefully using a scale for weight measures and standard measuring cups and measuring spoons for most other measures.

You will find that some recipes give a weight or cup measure, as well as a count measure, for the same ingredient. The measurement or count which precedes an item should be used in recipe preparation. The count or weight measure, appearing in parentheses after the ingredient, is given to help you estimate the amount to harvest or purchase. For best results, always use the measurement or count listed first.

How ingredients are prepared and how the recipe is cooked are important to the safe preservation of home canned foods. These factors are part of the equation when processing methods and processing times are developed. If a recipe gives exact guidelines for peeling, chopping, slicing, puréeing, etc., the instructions must be followed as directed. Any changes made in the preparation of the recipe may affect heat penetration and possibly yield an underprocessed product.

All of the ingredients listed in the recipe must be used as called for. Do not omit or substitute ingredients. Any changes made could affect the quality and safety of the food being canned.

Temperature is also an important element in the correct processing of home canned foods. The recipe will determine what temperature the food should be when packed into the jars. It may call for some ingredients to be packed into the jars while they are raw with hot brine, syrup, juice or water covering them or for the whole recipe to be cooked and packed while still hot. Maintaining the correct fill temperature is essential for the safe processing of the food.

After the recipe is prepared, filling and processing the jars must follow immediately. Process the jars using the method and time given by the specific recipe you have selected from this book.

Equipment Preparation

As with understanding the canning process, selection of produce and recipe preparation, special attention must be given to all canning equipment to ensure it is in proper, working condition. This includes both types of canners, boiling-water and pressure, and the home canning jars, lids and bands.

Canner Preparation

Check canners at the start of each canning session, making sure all parts are in proper, working condition.

Boiling-Water Canner—Occasionally, the rack for a boiling-water canner becomes corroded after repeated use. It should be replaced as needed. Check the canner base for dents or warping that might interfere with heat distribution. Also, check for pin-holes that can cause leaking. Replace defective parts.

Pressure Canner—Examine all parts of the canner. Canners fitted with replaceable gaskets and safety valves must be examined carefully and all parts that show signs of cracking or warping must be replaced. Clean the vent pipe of any residue that might block the passage of steam; check for any warping of the lid or canner base; make sure the canner lid locks securely. If using a dial gauge canner, have the gauge tested annually for accuracy before your first canning session.

Jar Preparation

The guidelines in this book must be followed for the safe handling and use of home canning jars.

Selection And Cleaning—All jars must be visually examined for nicks, cracks, uneven rims and other damage or defects. Once it has been determined the jars selected for use are in good condition, wash new and previously used jars in hot, soapy water. A dishwasher may be used for washing the jars. Do not use brushes with wire components, steel wool or abrasive materials or cleanser; they are likely to damage the glass.

Some jars accumulate a white film on the exterior surface. Film build-up can be caused by mineral deposits and may be easily removed by washing or soaking the jars in a solution of 1 cup vinegar to 1 gallon water. Rinse jars thoroughly. Add ¼ cup to ½ cup vinegar to the canner when processing jars to help prevent film build-up. If the film is not removed with the vinegar wash, it may have been caused by an etching of the glass. Etching results from friction on the surface of the jar which occurs with repeated cleaning and processing. Etching cannot be removed.

Heating—Jars must be heated for 10 minutes before filling to help prevent jar breakage. Submerge jars in enough water to cover. Bring water to a simmer (180°F), keeping jars in simmering water until ready for use. Remove jars one at a time as they are needed for filling. Jars can be heated in a saucepot on a cook-top. Or, in a slow cooker that has a temperature control that can maintain 180°F.

A dishwasher may also be used for heating jars. Jars should be washed and dried using a complete regular cycle. Keep jars in the closed dishwasher, removing one at a time as needed.

Note: The heating methods described above are the only methods recommended for heating jars before filling.

Lid And Band Preparation

The guidelines given in this book for preparing and using two-piece vacuum caps must be followed.

Selection And Cleaning—Choose the appropriate size caps for the jars you will be using. New lids with sealing compound must be used for each canning. Wash two-piece caps in hot, soapy water. Rinse in hot water. Do not use any abrasive materials or cleansers that might scratch or damage the coatings on the lids and bands. Dry bands and set aside. Lids must be heated.

Heating—Home canning lids with sealing compound must be heated for 10 minutes before using to help lids achieve a vacuum seal. Place lids in water to cover and bring water to a simmer (180°F), keeping lids in simmering water until ready for use. Remove lids one at a time as they are needed for canning. Lids can be heated in a saucepan on a cook-top. Or, in a slow cooker that has a temperature control that can maintain 180°F.

Note: Overheating lids by boiling can result in seal failure.

Preparing For Canning

Filling jars and adjusting caps properly is important to the overall success of canning. The basic steps outlined here will make it simple and efficient.

Filling Jars

There are two methods for packing particular food types and recipes into jars—hot pack and raw pack. Each recipe throughout this book designates the method to use. Some recipes will indicate either option is satisfactory. It is important to fill a single jar at a time, adjust the two-piece cap onto the jar immediately after it is filled and place the filled jar onto the canner rack in the canner. Repeat this procedure until the canner rack is full or the recipe is gone.

Hot Pack—The hot pack method is generally preferred when the food being canned is relatively firm and handles well. Precooking the food makes it more pliable, permits a tighter pack and requires fewer jars. Food is first cooked in brine, syrup, juice or water. Fruit canned without sweetening is always hot packed. The hot pack method is preferred for nearly all vegetables, meats, poultry, seafoods and most fruits.

In the boiling-water method, food that is hot packed usually requires less processing time than raw packed because it is already hot when it goes into the canner. However, with the pressure canner, there is no difference in processing time. During the time it takes for the pressure canner to reach 10 pounds and when you begin timing the processing, the raw packed food has become as hot as it would have been if it was initially packed hot.

Raw Pack—Foods that would be delicate after they are cooked, such as whole peaches, are usually easier to handle if they are raw packed. The food is placed into the jars while it is raw. It should be packed firmly but not crushed. Boiling brine, syrup, juice or water is added if additional liquid is needed. There may be some shrinkage when the food is processed, causing some foods to float to the top of the jar, or expanding the headspace.

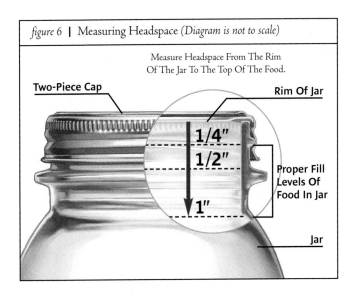

figure 6 | Measuring Headspace *(Diagram is not to scale)*

Measure Headspace From The Rim Of The Jar To The Top Of The Food.

Two-Piece Cap

Rim Of Jar

1/4"
1/2"
1"

Proper Fill Levels Of Food In Jar

Jar

Measuring Headspace

Headspace is the space in the jar between the top of the food or liquid and the inside of the lid. As a general rule, leave 1-inch headspace for low-acid foods, vegetables and meats; ½-inch headspace for high-acid foods, fruits, tomatoes, pickles and relishes; ¼-inch headspace for juices, jams and jellies. Care must be taken in filling the jars to the correct headspace (*see figure 6*).

Removing Air Bubbles

After the food has been packed into the jar, any air bubbles that are present must be removed. This can be done by placing a nonmetallic spatula inside the jar between the food and the side of the jar. Press spatula back against food to release trapped air. Repeat several times around the inside of the jar. Do not use metal knives or other metal utensils since they can scratch the glass and result in jar breakage. Even though air bubbles may not be visible, they can be trapped between pieces of food and must be removed.

Cleaning Jar Rims

The rim of the jar must be wiped with a clean, damp cloth. Particles of food remaining on the rim of a jar can prevent a vacuum seal.

Adjusting Lids And Bands

After each jar is filled and the jar rim is cleaned, place lid on jar rim, centering sealing compound on glass. Only the sealing compound should be touching the glass. Place a band over the lid and screw band until fingertip-tight. The adjustment of the band is firm and snug, but not as tight as you can make it. Using a jar lifter, place jar onto canner rack in the canner.

Processing

Heat processing food is essential to minimize the possibility of food spoilage due to microorganisms in sealed jars and deterioration from enzyme activity. Processing guidelines in this book are based on several factors such as pH of the food, food pack, heat penetration and jar size. The easy-to-follow steps for boiling-water and pressure processing described here will yield successful results when completed as instructed.

Note: Processing methods and processing times in this book are not interchangeable. Processing times in this book cannot be used with other heat processing methods.

Boiling-Water Processing

1. Fill boiling-water canner half-full with water and bring to a simmer (180°F). Position canner rack over simmering water.

2. Prepare recipe. Fill jars and adjust caps.

3. Place jars on canner rack immediately after each jar is filled. Carefully lower the rack into simmering water. Water level must cover jars and two-piece vacuum caps by 1 to 2 inches. Add boiling water, if needed.

4. Put the canner lid in place. Adjust heat to medium-high, bringing water to a rolling boil. Set timer according to the recipe processing time. Maintain water at a rolling boil for the entire processing period.

5. After the processing period is complete, turn off heat and remove canner lid. Let canner cool 5 minutes before removing jars.

6. Remove jars from canner, setting jars upright on a dry towel or cutting board to cool. Leave 1 to 2 inches of space between jars. Do not tighten bands if they loosened during processing. Let jars cool naturally 12 to 24 hours before checking for a seal.

Pressure Processing

1. Put canner rack inside canner base. Add approximately 2 inches of water, or follow canner instructions for adding water. Heat water to a simmer (180°F).

2. Prepare recipe. Fill jars and adjust caps.

3. Place jars on canner rack immediately after each jar is filled. Lock canner lid securely in place. Leave weight off vent pipe or open petcock. Adjust heat to medium-high setting until steam flows evenly from the vent pipe or petcock. Exhaust steam from the canner for 10 minutes.

4. Place weight on vent pipe or close petcock. The canner should pressurize in about 5 minutes. After gauge indicates recommended pounds of pressure has been reached, adjust the heat to maintain pressure for the entire processing period. Set timer according to the recipe processing time.

5. After the processing period is complete, turn off heat. Allow the canner to cool naturally. Do not remove the weighted gauge or open the petcock until the canner has depressurized and returned to zero pressure. Remove gauge or open petcock. Let canner cool 10 minutes before removing lid. Unlock lid and lift it off the canner base, being careful that steam escapes away from you. Let canner cool 10 minutes before removing jars.

6. Remove jars from canner, setting jars upright on a dry towel or cutting board to cool. Leave 1 to 2 inches of space between jars. Do not tighten bands if they loosened during processing. Let jars cool naturally 12 to 24 hours before checking for a seal.

After Processing

Cooling

Once the processing time is complete and the jars are ready to be removed from the canner, using a jar lifter, stand jars upright on a dry towel or cutting board. Space the jars 1 to 2 inches apart so they will cool at an even rate. Allow them to cool at room temperature 12 to 24 hours. Prevent exposure to extreme drafts or temperature changes that could cause jar breakage. Inverting jars, moving jars, or storing jars in a box while still warm are all factors that can cause seal failure or spoilage.

Occasionally bands loosen during the processing period. If this occurs, do not retighten them. Adjusting bands after processing may interfere with the seal already forming.

You may notice a slight decrease in the food and/or liquid levels. This happens as food shrinks from heat processing. It may also result from a siphoning of the liquid during processing. Should you notice a change, do not open the jars to add product or liquid. The sealed jars should be stored as is.

Testing Seals

After the jars have cooled 12 to 24 hours, test the lids to determine if a vacuum seal has formed. The best method for testing a seal is to press the center of the lid to determine if it is concave; then remove the band and gently try to lift the lid off with your fingertips. If the center does not flex up and down and you cannot lift the lid off, the lid has a good vacuum seal. Listening for a "ping" when the lid seals, tapping the lid with a spoon or visually examining the lid is not always an accurate test.

Reprocessing Unsealed Jars

If a lid does not seal within 24 hours, the product can be immediately reprocessed. To reprocess the product, remove the lid and reheat the food and/or liquid as recommended by the recipe. Pack food into clean, hot jars. Place a new, heated lid on the jar and adjust band. Reprocess the product using the canning method and full length of processing time recommended by the recipe.

If you determine the lid did not seal because of damage to the jar, dispose of the jar and its contents.

You may want to consider alternative storage methods for foods that did not seal, such as refrigerating or freezing.

Storage

Foods canned following tested recipes, correct processing methods and processing time can be safely stored for one year. After one year, natural chemical changes may occur that could lessen the quality. These changes may affect the flavor, color, texture or nutritional value. For this reason, food stored the longest period of time should be used first. Labeling each jar with the date the product was canned, as well as the type and variety of the product will help you easily identify inventory that needs to be rotated.

Before storing sealed jars, remove the bands and wash lids and entire surface of the jars to remove any food residue. Rinse and dry. Bands need not be replaced. If bands are stored on sealed jars, they may corrode and become difficult to remove.

Even foods that are properly processed will lose some of their nourishing qualities over an extended time. This loss may be accelerated if the food is stored at temperatures above 70°F. On the other hand, the food should not be stored where it might be subject to freezing since the food can expand and break the seal. The ideal temperature range for storing home canned foods is between 50° and 70°F.

Light hastens oxidation and destroys certain vitamins. Light will also cause certain foods to fade in color. To protect home canned foods from the deteriorating effects of light, store jars in a place that does not receive direct sunlight. It is best to keep home canned foods in a cool, dry, dark place.

Using Home Canned Foods

When up-to-date tested guidelines are followed, there should be little concern about the quality and safety of your home canned foods. However, it is always best to visually examine each jar before it is served to ensure no changes have occurred.

To minimize the risk of exposure to botulism in low-acid and tomato products the USDA recommends boiling the food 10 minutes for altitudes at or below 1,000 feet above sea level to destroy the toxin produced by Clostridium botulinum. Extend the boiling by 1 additional minute for each 1,000 foot increase in elevation.

Opening Jars

To open jars with vacuum sealed lids, release the vacuum with a can opener and lift off the lid. This method of removing lids will help prevent damage to the jar's sealing surface. The vacuum lids are not reusable. Do not serve any product which does not have a vacuum sealed lid or shows signs of spoilage.

Serving Home Canned Foods

Home canned foods may be used in all the same ways as commercially canned products. Commercially canned foods often come in containers sized differently than home canning jars. When a recipe gives a container size or weight for a commercially canned product, measure home canned foods according to the recipe measurement. Remember, home canned foods are fully cooked and may not be a suitable substitute for fresh ingredients.

Storing Opened Jars

Like commercially canned foods, once home canned foods are opened they have a shortened shelf expectancy. Leftover foods must be refrigerated or frozen until used again. However, they are best if used within a few days.

high-acid foods

Fruits, Juices & Tomatoes

When family and friends come together to share a meal, it's a celebration. Children scamper about; conversations ebb and flow; and the sound of laughter fills the air. At meal's end, the rich sweetness of Apple-Cranberry Pie is presented —a modern twist on an American classic. Flavors burst and blend together as walnuts, dates, cranberries and apples join to create a mouthwatering masterpiece.

Every flavorful bite hearkens back to each season, when trees were heavily laden with apples, peaches or pears, and vines rendered bushels of tomatoes for preserving. Memories flood the senses—families working in the kitchen—washing, preparing, cooking, preserving—as the sweet aromas fill the air. Tomatoes whole or simmered into thick, savory sauces. The fragrance of fruit mingled with cinnamon, clove and nutmeg spices. And the final reward —rows of jars all packed and ready to complement meals yet to come.

Tomatoes and fruits have always been the staple of fresh preserving—and no wonder. Whether hand-picked from your garden or carried home in bushels from the farmers' market, foods preserved at their peak stand ready to bring freshness and flavor to your table long after the harvest is over.

As you gaze with pride on the colorful jars in your pantry packed with nature's best, the sense of accomplishment you feel is rivaled only by the sumptuous goodness you'll enjoy when you unseal them—for one delicious meal after another.

Pictured, Apple-Cranberry Pie made with canned Apples.
Recipe for Apples for Baking found on page 17.
Apple-Cranberry Pie recipe found on page 23.

getting started

Foods among the easiest to preserve are those with naturally high levels of acid. The main concern when preserving high-acid foods is to control molds, yeasts and enzymes. These spoilers are destroyed or inactivated at a temperature of 212°F, which is easily reached when processing high-acid foods using the boiling-water method.

Soft spreads and pickled foods are also considered high-acid foods. Because preparation is somewhat different for these products, they are covered in separate sections.

In this section you will find recipes for preparing fruits and tomatoes in a variety of ways. You will also find some combination recipes that contain both high-acid and low-acid ingredients and have a pH of 4.6 or less. Because these recipes have the proper acid level, they are processed using the boiling-water canner. Each recipe will indicate the correct jar size and processing time to use.

The boiling-water processing times given for high-acid foods in this section are for processing at or below altitudes of 1,000 feet above sea level. For higher altitude areas, adjustments in processing time must be made, refer to Altitude Chart (see page 5).

Ingredients And Preparation

Fruits

Harvest or purchase only top-quality fruit at its peak of flavor, texture and color. Do not use overripe or diseased fruit.

Canning a few jars of fruit, prepared whole, sliced, as a sauce and juiced, makes them even more versatile for serving and cooking. Follow recipe guidelines for complete directions for preparing each fruit.

Fruits may be packed in a sweetened syrup, water, their own juice, or in a flavored liqueur. Fruits may be canned in a combination of two or more fruits. Some recipes require peeling, cutting and pitting while others may recommend the fruit be canned whole without peeling.

Fruit sauces make a wonderful accompaniment to entrées and add flavor to baked recipes. Sauces are easy to prepare. The sauce may be sweetened or spiced, if desired. Another way to preserve fruit is as a juice. Juice may be canned unsweetened or sweetened.

Tomatoes

Tomatoes are botanically classified as fruit. You will find tomato recipes for juices, sauces, pickles, relishes and even preserves. The amount of natural acid in tomatoes varies depending on the variety, growing conditions, maturity and handling. To ensure adequate amounts of acid are present when canning recipes using tomatoes, bottled lemon juice (not fresh) or vinegar labeled 5 percent acidity is added to acidify the recipe. By maintaining the correct pH level, tomatoes can be processed safely in a boiling-water canner.

Sweeteners

Fruits may be canned with or without a sweetener. Most often a syrup, sweetened with sugar or a combination of sugar and honey or corn syrup, is used. Sugar helps fruit retain a bright color and firm texture. The amount of sugar used can be adjusted to meet dietary needs and personal preference. Corn syrup or honey may also be used as a substitute for a portion of the sugar (see figure 7). To make syrup, measure sugar and liquid into a saucepot. Cook until syrup is hot throughout. Keep syrup hot until needed, but do not let it boil down. Usually 1 to 1½ cups of syrup is needed for each quart jar of fruit.

Any type of bottled or fresh fruit juice, sweetened or unsweetened, may be used instead of a sugar syrup. Water without sweetener may also be used. If unsweetened juice or water is used, the hot pack method must be followed.

These general guidelines for reducing sugar apply only to syrups used for canning fruits and not specific recipes. For additional information for canning without sugar or for using a sugar substitute, refer to the Special Diet section (see pages 72-77).

Antioxidants

Apples, apricots, peaches, pears and other light-color fruits tend to darken while being prepared for canning or after they are in the jar. To prevent darkening, use Ball Fruit-Fresh Produce Protector according to package instructions (see page 9).

Spices And Flavorings

A variety of spices, herbs, wines and liqueurs are used to add flavor and interest to fruits, sauces and juices. Ground spices are used unless the recipe calls for whole, crushed or slivered, etc. Use only the form called for in the recipe. Substituting ground spices for whole spices may affect the visual appearance and flavor of the product. Some spices are tied in a spice bag or several layers of cheesecloth, cooked with the syrup or fruit and removed before canning.

Wines, liqueurs and other flavorings impart their unique characteristics to the overall flavor of the recipe. It is not necessary to buy the most expensive brand of wine or liqueur; however, their natural characteristics, flavors and color should be considered to achieve a complementary blending with the fruit.

Syrups For Canning

A sugar syrup, juice or water is needed for canning whole, halved or sliced fruits. Figure 7 gives guidelines for preparing extra-light to heavy syrups. Honey and corn syrup can be used to substitute part of the sugar. Unsweetened fruit juice or water can be used in place of a sugar syrup. When fruits are canned without the addition of sugar, the hot pack method must be used.

figure 7 | Syrups For Canning					
Type of Syrup	Approx. % of Sugar	Sugar	Sweetener	Water	Yield of Syrup
Extra-Light	20	1¼ cups		5½ cups	6 cups
Light	30	2¼ cups		5¼ cups	6½ cups
Medium	40	3¼ cups		5 cups	7 cups
Heavy	50	4¼ cups		4¼ cups	7 cups
Corn Syrup		1½ cups	1 cup corn syrup	3 cups	6 cups
Honey		1 cup	1 cup honey	4 cups	5 cups

Equipment And Utensils

In addition to your home canning supplies and standard kitchen equipment, you may find a few other pieces of equipment helpful: pitting spoon for peaches and nectarines; zester for cutting small slivers of fruit peel; pear corer; apple corer; jelly bag for straining juice; and spice bag for infusing spice flavors in syrup or juice.

A food scale may be used to weigh fruit. Weight measurements are approximate. Factors that determine the amount of fruit needed include size of the fruit, preparation of the fruit and jar size. Weight measurements are given for quart size jars; reduce measurements by one-half for pint-size jars.

fruits

Apple Rings

Yield: about 6 pints or 3 quarts

10 pounds apples	4 cups sugar
Ball Fruit-Fresh Produce Protector	4 cups water
	Red food coloring (optional)

Wash and core apples; do not peel. Slice apples crosswise into ¼-inch rings. Treat with Fruit-Fresh to prevent darkening. Combine sugar and water in a large saucepot. Add a few drops of food coloring, if desired. Bring syrup mixture to a boil; boil 5 minutes. Remove from heat. Drain apple rings. Add apple rings to syrup; let stand 10 minutes. Bring mixture to a boil; reduce heat; simmer 30 minutes. Remove apple rings from syrup and cool. Return syrup to a boil. Pack apple rings loosely into hot jars, leaving ½-inch headspace. Ladle hot syrup over apple rings, leaving ½-inch headspace. Remove air bubbles. Adjust two-piece caps. Process pints 15 minutes, quarts 20 minutes, in a boiling-water canner.

Recipe Variation: Spiced apple rings may be made by adding stick cinnamon, whole cloves or other whole spices, tied in a spice bag, to the syrup during preparation. Remove spice bag before canning apple rings.

Note: Use a variety of eating apples good for cooking to help maintain shape and texture.

Apple Wedges In Cinnamon Red Hot Syrup

Yield: about 6 pints

8 to 10 pounds apples	2 teaspoons whole cloves
Ball Fruit-Fresh Produce Protector	1 teaspoon ginger
1½ cups sugar	2 cups water
½ cup cinnamon red hot candies	1½ cups vinegar
2 sticks cinnamon	⅔ cup light corn syrup
	2 tablespoons red food coloring (optional)

Wash, core and peel apples. Cut apples lengthwise into eighths. Treat with Fruit-Fresh to prevent darkening. Combine remaining ingredients in a large saucepot and bring slowly to a boil. Drain apple wedges. Add apple wedges to syrup mixture; cover and simmer 4 minutes. Pack hot apples into hot jars, leaving ½-inch headspace. Ladle hot syrup over apples, leaving ½-inch headspace. Remove air bubbles. Adjust two-piece caps. Process 15 minutes in a boiling-water canner.

Apples

2½ to 3 pounds apples per quart	Sugar
Ball Fruit-Fresh Produce Protector	Water

Wash, core and peel apples. Apples may be cut into ¼-inch slices, quartered or halved. Treat with Fruit-Fresh to prevent darkening. Make a light or medium syrup; keep syrup hot. Drain apples. Gently boil apples in syrup 5 minutes. Pack hot apples into hot jars, leaving ½-inch headspace. Ladle hot syrup over apples, leaving ½-inch headspace. Remove air bubbles. Adjust two-piece caps. Process pints and quarts 20 minutes in a boiling-water canner.

Note: Use a variety or combination of varieties of eating apples good for cooking to help maintain shape and texture.

Apples For Baking

Yield: about 4 quarts

10 to 12 pounds Granny Smith apples	1 cup sugar
Ball Fruit-Fresh Produce Protector	2 cups water
	1 tablespoon lemon juice

Wash, core and peel apples. Cut apples lengthwise into ½- to ¾-inch thick slices. Treat with Fruit-Fresh to prevent darkening. Combine sugar, water and lemon juice in a large saucepot, stirring to dissolve sugar. Bring mixture to a boil; reduce heat. Drain apples. Simmer apples 5 minutes in syrup. Pack hot apples into hot jars, leaving ½-inch headspace. Ladle hot syrup over apples, leaving ½-inch headspace. Remove air bubbles. Adjust two-piece caps. Process quarts 20 minutes in a boiling-water canner.

Note: Use any variety or combination of varieties of firm baking apples.

Applesauce

2½ to 3½ pounds apples per quart	Water
	Sugar (optional)

Wash apples; drain. Core, peel and quarter apples. Cook apples until soft in a large covered saucepot with just enough water to prevent sticking. Purée using a food processor or food mill. Return apple pulp to saucepot. Add ¼ cup sugar per pound of apples or to taste, if desired. Bring applesauce to a boil (212°F), stirring to prevent sticking. Maintain temperature at a boil (212°F) while filling jars. Ladle hot sauce into hot jars, leaving ½-inch headspace. Remove air bubbles. Adjust two-piece caps. Process pints and quarts 20 minutes in a boiling-water canner.

Recipe Variation: Spiced applesauce can be made by adding ground spices, such as cinnamon, nutmeg or allspice, to the sauce during the last 5 minutes of cooking. For a chunky sauce, coarsely crush half of the cooked apples; process remaining apples through a food processor or food mill. Combine crushed and sauced apple mixtures; continue as for Applesauce.

Apricots

2 to 2½ pounds apricots per quart	Sugar
Ball Fruit-Fresh Produce Protector	Water

Raw Pack: Wash apricots. Cut in half and pit; do not peel. Treat with Fruit-Fresh to prevent darkening. Make a light or medium syrup; keep syrup hot. Drain apricots. Pack apricots, cavity side down, into hot jars, leaving ½-inch headspace. Ladle hot syrup over apricots, leaving ½-inch headspace. Remove air bubbles. Adjust two-piece caps. Process pints 25 minutes, quarts 30 minutes, in a boiling-water canner.

Hot Pack: Wash and blanch apricots; remove peel. Cut in half and pit. Treat with Fruit-Fresh to prevent darkening. Make a light or medium syrup. Drain apricots. Cook apricots in syrup one layer at a time until hot throughout. Pack hot apricots, cavity side down, into hot jars, leaving ½-inch headspace. Ladle hot syrup over apricots, leaving ½-inch headspace. Remove air bubbles. Adjust two-piece caps. Process pints 20 minutes, quarts 25 minutes, in a boiling-water canner.

Note: If fruit is harvested before fully ripe, pits must be removed. Apricots may be canned with or without the peel.

Berries

Blackberries, Black Raspberries, Blueberries, Currants, Elderberries, Huckleberries, Red Raspberries, etc.

1½ to 3 pounds berries per quart	Sugar Water

Raw Pack: Wash berries; drain. Make a light or medium syrup; keep syrup hot. Ladle ½ cup hot syrup into hot jar. Fill jar with berries. Gently shake jar to pack berries closely without crushing, leaving ½-inch headspace. Add hot syrup to cover berries, if needed, leaving ½-inch headspace. Remove air bubbles. Adjust two-piece caps. Process pints 15 minutes, quarts 20 minutes, in a boiling-water canner.

Hot Pack: Wash, drain and measure berries. Put berries in a large saucepot. For each quart of berries measured, add ¼ to ½ cup sugar; stir. Let stand 2 hours in a cool place. Cook mixture slowly until sugar dissolves and berries are hot throughout. Ladle hot berries and syrup into hot jars, leaving ½-inch headspace. If there is not enough syrup to cover berries, add boiling water, leaving ½-inch headspace. Remove air bubbles. Adjust two-piece caps. Process pints and quarts 15 minutes in a boiling-water canner.

Note: Use Raw Pack for red raspberries and other berries that do not hold their shape well when heated. Use Hot Pack for blackberries and other berries that hold their shape when heated.

Add 1 to 2 tablespoons lemon juice for each quart of elderberries to improve flavor, if desired.

Berries For Baking: Wash berries. Simmer berries until hot throughout, adding just enough water to prevent sticking. Process as for Berries, Hot Pack.

Note: If there is not enough liquid to cover berries, add boiling water.

Brandied Cherries

Yield: about 6 pints

6 pounds dark, sweet cherries	1 cup water ½ cup lemon juice
1 cup sugar	1¼ cups brandy

Wash and pit cherries. Combine sugar, water and lemon juice in a large saucepot. Bring mixture to a boil; reduce heat to a simmer. Add cherries and simmer until hot throughout. Remove from heat; stir in brandy. Pack hot cherries into hot jars, leaving ½-inch headspace. Ladle hot syrup over cherries, leaving ½-inch headspace. Remove air bubbles. Adjust two-piece caps. Process 10 minutes in a boiling-water canner.

Brandied Peaches

Yield: about 3 pints

4 pounds small peaches	1 teaspoon salt
Ball Fruit-Fresh Produce Protector	1 quart water ¾ cup peach brandy
6 cups sugar, divided	

Wash and peel peaches (*see page 20*). Leave peaches whole. Treat with Fruit-Fresh to prevent darkening. Combine 3 cups sugar, salt and water in a large saucepot; bring to a boil. Drain peaches. Gently boil peaches in syrup one layer at a time 5 minutes or until hot throughout. Peaches will darken if undercooked, but do not cook until soft. Place peaches in a deep bowl. Boil syrup 5 minutes; pour over peaches. Cover and let stand 12 to 18 hours in a cool place. Remove peaches from syrup. Add remaining 3 cups sugar to syrup. Boil syrup 5 minutes; pour over peaches. Cover and let stand 12 to 18 hours in a cool place. Remove peaches from syrup. Boil syrup.

Pack peaches into hot jars, leaving ½-inch headspace. Add 3 to 4 tablespoons of peach brandy to each jar. Ladle hot syrup over peaches, leaving ½-inch headspace. Remove air bubbles. Adjust two-piece caps. Process 10 minutes in a boiling-water canner. Peaches should be ready to use in approximately 4 weeks.

Brandied Pears

Yield: about 4 quarts

10 pounds pears	6 cups sugar
Ball Fruit-Fresh Produce Protector	4 cups water 3 cups brandy

Wash, peel, halve and core pears. Treat with Fruit-Fresh to prevent darkening. Combine sugar and water in a large saucepot; bring to a boil. Cook pears in syrup one layer at a time until just tender, about 5 minutes. Place cooked pears in a large bowl; set aside. After all pears are cooked, continue cooking syrup until thickened, about 15 minutes. Remove from heat; add brandy. Pack pears into hot jars, leaving ½-inch headspace. Ladle hot syrup over pears, leaving ½-inch headspace. Remove air bubbles. Adjust two-piece caps. Process 15 minutes in a boiling-water canner.

Note: Use white brandy for a clear syrup; however, any brandy will flavor the fruit.

Cherries

2 to 2½ pounds cherries per quart	Sugar Water

Raw Pack: Wash cherries and drain. Make a light or medium syrup for sweet cherries, a medium or heavy syrup for sour cherries; keep syrup hot. Ladle ½ cup hot syrup into hot jar. Fill jar with cherries. Gently shake jar to pack cherries closely without crushing, leaving ½-inch headspace. Add hot syrup to cover cherries, if needed, leaving ½-inch headspace. Remove air bubbles. Adjust two-piece caps. Process pints and quarts 25 minutes in a boiling-water canner.

Hot Pack: Wash cherries and drain. Measure cherries. Put cherries in a large saucepot. For each quart of cherries measured, add ½ to ¾ cup sugar; stir. Cook mixture slowly until sugar dissolves and cherries are hot throughout. If cherries are unpitted, add just enough water to prevent sticking. Ladle hot cherries and juice into hot jars, leaving ½-inch headspace. Add boiling water to cover cherries, if needed, leaving ½-inch headspace. Remove air bubbles. Adjust two-piece caps. Process pints 15 minutes, quarts 20 minutes, in a boiling-water canner.

Note: Pits may be left in or taken out. If pit is left in, prick each cherry to prevent bursting and shrinking. When canning without the pits, measure cherries after pits are removed.

Cherries For Baking: Wash and pit cherries. Heat cherries in an extra-light syrup or water until hot throughout. Process as for Cherries, Hot Pack.

Note: A sugar syrup will help retain color.

Cranberry Sauce—Jellied

Yield: about 2 pints

4¼ cups cranberries	2 cups sugar
1¾ cups water	

Wash cranberries; drain. Combine cranberries and water in a large saucepot. Boil until skins burst. Purée using a food processor or food mill. Add sugar to cranberry pulp and juice. Boil mixture almost to gelling point (*see page 29*). Ladle hot sauce into hot jars, leaving ½-inch headspace. Adjust two-piece caps. Process 15 minutes in a boiling-water canner.

Recipe Variation: Stick cinnamon and whole cloves tied in a spice bag may be cooked with the sauce to give a spicy flavor. Remove spice bag before canning sauce.

Note: To serve jellied sauce as a mold, pack sauce in straight-sided canning jars for easy removal.

Cranberry Sauce—Whole Berry

Yield: about 6 pints

8 cups cranberries	4 cups water
4 cups sugar	

Wash cranberries; drain. Combine sugar and water in a large saucepot. Boil 5 minutes. Add cranberries. Continue boiling, without stirring, until skins burst. Ladle hot sauce into hot jars, leaving ½-inch headspace. Adjust two-piece caps. Process 15 minutes in a boiling-water canner.

Figs

2½ pounds figs per quart	Water
Sugar	Bottled lemon juice

Wash figs and drain. Do not stem, peel or cut. Blanch whole figs 2 minutes in boiling water. Drain. Gently boil figs in a light or medium syrup for 5 minutes. Add 1 tablespoon bottled lemon juice to each pint, 2 tablespoons bottled lemon juice to each quart jar. Pack hot figs into hot jars, leaving ½-inch headspace. Ladle hot syrup over figs, leaving ½-inch headspace. Remove air bubbles. Adjust two-piece caps. Process pints 45 minutes, quarts 50 minutes, in a boiling-water canner.

Gooseberries

1½ to 3 pounds gooseberries per quart	Sugar
	Water

Wash gooseberries; drain. Use scissors to snip off stem and blossom ends. Make a medium or heavy syrup; keep syrup hot. Ladle ½ cup hot syrup into hot jar. Fill jar with gooseberries. Gently shake jar to pack gooseberries closely without crushing, leaving ½-inch headspace. Add hot syrup to cover gooseberries, if needed, leaving ½-inch headspace. Remove air bubbles. Adjust two-piece caps. Process pints 15 minutes, quarts 20 minutes, in a boiling-water canner.

Grapefruit

2 to 2½ pounds grapefruit per quart	Sugar
	Water

Wash grapefruit; drain. Peel grapefruit, cutting deep enough to remove white pith. Cut membrane away from pulp for each section; lift out the pulp without breaking the cell structure. Discard seeds. Make a light syrup; keep syrup hot. Pack grapefruit into hot jars, leaving ½-inch headspace. Ladle hot syrup over grapefruit, leaving ½-inch headspace. Remove air bubbles. Adjust two-piece caps. Process pints and quarts 10 minutes in a boiling-water canner.

Grapes—Ripe

2 pounds grapes per quart	Water
Sugar	

Wash grapes; drain. Make a light or medium syrup; keep syrup hot. Ladle ½ cup hot syrup into hot jar. Fill jar with grapes. Gently shake jar to pack grapes closely without crushing, leaving ½-inch headspace. Add hot syrup to cover grapes, if needed, leaving ½-inch headspace. Remove air bubbles. Adjust two-piece caps. Process pints 15 minutes, quarts 20 minutes, in a boiling-water canner.

Grapes—Unripe

2 pounds grapes per quart	Water
Sugar	

Wash grapes; drain. Make a medium or heavy syrup; keep syrup hot. Ladle ½ cup hot syrup into hot jar. Fill jar with grapes. Gently shake jar to pack grapes closely without crushing, leaving ½-inch headspace. Add hot syrup to cover grapes, if needed, leaving ½-inch headspace. Remove air bubbles. Adjust two-piece caps. Process pints and quarts 20 minutes in a boiling-water canner.

Note: Green grapes used for pies should be canned before seeds harden.

Guavas

2 pounds guavas per quart	Water
Sugar	

Wash guavas; drain. Peel, cut in half and remove seeds. Make a light syrup; heat syrup to boiling. Pour hot syrup over guavas; let stand 30 minutes. Remove guavas from syrup. Bring syrup to a boil. Pack guavas into hot jars, leaving ½-inch headspace. Ladle hot syrup over guavas, leaving ½-inch headspace. Remove air bubbles. Adjust two-piece caps. Process pints 15 minutes, quarts 20 minutes, in a boiling-water canner.

Honey-Orange Slices

Yield: about 3 half-pints

2½ pounds oranges (about 4 large)	1 lemon, juiced
	3 sticks cinnamon
1¼ cups sugar	1½ teaspoons whole cloves
1¼ cups honey	1½ teaspoons whole allspice

Wash oranges; drain. Slice oranges, discarding ends and seeds. Cut orange slices in half. Place in saucepot, adding enough water to cover. Bring to a boil. Reduce heat and simmer until peel is tender. Drain. Combine sugar, honey and lemon juice in a saucepot; bring to a boil. Tie whole spices in a spice bag. Add orange slices and spice bag to syrup. Simmer 40 minutes. Remove spice bag. Pack hot oranges into hot jars, leaving ½-inch headspace. Ladle hot syrup over oranges, leaving ½-inch headspace. Remove air bubbles. Adjust two-piece caps. Process 10 minutes in a boiling-water canner.

Honey-Spiced Peaches

Yield: about 3 quarts

8 pounds small peaches	2 cups honey
Ball Fruit-Fresh	3 sticks cinnamon
Produce Protector	1½ teaspoons whole allspice
1 cup sugar	¾ teaspoon whole cloves
4 cups water	

Wash peaches; drain. Peel peaches, refer to Peaches recipe. Leave peaches whole. Treat with Fruit-Fresh to prevent darkening. Combine sugar, water and honey in a large saucepot. Cook until sugar dissolves. Drain peaches. Cook peaches one layer at a time in syrup 3 minutes or until hot throughout. Pack hot peaches into hot jars, leaving ½-inch headspace. Add 1 cinnamon stick, ½ teaspoon allspice and ¼ teaspoon cloves to each jar. Ladle hot syrup over peaches, leaving ½-inch headspace. Remove air bubbles. Adjust two-piece caps. Process 25 minutes in a boiling-water canner.

Loquats

2 to 2½ pounds loquats	Sugar
per quart	Water

Wash loquats; drain. Remove stem and blossom ends, cut in half and remove seeds. Make a light syrup. Cook loquats in syrup until hot throughout. Pack hot loquats into hot jars, leaving ½-inch headspace. Ladle hot syrup over loquats, leaving ½-inch headspace. Remove air bubbles. Adjust two-piece caps. Process pints 15 minutes, quarts 20 minutes, in a boiling-water canner.

Mangoes, Green

3 to 3½ pounds firm,	Sugar
non-fibrous green	Water
mangoes per quart	

Wash green mangoes; drain. Make four lengthwise cuts through peel and flesh of mangoes to remove from pit. Allow about ¼-inch around pit to avoid fibrous flesh. Peel and slice mangoes. Make a light or medium syrup. Bring syrup to a boil. Add mango slices and cook 2 minutes. Pack hot mangoes into hot jars, leaving ½-inch headspace. Ladle hot syrup over mangoes, leaving ½-inch headspace. Remove air bubbles. Adjust two-piece caps. Process pints 15 minutes, quarts 20 minutes, in a boiling-water canner.

Mixed Fruits

Apricots, Cherries, Grapefruit, Peaches, Pears, Pineapple, Plums, White Grapes, etc.

2 to 3 pounds mixed fruit	Sugar
per quart	Water

Use three or more varieties of fruit. Prepare fruit as directed for individual recipe for the type of fruit used. Make a light syrup. Bring syrup to a boil and add fruit. Cook fruit until hot throughout. Pack hot fruit into hot jars, leaving ½-inch headspace. Ladle hot syrup over fruit, leaving ½-inch headspace. Remove air bubbles. Adjust two-piece caps. Process pints 20 minutes, quarts 25 minutes, in a boiling-water canner.

Note: If fruit is to be used for salad or dessert, leave in large pieces; cut fruit into small pieces for cocktail.

Nectarines

2 to 2½ pounds nectarines	Sugar
per quart	Water
Ball Fruit-Fresh	
Produce Protector	

Raw Pack: Wash nectarines; drain. Cut in half and pit; do not peel. Treat with Fruit-Fresh to prevent darkening. Make a light or medium syrup; keep syrup hot. Drain nectarines. Pack nectarines, cavity side down, into hot jars, leaving ½-inch headspace. Ladle hot syrup over nectarines, leaving ½-inch headspace. Remove air bubbles. Adjust two-piece caps. Process pints 25 minutes, quarts 30 minutes, in a boiling-water canner.

Hot Pack: Wash nectarines; drain. Cut in half and pit; do not peel. Treat with Fruit-Fresh to prevent darkening. Make a light or medium syrup. Drain nectarines. Cook nectarines in syrup one layer at a time until hot throughout. Pack hot nectarines, cavity side down, into hot jars, leaving ½-inch headspace. Ladle hot syrup over nectarines, leaving ½-inch headspace. Remove air bubbles. Adjust two-piece caps. Process pints 20 minutes, quarts 25 minutes, in a boiling-water canner.

Papayas

3 to 3½ pounds papaya	Water
per quart	Bottled lemon juice
Sugar	

Wash papayas; drain. Peel and seed papayas. Cube papayas. Make a medium or heavy syrup. Bring syrup to a boil; reduce heat. Add papaya cubes and gently cook 2 to 3 minutes. Pack hot papayas into hot jars, leaving ½-inch headspace. Add 1 tablespoon bottled lemon juice to each quart jar. Ladle hot syrup over papayas, leaving ½-inch headspace. Remove air bubbles. Adjust two-piece caps. Process pints 15 minutes, quarts 20 minutes, in a boiling-water canner.

Peaches

2 to 3 pounds peaches	Sugar
per quart	Water
Ball Fruit-Fresh	
Produce Protector	

Raw Pack: Wash peaches; drain. Peel peaches; cut in half and pit. Treat with Fruit-Fresh to prevent darkening. Make a light or medium syrup; keep syrup hot. Drain peaches. Pack peaches cavity side down, layers overlapping, into hot jars, leaving ½-inch headspace. Ladle hot syrup over peaches, leaving ½-inch headspace. Remove air bubbles. Adjust two-piece caps. Process pints 25 minutes, quarts 30 minutes, in a boiling-water canner.

Hot Pack: Wash peaches; drain. Peel peaches; cut in half and pit. Treat with Fruit-Fresh to prevent darkening. Make a medium or heavy syrup. Drain peaches. Cook peaches one layer at a time in syrup until peaches are hot throughout. Pack hot peaches, cavity side down, into hot jars, leaving ½-inch headspace. Ladle hot syrup over peaches, leaving ½-inch headspace. Remove air bubbles. Adjust two-piece caps. Process pints 20 minutes, quarts 25 minutes, in a boiling-water canner.

Note: To peel peaches, dip in boiling water for 30 to 60 seconds. Immediately drain and place peaches in cold water. Slip off peel. Cut in half, pit and scrape cavity to remove fibrous flesh.

fruits, fruit juices, nectars & purées

Pears

2 to 3 pounds pears	Sugar
per quart	Water
Ball Fruit-Fresh	
Produce Protector	

Hot Pack: Wash pears; drain. Cut into halves; core and peel. Treat with Fruit-Fresh to prevent darkening. Make a light syrup; keep syrup hot. Drain pears. Cook pears one layer at a time in syrup until hot throughout. Pack hot pears into hot jars, leaving ½-inch headspace. Ladle hot syrup over pears, leaving ½-inch headspace. Remove air bubbles. Adjust two-piece caps. Process pints 20 minutes, quarts 25 minutes, in a boiling-water canner.

Note: Pears should be harvested when full grown and stored in a cool place (60° to 65°F) until ripe but not soft. Bartlett pears are considered best for canning. Kieffer pears and similar varieties are satisfactory if properly ripened and cooked in water until almost tender.

Pear Mincemeat

Yield: about 9 pints

7 pounds Bartlett pears	1 tablespoon cinnamon
1 lemon	1 tablespoon nutmeg
2 pounds raisins	1 tablespoon allspice
6¾ cups sugar	1 teaspoon ginger
1 tablespoon cloves	1 cup vinegar

Wash pears; drain. Cut into halves and core. Coarsely chop pears. Cut lemon into quarters, removing seeds. Finely chop lemon. Combine all ingredients in a large saucepot. Bring mixture to a boil over medium heat; reduce heat; simmer 30 minutes. Ladle hot mincemeat into hot jars, leaving ½-inch headspace. Remove air bubbles. Adjust two-piece caps. Process 25 minutes in a boiling-water canner.

Pineapple

3 pounds pineapple	Sugar
per quart	Water

Scrub pineapple; drain. Peel and core pineapple. Cut into ½-inch slices. Pineapple may also be cut lengthwise into wedges or 1-inch chunks. Make a light syrup. Simmer pineapple in syrup until tender. Pack hot pineapple into hot jars, leaving ½-inch headspace. Ladle hot syrup over pineapple, leaving ½-inch headspace. Remove air bubbles. Adjust two-piece caps. Process pints 15 minutes, quarts 20 minutes, in a boiling-water canner.

Plums Or Fresh Prunes

1½ to 2½ pounds plums	Sugar
or prunes per quart	Water

Raw Pack: Wash plums; drain. Prick whole plums in several places. Make a light or medium syrup; keep syrup hot. Firmly pack plums into hot jars, leaving ½-inch headspace. Ladle hot syrup over plums, leaving ½-inch headspace. Remove air bubbles. Adjust two-piece caps. Process pints 20 minutes, quarts 25 minutes, in a boiling-water canner.

Hot Pack: Wash plums; drain. Prick whole plums in several places. Make a medium or heavy syrup. Bring syrup to a boil. Reduce heat and simmer syrup 5 minutes. Cook plums in syrup one layer at a time, remove plums from pot and keep hot. After all plums are cooked, remove syrup from heat. Return plums to syrup and cover. Let stand 30 minutes. Remove plums and bring syrup to a simmer. Pack hot plums into hot jars, leaving ½-inch headspace. Ladle hot syrup over plums, leaving ½-inch headspace. Remove air bubbles. Adjust two-piece caps. Process pints 20 minutes, quarts 25 minutes, in a boiling-water canner.

Note: Green Gage and other meaty plums are better for canning than the more juicy varieties. Plums may be blanched and peeled, but they are usually canned unpeeled. Plums may be cut in half and pit removed or left whole. Pricking whole plums does not prevent peel from cracking but helps to prevent fruit from bursting.

Rhubarb

1½ to 2 pounds rhubarb	Sugar
per quart	

Wash rhubarb; drain. Discard leafy tops. Cut stalks into 1-inch pieces. Measure. Put rhubarb in a large saucepot. For each quart rhubarb measured, add ½ to 1 cup sugar. Stir to coat rhubarb with sugar; let stand 3 to 4 hours in a cool place. Place mixture in a large saucepot. Bring slowly to a boil; boil 30 seconds. Pack hot rhubarb and syrup into hot jars, leaving ½-inch headspace. Remove air bubbles. Adjust two-piece caps. Process pints and quarts 15 minutes in a boiling-water canner.

Strawberries

2½ to 3 pounds strawberries	Sugar
per quart	

Wash strawberries; drain. Remove caps from strawberries. Measure strawberries. Put strawberries in a large saucepot. For each quart of strawberries measured, add ½ to ¾ cup sugar. Gently stir to evenly coat strawberries with sugar. Let stand 5 to 6 hours in a cool place. Cook slowly until sugar dissolves and strawberries are hot throughout. Pack hot strawberries and syrup into hot jars, leaving ½-inch headspace. Remove air bubbles. Adjust two-piece caps. Process pints 10 minutes, quarts 15 minutes, in a boiling-water canner.

Note: Use firm, red-ripe berries which have neither white flesh nor hollow centers. Strawberries tend to fade and lose flavor when canned.

fruit juices, nectars & purées

Apple Juice

Yield: about 6 quarts

24 pounds apples	2 quarts water

Wash apples; drain. Remove stem and blossom ends. Chop apples and place in a large saucepot. Add water and cook until tender, stirring to prevent sticking. Strain through a damp jelly bag or several layers of cheesecloth. Heat juice 5 minutes at 190°F. Do not boil. Ladle hot juice into hot jars, leaving ¼-inch headspace. Adjust two-piece caps. Process 10 minutes in a boiling-water canner.

Berry Juice

Boysenberry, Loganberry, Raspberry, etc.

Wash, crush and simmer berries until soft. Add a small amount of water to prevent sticking, if necessary. Strain through a damp jelly bag or several layers of cheesecloth. Measure juice; add 1 to 2 cups sugar for each gallon of juice. Heat juice 5 minutes at 190°F. Do not boil. Ladle hot juice into hot jars, leaving ¼-inch headspace. Adjust two-piece caps. Process pints and quarts 15 minutes in a boiling-water canner.

Note: If clear juice is desired, let strained juice stand for 24 hours in refrigerator. Ladle juice from pan, being careful not to disturb sediment. Proceed as above.

Cranberry Juice

Wash cranberries; drain. Combine an equal measure of cranberries and water in a large saucepot. Bring to a boil. Reduce heat; cook until cranberries burst. Strain juice through a damp jelly bag or several layers of cheesecloth. Combine cranberry juice with sugar to taste, if desired. Heat juice 5 minutes at 190°F. Do not boil. Ladle hot juice into hot jars, leaving ¼-inch headspace. Adjust two-piece caps. Process pints and quarts 15 minutes in a boiling-water canner.

Note: If clear juice is desired, let strained juice stand for 24 hours in refrigerator. Ladle juice from pan, being careful not to disturb sediment. Proceed as above.

Four Fruit Juice

Yield: about 4 quarts

4 cups peach purée	4 cups grapefruit juice
4 cups orange juice	2 cups water
4 cups pineapple juice	½ cup honey (optional)

Combine all ingredients in a large saucepot. Heat juice 5 minutes at 190°F. Do not boil. Remove from heat. Skim foam, if necessary. Ladle hot juice into hot jars, leaving ¼-inch headspace. Adjust two-piece caps. Process pints and quarts 20 minutes in a boiling-water canner.

Fruit Purée Or Nectar

4 to 6 pounds fruit per quart	Sugar (optional)
Water	

Wash fruit; drain. Peel, pit or core and coarsely chop fruit. Measure fruit. Put fruit in a large saucepot. For each quart of fruit measured, add 1 cup water. Cook fruit until soft. Purée fruit and liquid using a food processor or food mill. Combine fruit purée with sugar to taste, if desired. Bring purée to a boil. Stir to prevent sticking. Ladle hot purée into hot jars, leaving ¼-inch headspace. Remove air bubbles. Adjust two-piece caps. Process pints and quarts 15 minutes in a boiling-water canner.

Note: Add 2 tablespoons bottled lemon juice per quart pureed figs.

Golden Nectar

Yield: about 6 quarts

2 quarts sliced peaches	1½ cups honey
6 cups cubed cantaloupe	1 cup pineapple juice
1 quart water	½ cup lemon juice
7 cups orange juice	

Cook sliced peaches and cubed cantaloupe in water until fruit is soft. Purée fruit and cooking liquid using a food processor or food mill. Add remaining ingredients to nectar. Bring nectar to a boil, stirring to prevent sticking. Ladle hot nectar into hot jars, leaving ¼-inch headspace. Remove air bubbles. Adjust two-piece caps. Process pints and quarts 20 minutes, in a boiling-water canner.

Grape Juice

Wash grapes; drain. Stem, crush and measure grapes. Add 1 cup water to each gallon crushed grapes. Heat grapes 10 minutes at 190°F. Do not boil. Strain juice through a damp jelly bag or several layers of cheesecloth. Let juice stand 24 hours in refrigerator. Ladle juice from pan, being careful not to disturb sediment. Strain juice again. Measure juice; add 1 to 2 cups sugar to each gallon juice. Reheat juice for 5 minutes at 190°F. Do not boil. Ladle hot juice into hot jars, leaving ¼-inch headspace. Adjust two-piece caps. Process pints and quarts 15 minutes in a boiling-water canner.

Grapefruit Juice

Wash grapefruit; drain. Extract and strain juice. Combine juice with sugar to taste, if desired. Heat juice 5 minutes at 190°F. Do not boil. Ladle hot juice into hot jars, leaving ¼-inch headspace. Adjust two-piece caps. Process pints and quarts 15 minutes in a boiling-water canner.

tomatoes

Tomatoes—Packed In Water

Whole, Halved Or Quartered

2½ to 3½ pounds tomatoes per quart	Ball Citric Acid or bottled lemon juice
	Salt (optional)

Raw Pack: Prepare tomatoes *(see steps 5-7, page 24)*. Add ¼ teaspoon citric acid or 1 tablespoon bottled lemon juice to each pint jar, ½ teaspoon citric acid or 2 tablespoons bottled lemon juice to each quart jar. Pack tomatoes into hot jars, leaving ¼-inch headspace. Ladle hot water over tomatoes, leaving ½-inch headspace. Add ½ teaspoon salt to each pint jar, 1 teaspoon salt to each quart jar, if desired. Remove air bubbles. Adjust two-piece caps. Process pints 40 minutes, quarts 45 minutes, in a boiling-water canner.

Hot Pack: Prepare tomatoes *(see steps 5-7, page 24)*. Place tomatoes in a large saucepot; add enough water to cover tomatoes. Boil gently 5 minutes, stirring to prevent sticking. Add ¼ teaspoon citric acid or 1 tablespoon bottled lemon juice to each pint jar, ½ teaspoon citric acid or 2 tablespoons bottled lemon juice to each quart jar. Pack hot tomatoes into hot jars, leaving ½-inch headspace. Ladle hot cooking liquid over tomatoes, leaving ½-inch headspace. Add ½ teaspoon salt to each pint jar, 1 teaspoon salt to each quart jar, if desired. Remove air bubbles. Adjust two-piece caps. Process pints 40 minutes, quarts 45 minutes, in a boiling-water canner.

Tomatoes—Packed In Own Juice

Whole, Halved Or Quartered

2½ to 3½ pounds tomatoes per quart	Ball Citric Acid or bottled lemon juice
	Salt (optional)

Prepare tomatoes *(see steps 5-7, page 24)*. Add ¼ teaspoon citric acid or 1 tablespoon bottled lemon juice to each pint jar, ½ teaspoon citric acid or 2 tablespoons bottled lemon juice to each quart jar. Pack tomatoes into hot jars, pressing gently on tomatoes until the natural juice fills the spaces between tomatoes, leaving ½-inch headspace. Add ½ teaspoon salt to each pint jar, 1 teaspoon salt to each quart jar, if desired. Remove air bubbles. Adjust two-piece caps. Process pints and quarts 1 hour and 25 minutes in a boiling-water canner.

Tomato Juice

3 to 3½ pounds tomatoes per quart	Ball Citric Acid or bottled lemon juice

Wash tomatoes; drain. Remove core and blossom ends. Cut tomatoes into quarters and simmer until soft, stirring to prevent sticking. Juice tomatoes in a food processor or food mill. Strain juice to remove peels and seeds. Heat juice 5 minutes at 190°F. Do not boil. Add ¼ teaspoon citric acid or 1 tablespoon bottled lemon juice to each pint jar, ½ teaspoon citric acid or 2 tablespoons bottled lemon juice to each quart jar. Ladle hot juice into hot jars, leaving ¼-inch headspace. Adjust two-piece caps. Process pints 35 minutes, quarts 40 minutes, in a boiling-water canner.

fruit juice, nectars & purées, tomatoes

Recipe Variation: For herb tomato juice, add one or two sprigs fresh herbs, such as dill, parsley or basil, to juice during the last 5 minutes of cooking. Remove herbs before canning. Fresh herbs may be canned with the tomato juice, but the flavoring will become stronger during storage. Tomato juice may be seasoned to taste with salt, sugar, spices and hot pepper sauce.

Tomato Garden Juice Blend

Yield: about 14 pints or 7 quarts

22 pounds tomatoes	½ cup chopped onion
¾ cup diced carrots	¼ cup chopped parsley
¾ cup chopped celery	1 tablespoon salt
¾ cup chopped green pepper	Ball Citric Acid or bottled lemon juice

Wash tomatoes; drain. Remove core and blossom ends. Cut into quarters. Combine tomatoes and vegetables in a large saucepan; simmer 20 minutes, stirring to prevent sticking. Juice tomatoes in a food processor or food mill. Strain juice to remove peels and seeds. Stir in salt, if desired. Heat juice 5 minutes at 190°F. Do not boil. Add ¼ teaspoon citric acid or 1 tablespoon bottled lemon juice to each pint jar, ½ teaspoon citric acid or 2 tablespoons bottled lemon juice to each quart jar. Ladle hot juice into hot jars, leaving ¼-inch headspace. Adjust two-piece caps. Process pints 35 minutes, quarts 40 minutes, in a boiling-water canner.

Tomato Sauce

Yield: about 14 pints or 7 quarts

45 pounds tomatoes	Ball Citric Acid or bottled lemon juice

Wash tomatoes; drain. Remove core and blossom ends. Cut into quarters; simmer 20 minutes in a large saucepot, stirring occasionally. Purée tomatoes in a food processor or food mill. Strain purée to remove seeds and peels. Cook pulp in a large, uncovered saucepot over medium-high heat until sauce thickens, stirring to prevent sticking. Reduce volume by one-half. Add ¼ teaspoon citric acid or 1 tablespoon bottled lemon juice to each pint jar, ½ teaspoon citric acid or 2 tablespoons bottled lemon juice to each quart jar. Ladle hot sauce into hot jars, leaving ½-inch headspace. Adjust two-piece caps. Process pints 35 minutes, quarts 40 minutes, in a boiling-water canner.

Seasoned Tomato Sauce

Yield: about 14 pints or 7 quarts

45 pounds tomatoes	1 tablespoon black pepper
6 cups chopped onions	1½ tablespoons sugar
12 cloves garlic, minced	¼ cup salt
½ cup olive oil	2 teaspoons crushed red pepper (optional)
2 tablespoons oregano	
6 bay leaves	Ball Citric Acid or bottled lemon juice

Wash tomatoes; drain. Remove core and blossom ends. Cut into quarters; set aside. Sauté onions and garlic in olive oil in a large saucepot. Add tomatoes, oregano, bay leaves, black pepper and sugar. Stir in salt and crushed red pepper, if desired. Simmer 20 minutes, stirring occasionally. Remove bay leaves. Purée tomatoes using a food processor or food mill. Strain purée to remove peels and seeds. Cook pulp in a large, uncovered saucepot over medium-high heat until sauce thickens, stirring to prevent sticking. Reduce volume by one-half. Add ¼ teaspoon citric acid or

1 tablespoon bottled lemon juice to each pint jar, ½ teaspoon citric acid or 2 tablespoons bottled lemon juice to each quart jar. Ladle hot sauce into hot jars, leaving ½-inch headspace. Adjust two-piece caps. Process pints 35 minutes, quarts 40 minutes, in a boiling-water canner.

featured prepared recipe
Apple-Cranberry Pie

Makes one 9-inch pie

Crust

2½ cups all-purpose flour	¾ cup vegetable shortening
2 tablespoons sugar	⅔ cup cold water
1 teaspoon salt	

Filling

2 quart jars Apples for Baking *(recipe on page 17)*	¾ cup sweetened dried cranberries
½ cup sugar	¾ cup chopped dates
2 tablespoons all-purpose flour	¾ cup chopped walnuts
¼ teaspoon salt	1 tablespoon freshly grated orange zest
¼ teaspoon cinnamon	2 tablespoons unsalted butter
⅛ teaspoon allspice	

Crust: Combine flour, sugar and salt in a medium bowl. Cut shortening into dry ingredients using a pastry blender just until mixture is uniformly coarse. Add water one tablespoon at a time, stirring gently with a fork after each addition. Use just enough water for dough to hold together in a ball. Divide dough into two portions with one slightly larger. Cover each portion of dough with plastic wrap and refrigerate.

Filling: Drain apples, reserving liquid. Combine sugar, flour, salt, cinnamon, and allspice in a medium bowl. Add drained apples and stir gently to coat evenly with sugar mixture; set aside. Combine cranberries, dates, walnuts and orange zest in a small bowl. Stir in two tablespoons reserved liquid from apples; let stand 10 minutes.

To Assemble Pie: Remove dough from refrigerator. Roll out larger portion of dough on a lightly floured surface to ⅛-inch thick and 2 inches larger than pie pan. Place rolled dough into pie pan and gently work the dough to fit pan. Trim edge even with pie pan. Roll out remaining dough to ⅛-inch thick and 1 inch larger than pie pan. Cut steam vents into crust; set aside. Spread cranberry mixture evenly over bottom of pie crust. Spoon the apple mixture evenly over cranberries to cover. Cut butter into small pieces and place evenly over apples. Center top crust over pie and trim edge allowing ½-inch overhang. Fold edge of top crust under bottom crust; flute the edge to seal. Bake pie at 450°F for 20 minutes, reduce heat to 350°F and continue baking 40 minutes, or until crust is lightly browned and fruit is tender.

canning tomatoes step-by-step

1. Read recipe instructions; assemble equipment and ingredients before starting. Follow guidelines for recipe preparation, jar size, canning method and processing time. Do not make changes in recommended guidelines.

2. Visually examine canning jars for nicks, cracks, uneven rims or sharp edges that may prevent sealing or cause breakage. Examine canning lids to ensure they are free of dents and sealing compound is even and complete. Check bands for proper fit.

3. Wash jars and two-piece caps in hot, soapy water. Rinse well. Dry bands; set aside. Heat jars and lids in a saucepot of simmering water (180°F). DO NOT BOIL LIDS. Allow jars and lids to remain in hot water until ready for use, removing one at a time as needed.

4. Fill boiling-water canner half-full with hot water. Elevate rack in canner. Put canner lid in place. Heat water just to a simmer (180°F). Keep water hot until used for processing.

5. Select fresh tomatoes at their peak of quality and flavor. Use firm tomatoes free of cracks, spots and growths. Prepare only enough for one canner load. Wash tomatoes; drain.

6. Place tomatoes in wire basket and lower into a large saucepot of boiling water. Blanch tomatoes 30 to 60 seconds or until skins start to crack. Remove from boiling water. Dip immediately into cold water.

7. Slip off skins; trim away any green areas; cut out core. Leave tomatoes whole or cut into halves or quarters.

8. For tomatoes packed in water, place tomatoes in a large saucepot, adding just enough water to cover. Boil gently 5 minutes. Or follow recipe directions on page 22 for Tomatoes-Packed In Own Juice.

9. Remove canning jar from hot water with a jar lifter; set jar on towel. Add ¼ teaspoon citric acid or 1 tablespoon bottled lemon juice to each pint jar, ½ teaspoon citric acid or 2 tablespoons bottled lemon juice to each quart jar.

10. Carefully pack tomatoes into hot jar, leaving ½-inch headspace. Ladle boiling water or cooking liquid over tomatoes, leaving ½-inch headspace. Add ½ teaspoon salt per pint jar or 1 teaspoon salt per quart jar, if desired.

11. Slide a nonmetallic spatula between tomatoes and jar; press back gently on tomatoes to release trapped air bubbles. Repeat procedure 2 to 3 times around inside of jar.

12. Wipe rim and threads of jar with a clean, damp cloth. Remove lid from hot water using a lid wand. Place lid on jar, centering sealing compound on rim. Screw band down evenly and firmly, just until resistance is met—fingertip tight.

13. As each jar is filled, set it onto the elevated rack in the boiling-water canner. Water in canner should be kept at a simmer (180°F). After all jars are filled and placed onto the rack, lower rack into canner. Water level must cover the two-piece caps on the jars by 1 to 2 inches. Add boiling water, if necessary.

14. Put lid on canner. Bring water to a boil. Start counting processing time after water comes to a rolling boil. Process pints 40 minutes, quarts 45 minutes, at a gentle but steady boil for altitudes at or below 1,000 feet above sea level. For higher altitude areas, refer to Altitude Chart (*see page 5*).

15. When processing time is complete, turn off heat and remove canner lid. Let canner cool 5 minutes before removing jars. Remove jars from canner and set them upright, 1 to 2 inches apart, on a dry towel to cool. Do not retighten bands. Let jars cool 12 to 24 hours.

16. After jars have cooled, check lids for a seal by pressing on the center of each lid. If the center is pulled down and does not flex, remove the band and gently try to lift the lid off with your fingertips. If the lid does not flex and you cannot lift it off, the lid has a good vacuum seal. Wipe lid and jar surface with a clean, damp cloth to remove food particles or residue. Label. Store jars in a cool, dry, dark place (*see page 12*).

soft spreads

Jams, Jellies & Fruit Spreads

Leisurely weekends are all too few—so when a free Saturday morning magically appears, savor every minute. Sip a steaming cup of coffee, peruse your favorite magazine and reconnect with a friend you haven't called in some time. Sunrise Muffins complete the scene, with the chunky goodness of Carrot-Pineapple-Orange Marmalade baked right in to yield an extra burst of flavor and a blush of color.

Jams, jellies, conserves, preserves and sunny marmalades—every spoonful a delight. Easy to make and hard to resist, these delectable spreads are perfect for any meal. For family gatherings, think crepes filled with Elderberry Jam and garnished with freshly whipped cream. Or cook up a batch of French toast that will be forever remembered for the Apple Preserves that adorn it. And what better to top that juicy pork roast than a shimmering Currant Jelly?

Preserving is about more than food. When your home is filled with the fragrant aroma of sweet spreads simmering on the stove, you are preserving memories that last a lifetime.

So, the next time you are sipping your coffee and wondering what the day will bring, go ahead. Spread another dollop of marmalade on your muffin. Make your day.

Pictured, Sunrise Muffins made with
Carrot-Pineapple-Orange Marmalade.
Carrot-Pineapple-Orange Marmalade
recipe found on page 37.
Recipe for Sunrise Muffins
found on page 41.

getting started

Soft spreads produce the most satisfaction and pride of all home canning recipes. They make charming gifts when tied with a ribbon or tucked in a basket filled with baked goods. There are four main ingredients in all soft spreads: fruit, sugar, pectin and acid. However, the consistency of soft spreads ranges from a firm set for jellies to a soft, honey-like consistency for preserves. Each type of soft spread requires slightly different cooking techniques. The general information that follows applies to the type of spread it is describing. Specific preparation instructions are given in each recipe.

Butter

Fruit Butter is made by cooking fruit pulp and sugar to a thick consistency that will spread easily. Spices may be added. Butters are cooked slowly until thick enough to round up on a spoon.

Conserve

Conserves are jam-like products made with a combination of two or more fruits, nuts and raisins. Conserves are cooked until they round up on a spoon. If nuts are used, they can be added during the last five minutes of cooking.

Jam

Jams are made by cooking crushed or chopped fruits with sugar until the mixture will round up on a spoon. Jams can be made of one fruit or a combination of fruits. They should be firm but spreadable; jams do not hold the shape of the jar.

Jelly

Juice strained from fruit is used to make jelly. It is usually prepared in a way that keeps the juice crystal clear and shimmering. Jelly is gelatinized enough to hold its shape when removed from the jar, yet soft enough to spread easily.

Marmalade

Marmalade is a soft jelly containing small pieces of fruit and peel evenly suspended in the transparent jelly. Marmalade is cooked in small batches and brought rapidly to (or almost to) the gelling point. Marmalades are similar in structure to jam.

Preserve

Fruit is preserved with sugar so it retains its shape, is transparent, shiny, tender and plump. The syrup varies from the thickness of honey to that of soft jelly. A true preserve does not hold its shape when spooned from the jar.

Ingredients And Preparation

Fruit

Fruit provides the flavor and color for soft spreads. It is also an important factor in achieving the desired gel. Use only top quality fruit for best results. Fruit selection should include some fruit that is slightly under-ripe (but not green) for added pectin and acid, along with some fruit that is at the peak of ripeness for flavor.

Wash fruit thoroughly under cold running water. Dry fruit. Remove scarred or bruised areas. Discard all diseased fruit and any fruit past its peak of ripeness. Peel, pit or core, crush or chop fruit as instructed by the recipe. Crushing or chopping fruit too finely will add too much fruit and juice to the recipe, causing an imbalance of ingredients that may not allow the spread to gel. To prepare juice for jelly, refer to Juice for Jelly (*see page 30*).

Unsweetened bottled or frozen juice may be used for making jellies; unsweetened frozen fruit may also be used for making other soft spreads. The acid and pectin level of bottled or frozen juice and frozen fruit may be less than in fresh fruit juice or fresh fruit. For this reason, it is best to follow recipes calling for a commercial pectin when using these products.

Pectin

Pectin is a natural substance of high molecular weight found in varying amounts in fruits. It is pectin that causes fruit to gel. Fruit that is slightly under-ripe contains more pectin than fully-ripe fruit. Overripe fruit used in spreads will likely cause a runny final product. Many recipes call for the peel and core to be included when preparing fruit for juice or pulp. This is because the pectin is concentrated in these areas. In preparing oranges, lemons and grapefruit for marmalade, part of the pith (white portion of the peel) should be cooked with the outer peel; the pith contains most of the pectin found in citrus fruit. Using too much of the pith may cause the spread to be bitter.

Recipes made without added pectin rely on the natural pectin in fruit to set the gel. These recipes use less sugar than recipes with added pectin, but they require a longer cooking time to reach the gelling point. The longer cooking time may cause the fruit to have a cooked flavor and yield less spread.

Commercial pectin, liquid or powdered, is required for some soft spread recipes. The two forms are not interchangeable; so, the type of pectin called for in the recipe must be used. Generally, powdered pectin is stirred into the fruit and brought to a boil before the sugar is added. Liquid pectin is added to the mixture after all other ingredients have been brought to a boil. Commercial pectin helps reduce the cooking time, resulting in a truer fruit flavor and greater yield.

Use Ball RealFruit Pectin to make jams and jellies having a truer fruit flavor and perfect gel every time. Ball RealFruit Pectin is available in: Classic, Liquid, Low and No-Sugar Needed, and Instant varieties. Each recipe in this guide will indicate the correct type and amount of pectin to use. Use only the type of pectin indicated in the recipe as they are not interchangeable.

Acid

Acid adds flavor and helps with the gel formation of soft spreads. Like pectin, the acid content varies in different fruits but is higher in slightly under-ripe fruit than in fruit that is fully-ripe. If acid is needed in the recipe, it will be listed as an ingredient. Generally lemon juice is used for additional acid. One tablespoon lemon juice to each cup fruit juice or pulp usually will supply the needed acid.

Sugar

Sugar helps in gel formation, contributes to flavor and serves as a preserving agent. Beet and cane sugar may be used with equal success.

Light corn syrup can be used to replace part of the sugar in recipes. In recipes without added pectin, one-fourth of the sugar can be replaced with corn syrup. When commercial pectin is used, corn syrup can replace one-half of the sugar.

Honey can also be used to replace sugar. Light, mild-flavored honey generally is the best kind to use. In recipes without added pectin, honey can replace one-half of the sugar. When pectin is added, 2 cups honey can replace 2 cups sugar in most recipes; ¾ to 1 cup sugar can be replaced by honey in recipes with a smaller yield, up to 6 half-pints.

Other Ingredients

A variety of spices, nuts and flavorings are used to enhance the flavor and texture of soft spreads. In most recipes, nuts are added during the last 5 minutes of cooking. Flavorings containing alcohol are usually added after the product has been cooked and removed from the heat. Soft spreads such as Jalapeño Jelly may call for vinegar. All recipes in this book requiring vinegar are developed using 5 percent acidity vinegar.

Equipment And Utensils

Some specialized equipment may be helpful in achieving successful results when making soft spreads. This equipment is readily available at grocery, kitchen or housewares stores.

Large Saucepot—An 8- or 10-quart heavy saucepot is essential for making soft spreads. The saucepot must have a broad, flat bottom for good heat distribution and deep sides to prevent the recipe from boiling over.

Food Scale—A weighted scale may be required to measure fruit and sugar. When cup and spoon measurements are given, standard measuring cups and measuring spoons should be used.

Candy/Jelly Thermometer—To accurately determine the gelling point for long-cooking spreads, a candy/jelly thermometer may be used. The bulb of the thermometer must be completely covered with the hot mixture but must not touch the bottom or sides of the pan. Hold the thermometer vertical in the saucepot and bring eyes level with the thermometer markings to read the temperature.

Jelly Bag—A jelly bag is a convenient tool to use when straining juice to make jelly. If one is not available, a strainer lined with several layers of cheesecloth works well. The jelly bag or cheesecloth must be dampened before using.

Spice Bag—A small muslin bag used for holding whole spices during the cooking period aids in removal of the spices before the spread is put into the jars. If a spice bag is not available, tie whole spices in several layers of cheesecloth.

Skimmer Or Slotted Spoon—Some soft spreads develop a layer of foam on the top during cooking. This is caused by the air in the fruit and air that is incorporated during boiling. The foam should be removed with a skimmer or slotted spoon before filling jars.

General Information

Prepare all soft spreads in single recipe batches. Never double recipes since double-size mixtures will not cook in the same manner as single batches. Doubling the recipe may prevent the spread from gelling.

Measure all ingredients accurately. Do not reduce or increase the measurement for any ingredient. If a low-sugar spread is desired, use only those recipes developed for less sugar (*see pages 75-76*).

The actual cooking time for soft spreads without added pectin will vary according to the recipe, ingredients, saucepot size, humidity and altitude. In making soft spreads without added pectin, the temperature, sheet test and plate test are used to help determine the correct cooking time (*see Gelling Test*).

Recipes requiring commercial pectin are not cooked to the gelling point. They are brought to a final rolling boil and boiled for 1 minute, or boiled the length of time stated in the recipe.

Soft spreads continue to thicken as they cool. Exactly how thick the finished product will be cannot be determined until the mixture is cooled to room temperature. For a softer spread, shorten the cooking time; for a firmer product, extend the cooking time. Most recipes will develop the desired gel structure within 24 hours. However, some recipes may require up to two weeks to gel.

Gelling Test

When preparing a soft spread recipe that does not require the addition of a commercial pectin product, you will need to test for doneness. Remove the saucepot from heat so the soft spread does not continue to cook while you are testing the gel. Testing jelly for the gelling point can be done using the sheet test, plate test or a thermometer. Jams, marmalades and preserves can be tested using a plate test or a thermometer. Butters and conserves are cooked until they round up on a spoon.

Using the sheet test, dip a cool, metal spoon into the boiling jelly (*see figure 8*). Lift out a spoonful of the mixture; moving the spoon away from the steam. Tip the spoon over a dish so the juice will drop off. When the jelly mixture first begins to boil, the drops will be light and syrupy. After continued cooking, the drops will become larger and will drop off the spoon in a sheet or flake. The gelling point has been reached when the jelly sheets off the spoon.

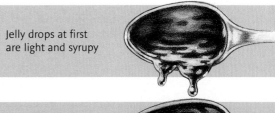

| figure 8 | Sheeting Test For Gelling Point Without Added Pectin |

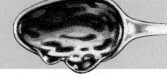

Jelly drops at first are light and syrupy

Then they become larger and show signs of sheeting

When gelling point is reached, jelly breaks from spoon in a sheet or flake

To complete the plate test, place a small amount of the hot spread on a chilled plate; set plate in a freezer until spread is cooled to room temperature. Gently run your finger through the cooled spread, if it separates then slowly returns to its original form, it is ready to process.

To use a candy/jelly thermometer for testing the gelling point, first determine the exact gelling point for your elevation. Hold the candy/jelly thermometer in boiling water; add 8°F to establish the gelling point. Once the gelling point is determined, prepare recipe. When reading the candy/jelly thermometer hold vertical in the mixture and read the markings at eye level. Once the spread has reached the gelling point, remove it from the heat.

Juice For Jelly

Hard Fruits—Apples, Pears, Nectarines, etc. Select top-quality fruit. Wash; remove stem and blossom ends; do not peel or core. Chop or quarter fruit; measure. Add 1 cup water for each slightly heaped quart prepared fruit in a large saucepot. Cover; simmer fruit until soft. Strain mixture through a damp jelly bag or several layers of cheesecloth to extract juice. Juice may be used fresh, canned or frozen for later use.

Soft Fruits—Grapes, Cherries, Berries, etc. Select top-quality fruit. Wash and stem fruit. Slightly crush fruit or follow recipe guidelines for preparing fruit; measure. Add ¼ to ½ cup water for each quart prepared fruit in a large saucepot. Cover; simmer fruit until soft. Strain mixture through a damp jelly bag or several layers of cheesecloth to extract juice. Juice may be used fresh, canned or frozen for later use.

Note: If juice is to be canned, heat juice just to a boil. Ladle hot juice into hot jars, leaving ¼-inch headspace. Adjust two-piece caps. Process pints and quarts 10 minutes in a boiling-water canner.

butters

Apple Butter

Yield: about 3 pints

4 pounds apples (about 16 medium)	2 teaspoons cinnamon
4 cups sugar	¼ teaspoon cloves

To Prepare Pulp: Wash apples. Core, peel and quarter apples. Combine apples and 2 cups water in a large saucepot. Simmer until apples are soft. Purée using a food processor or food mill, being careful not to liquefy. Measure 2 quarts apple pulp.

To Make Butter: Combine apple pulp, sugar and spices in a large saucepot. Cook slowly until thick enough to round up on a spoon. As mixture thickens, stir frequently to prevent sticking. Ladle hot butter into hot jars, leaving ¼-inch headspace. Remove air bubbles. Adjust two-piece caps. Process 10 minutes in a boiling-water canner.

Note: If butter becomes too thick, add water or apple juice for desired consistency.

Apricot Butter

Yield: about 3 pints

2 pounds apricots (about 24 medium)	3 cups sugar
	2 tablespoons lemon juice

To Prepare Pulp: Wash and blanch apricots. Put apricots in cold water. Peel, halve and pit apricots. Combine apricots and ½ cup water in a large saucepot. Simmer until apricots are soft. Purée using a food processor or food mill, being careful not to liquefy. Measure 1½ quarts apricot pulp.

To Make Butter: Combine apricot pulp and sugar in a large saucepot. Cook until thick enough to round up on a spoon. As mixture thickens, stir frequently to prevent sticking. Add lemon juice. Ladle hot butter into hot jars, leaving ¼-inch headspace. Remove air bubbles. Adjust two-piece caps. Process 10 minutes in a boiling-water canner.

Cranapple Butter

Yield: about 6 pints

6 pounds apples (about 24 medium)	4 cups sugar
2 quarts cranberry juice cocktail	2 teaspoons cinnamon
	½ teaspoon nutmeg

To Prepare Pulp: Wash apples. Core, peel and quarter apples. Combine apples and cranberry juice cocktail in a large saucepot. Simmer until apples are soft. Purée using a food processor or food mill, being careful not to liquefy.

To Make Butter: Combine apple pulp, sugar and spices in a large saucepot. Cook until thick enough to round up on a spoon. As mixture thickens, stir frequently to prevent sticking. Ladle hot butter into hot jars, leaving ¼-inch headspace. Remove air bubbles. Adjust two-piece caps. Process 10 minutes in a boiling-water canner.

Honeyed-Yellow Tomato Butter

Yield: about 3 half-pints

5 pounds yellow tomatoes (about 15 medium)	1 1-inch piece fresh ginger, peeled
2 cups sugar	1 tablespoon whole allspice
1 cup honey	2 sticks cinnamon

To Prepare Pulp: Wash tomatoes; drain. Remove core and blossom ends. Cut into quarters. Cook tomatoes in a large saucepot until soft. Press through a sieve or food mill; discard seeds and peel. Measure 2 quarts tomato pulp.

To Make Butter: Combine tomato pulp, sugar and honey in a large saucepot. Tie ginger and spices in a spice bag. Add spice bag to tomato mixture. Cook slowly until thick enough to round up on a spoon. As mixture thickens, stir frequently to prevent sticking. Ladle hot butter into hot jars, leaving ¼-inch headspace. Remove air bubbles. Adjust two-piece caps. Process 10 minutes in a boiling-water canner.

Peach Butter

Yield: about 4 pints

4 to 4½ pounds peaches (about 18 medium)	4 cups sugar

To Prepare Pulp: Wash and blanch peaches. Put peaches in cold water. Peel, pit and slice peaches. Combine peaches and ½ cup water in a large saucepot. Simmer until peaches are soft. Purée using a food processor or food mill, being careful not to liquefy. Measure 2 quarts peach pulp.

To Make Butter: Combine peach pulp and sugar in a large saucepot. Cook until thick enough to round up on a spoon. As mixture thickens, stir frequently to prevent sticking. Ladle hot butter into hot jars, leaving ¼-inch headspace. Remove air bubbles. Adjust two-piece caps. Process 10 minutes in a boiling-water canner.

Recipe Variation: For spiced peach butter add ½ to 1 teaspoon of ginger, nutmeg and cinnamon or any combination of these spices when adding sugar.

Pear Butter

Yield: about 4 pints

6 to 7 pounds pears (about 20 medium)	½ teaspoon nutmeg
4 cups sugar	⅓ cup orange juice
1 teaspoon grated orange peel	

To Prepare Pulp: Wash pears. Core, peel and slice pears. Combine pears and ½ cup water in a large saucepot. Simmer until pears are soft. Purée using a food processor or food mill, being careful not to liquefy. Measure 2 quarts pear pulp.

To Make Butter: Combine pear pulp and sugar in a large saucepot, stirring until sugar dissolves. Add remaining ingredients. Cook until thick enough to round up on a spoon. As mixture thickens, stir frequently to prevent sticking. Ladle hot butter into hot jars, leaving ¼-inch headspace. Remove air bubbles. Adjust two-piece caps. Process 10 minutes in a boiling-water canner.

Sweet Cider Apple Butter

Yield: about 4 pints

6 pounds apples (about 24 medium)	3 cups sugar
2 cups sweet cider	1½ teaspoons cinnamon
	½ teaspoon cloves

To Prepare Pulp: Wash apples. Core, peel and quarter apples. Combine apples and sweet cider in a large saucepot. Simmer until apples are soft. Purée using a food processor or food mill, being careful not to liquefy. Measure 3 quarts apple pulp.

To Make Butter: Combine apple pulp, sugar and spices in a large saucepot, stirring until sugar dissolves. Cook slowly until thick enough to round up on a spoon. As mixture thickens, stir frequently to prevent sticking. Ladle hot butter into hot jars, leaving ¼-inch headspace. Remove air bubbles. Adjust two-piece caps. Process 15 minutes in a boiling-water canner.

conserves

Ambrosia Conserve

Yield: about 6 half-pints

1 fresh pineapple, peeled, cored, chopped (about 5 pounds)	5 cups sugar
	1 cup coconut
⅓ cup grated orange peel (about 2 medium)	1 cup chopped maraschino cherries
1 cup orange juice (about 2 medium)	½ cup slivered almonds

Combine pineapple, orange peel and juice in a large saucepot. Simmer 10 minutes. Add sugar, stirring until dissolved. Cook rapidly almost to gelling point. As mixture thickens, stir frequently to prevent sticking. Remove from heat; stir in coconut, cherries and almonds. Ladle hot conserve into hot jars, leaving ¼-inch headspace. Remove air bubbles. Adjust two-piece caps. Process 15 minutes in a boiling-water canner.

Apricot-Orange Conserve

Yield: about 6 half-pints

3½ cups chopped, pitted, peeled apricots (about 12 medium)	1½ cups orange juice (about 3 medium)
	2 tablespoons lemon juice
2 tablespoons finely grated orange peel	3½ cups sugar
	½ cup chopped walnuts

Combine apricots, orange peel, orange juice and lemon juice in a large saucepot. Add sugar, stirring until dissolved. Cook rapidly almost to gelling point. As mixture thickens, stir frequently to prevent sticking. Add nuts the last 5 minutes of cooking; stir well. Remove from heat. Ladle hot conserve into hot jars, leaving ¼-inch headspace. Remove air bubbles. Adjust two-piece caps. Process 10 minutes in a boiling-water canner.

Blueberry Conserve

Yield: about 4 half-pints

2 cups water	½ cup thinly sliced orange (about ½ medium)
4 cups sugar	
⅓ cup thinly sliced lemon (about ½ large)	½ cup raisins
	1 quart blueberries

Bring water and sugar to a boil; add lemon, orange and raisins. Simmer 5 minutes. Stir in blueberries. Cook rapidly almost to gelling point. As mixture thickens, stir frequently to prevent sticking. Ladle hot conserve into hot jars, leaving ¼-inch headspace. Remove air bubbles. Adjust two-piece caps. Process 15 minutes in a boiling-water canner.

Cherry-Raspberry Conserve

Yield: about 4 half-pints

3 cups raspberry pulp	4 cups sugar
3 cups pitted sweet cherries	

To Prepare Pulp: Press raspberries through a sieve or food mill to remove seeds. Measure 3 cups raspberry pulp.

To Make Conserve: Simmer cherries until tender; stir in raspberry pulp. Add sugar, stirring until dissolved. Cook rapidly almost to gelling point. As mixture thickens, stir frequently to prevent sticking. Ladle hot conserve into hot jars, leaving ¼-inch headspace. Remove air bubbles. Adjust two-piece caps. Process 15 minutes in a boiling-water canner.

Cranberry Conserve

Yield: about 4 half-pints

¾ cup chopped and seeded orange (about 1 medium)	½ cup raisins
	3 cups sugar
2 cups water	½ cup chopped walnuts or other nuts
1 quart cranberries	

Combine orange and water in a large saucepot. Cook rapidly until peel is tender. Stir in cranberries and raisins. Add sugar, stirring until dissolved. Bring slowly to a boil. Cook rapidly almost to gelling point. As mixture thickens, stir frequently to prevent sticking. Add nuts the last 5 minutes of cooking; stir well. Ladle hot conserve into hot jars, leaving ¼-inch headspace. Remove air bubbles. Adjust two-piece caps. Process 15 minutes in a boiling-water canner.

Peach Conserve With Rum

Yield: about 2 pints

3 tablespoons slivered orange peel	¾ cup crushed pineapple
⅔ cup chopped and seeded orange pulp (about 1 medium)	½ cup chopped maraschino cherries
½ cup light rum	3 tablespoons lime juice
2 cups chopped, pitted, peeled peaches (about 3 large)	6½ cups sugar
	½ teaspoon salt
	½ teaspoon ginger
	¼ teaspoon mace

Combine orange peel and pulp with just enough water to cover in a small saucepan. Cook until peel is tender; set aside. Put opened container of rum in hot water; set aside. Combine reserved orange mixture with peaches, pineapple, cherries and lime juice in a large saucepot. Add sugar and spices, stirring until sugar dissolves. Cook rapidly almost to gelling point. As mixture thickens, stir frequently to prevent sticking. Remove from heat. Stir in hot rum. Ladle hot conserve into hot jars, leaving ¼-inch headspace. Remove air bubbles. Adjust two-piece caps. Process 15 minutes in a boiling-water canner.

Plum Conserve

Yield: about 5 half-pints

5 cups chopped and pitted plums (about 2 pounds)	1 cup raisins
3 cups sugar	⅓ cup thinly sliced orange peel
1 cup chopped and seeded orange pulp (about 1 large)	1 cup chopped pecans

Combine all ingredients, except pecans, in a large saucepot. Bring slowly to a boil, stirring until sugar dissolves. Cook rapidly almost to gelling point, about 15 minutes. As mixture thickens, stir frequently to prevent sticking. Add nuts the last 5 minutes of cooking. Ladle hot conserve into hot jars, leaving ¼-inch headspace. Remove air bubbles. Adjust two-piece caps. Process 15 minutes in a boiling-water canner.

Rhubarb Conserve

Yield: about 7 half-pints

2 pounds rhubarb	1 cup raisins
¼ cup water	1¼ teaspoons mace
5 cups sugar	2 pouches Ball Liquid Pectin
2 oranges, seeded and finely chopped	½ cup walnuts
1 lemon, seeded and finely chopped	

Wash rhubarb and remove leaves. Dice rhubarb. Combine rhubarb and water in a large saucepot. Simmer 2 minutes. Add sugar, oranges, lemon, raisins and mace, stirring until sugar dissolves. Bring to a rolling boil over medium-high heat. Stir in liquid pectin. Return to a boil. Boil hard 1 minute, stirring constantly. Remove from heat. Stir in walnuts. Ladle hot conserve into hot jars, leaving ¼-inch headspace. Remove air bubbles. Adjust two-piece caps. Process 10 minutes in a boiling-water canner.

Spring Conserve

Yield: about 7 half-pints

1½ cups crushed pineapple	1 tablespoon grated lemon peel
1½ cups crushed strawberries	2 tablespoons lemon juice
1¼ cups diced rhubarb	6½ cups sugar
6 tablespoons Ball Classic Pectin	½ cup chopped pecans
	½ cup light raisins (optional)

Combine pineapple, strawberries, rhubarb, classic pectin, lemon peel and lemon juice in a large saucepot. Bring to a boil over medium-high heat. As mixture thickens, stir frequently to prevent sticking. Add sugar, stirring until sugar dissolves. Return to a rolling boil. Boil hard 1 minute, stirring constantly. Remove from heat. Stir in nuts and raisins, if desired. Ladle hot conserve into hot jars, leaving ¼-inch headspace. Remove air bubbles. Adjust two-piece caps. Process 15 minutes in a boiling-water canner.

jams

Apricot Jam

Yield: about 5 pints

2 quarts crushed and peeled apricots	¼ cup lemon juice
	6 cups sugar

Combine apricots and lemon juice in a large saucepot. Add sugar, stirring until sugar dissolves. Bring slowly to a boil. Cook rapidly to gelling point. As mixture thickens, stir frequently to prevent sticking. Remove from heat. Skim foam if necessary. Ladle hot jam into hot jars, leaving ¼-inch headspace. Adjust two-piece caps. Process 15 minutes in a boiling-water canner.

Berry Jam

Blackberry, Blueberry, Boysenberry, Dewberry, Gooseberry, Loganberry, Raspberry, Youngberry

Yield: about 3 pints

9 cups crushed berries	6 cups sugar

Combine berries and sugar in a large saucepot. Bring slowly to a boil, stirring until sugar dissolves. Cook rapidly to gelling point. As mixture thickens, stir frequently to prevent sticking. Remove from heat. Skim foam if necessary. Ladle hot jam into hot jars, leaving ¼-inch headspace. Adjust two-piece caps. Process 15 minutes in a boiling-water canner.

Note: If seedless jam is preferred, crushed berries may be heated until soft and pressed through a sieve or food mill; measure pulp and proceed as above.

Bing Cherry Jam

Yield: about 6 half-pints

1 quart chopped and pitted Bing cherries	½ teaspoon cinnamon
6 tablespoons Ball Classic Pectin	½ teaspoon cloves
	¼ cup lemon juice
	¼ cup almond liqueur
	4½ cups sugar

Combine all ingredients, except sugar, in a large saucepot. Bring to a boil, stirring constantly. Add sugar, stirring until dissolved. Return to a rolling boil. Boil 2 minutes, stirring constantly. Remove from heat. Skim foam if necessary. Ladle hot jam into hot jars, leaving ¼-inch headspace. Adjust two-piece caps. Process 10 minutes in a boiling-water canner.

Blueberry-Lime Jam

Yield: about 6 half-pints

4½ cups blueberries	5 cups sugar
6 tablespoons Ball Classic Pectin	1 tablespoon grated lime peel
	⅓ cup lime juice

Crush blueberries one layer at a time. Combine crushed blueberries and classic pectin in a large saucepot. Bring to a boil, stirring frequently. Add sugar, stirring until dissolved. Stir in grated lime peel and lime juice. Return to a rolling boil. Boil hard 1 minute, stirring constantly. Remove from heat. Skim foam if necessary. Ladle hot jam into hot jars, leaving ¼-inch headspace. Adjust two-piece caps. Process 15 minutes in a boiling-water canner.

Cherry Jam

Yield: about 8 half-pints

1 quart chopped and pitted sweet or sour cherries	2 tablespoons lemon juice (use only with sweet cherries)
6¼ cups sugar	2 pouches Ball Liquid Pectin

Combine cherries, sugar and lemon juice (if needed) in a large saucepot. Bring to a boil, stirring until sugar dissolves. Stir in liquid pectin. Return to a rolling boil. Boil hard 1 minute, stirring constantly. Remove from heat. Skim foam if necessary. Ladle hot jam into hot jars, leaving ¼-inch headspace. Adjust two-piece caps. Process 10 minutes in a boiling-water canner.

Damson Plum Jam

Yield: about 3 pints

5 cups coarsely chopped Damson plums (about 2 pounds)	3 cups sugar
	¾ cup water

Combine plums, sugar and water in a large saucepot. Bring slowly to a boil, stirring until sugar dissolves. Cook rapidly to gelling point. As mixture thickens, stir frequently to prevent sticking. Remove from heat. Skim foam if necessary. Ladle hot jam into hot jars, leaving ¼-inch headspace. Adjust two-piece caps. Process 15 minutes in a boiling-water canner.

Elderberry Jam

Yield: about 3 pints

2 quarts crushed elderberries	6 cups sugar
	¼ cup vinegar

Combine elderberries, sugar and vinegar in a large saucepot. Bring slowly to a boil, stirring until sugar dissolves. Cook rapidly to gelling point. As mixture thickens, stir frequently to prevent sticking. Remove from heat. Skim foam if necessary. Ladle hot jam into hot jars, leaving ¼-inch headspace. Adjust two-piece caps. Process 15 minutes in a boiling-water canner.

Fig Jam

Yield: about 5 pints

5 pounds figs	¾ cup water
6 cups sugar	¼ cup lemon juice

To Prepare Figs: Completely cover figs with boiling water. Let stand 10 minutes. Drain, stem and chop figs. Measure 2 quarts chopped figs.

To Make Jam: Combine figs, sugar and water in a large saucepot. Bring slowly to a boil, stirring until sugar dissolves. Cook rapidly to gelling point. As mixture thickens, stir frequently to prevent sticking.

Add lemon juice and cook 1 minute longer. Remove from heat. Skim foam if necessary. Ladle hot jam into hot jars, leaving ¼-inch headspace. Adjust two-piece caps. Process 15 minutes in a boiling-water canner.

Grape Jam

Concord, Muscadine, Scuppernong
Yield: about 3 pints

2 quarts grapes	6 cups sugar

To Prepare Pulp: Separate pulp from skins of grapes. Chop skins, if desired. Cook skins gently 15 to 20 minutes, adding only enough water to prevent sticking (about ½ cup). Cook pulp without water until soft. Press through a sieve or food mill to remove seeds.

To Make Jam: Combine pulp, skins and sugar in a large saucepot. Bring slowly to a boil, stirring until sugar dissolves. Cook rapidly to gelling point. As mixture thickens, stir frequently to prevent sticking. Remove from heat. Skim foam if necessary. Ladle hot jam into hot jars, leaving ¼-inch headspace. Adjust two-piece caps. Process 15 minutes in a boiling-water canner.

Kiwi Jam

Yield: about 4 half-pints

3 cups chopped and peeled kiwi	1 cup unsweetened pineapple juice
6 tablespoons Ball Classic Pectin	4 cups sugar

Combine kiwi, classic pectin and pineapple juice in a large saucepot. Bring to a boil, stirring constantly. Add sugar, stirring until dissolved. Return to a rolling boil. Boil hard 1 minute, stirring constantly. Remove from heat. Skim foam if necessary. Ladle hot jam into hot jars, leaving ¼-inch headspace. Adjust two-piece caps. Process 10 minutes in a boiling-water canner.

Mango-Raspberry Jam

Yield: about 7 half-pints

3 cups finely chopped, peeled, pitted mangoes (about 3 pounds)	2 tablespoons lemon juice
	6 tablespoons Ball Classic Pectin
1½ cups crushed red raspberries (about 1½ pints)	5½ cups sugar

Combine mangoes, raspberries, lemon juice and classic pectin in a large saucepot. Bring slowly to a boil over high heat, stirring frequently. Add sugar, stirring until dissolved. Return to a rolling boil. Boil hard 1 minute, stirring constantly. Remove from heat. Skim foam if necessary. Ladle hot jam into hot jars, leaving ¼-inch headspace. Adjust two-piece caps. Process 10 minutes in a boiling-water canner.

Peach Or Pear Jam

Yield: about 8 half-pints

1 quart finely chopped, pitted/cored, peeled peaches or pears	7½ cups sugar ¼ cup lemon juice 1 pouch Ball Liquid Pectin

Combine fruit, sugar and lemon juice in a large saucepot. Bring slowly to a boil, stirring until sugar dissolves. Stir in liquid pectin. Return to a rolling boil. Boil hard 1 minute, stirring constantly. Remove from heat. Skim foam if necessary. Ladle hot jam into hot jars, leaving ¼-inch headspace. Adjust two-piece caps. Process 10 minutes in a boiling-water canner.

Recipe Variation: Add 1 teaspoon whole cloves, ½ teaspoon whole allspice and 1 cinnamon stick tied in a spice bag to jam during cooking. Remove spice bag before filling jars.

Pineapple Jam

Yield: about 3 half-pints

1 quart finely chopped, cored, peeled pineapple (about 5 pounds) 2½ cups sugar	½ lemon, thinly sliced and seeded 1 cup water

Combine all ingredients in a large saucepot. Bring slowly to a boil, stirring until sugar dissolves. Cook rapidly to gelling point. As mixture thickens, stir frequently to prevent sticking. Remove from heat. Skim foam if necessary. Ladle hot jam into hot jars, leaving ¼-inch headspace. Adjust two-piece caps. Process 15 minutes in a boiling-water canner.

Raspberry-Currant Jam

Yield: about 2 pints

2 cups red currant pulp 2 cups crushed red raspberries	3 cups sugar

To Prepare Pulp: Cook currants until soft, adding only enough water to prevent sticking (about ¼ cup). Press through a sieve or food mill.

To Make Jam: Combine currant pulp and raspberries in a large saucepot. Add sugar, stirring until dissolved. Cook rapidly to gelling point. As mixture thickens, stir frequently to prevent sticking. Remove from heat. Skim foam if necessary. Ladle hot jam into hot jars, leaving ¼-inch headspace. Adjust two-piece caps. Process 15 minutes in a boiling-water canner.

Raspberry Jam

Yield: about 8 half-pints

1 quart crushed red raspberries	6½ cups sugar 1 pouch Ball Liquid Pectin

Combine raspberries and sugar in a large saucepot. Bring to a boil over high heat, stirring until sugar dissolves. Stir in liquid pectin. Return to a rolling boil. Boil hard 1 minute, stirring constantly. Remove from heat. Skim foam if necessary. Ladle hot jam into hot jars, leaving ¼-inch headspace. Adjust two-piece caps. Process 10 minutes in a boiling-water canner.

Red Tomato Jam

Yield: about 5 half-pints

6 pounds red tomatoes (about 18 medium) 6 tablespoons Ball Classic Pectin	1 teaspoon grated lemon peel ½ teaspoon salt 2 teaspoons lemon juice 3½ cups sugar

To Prepare Pulp: Wash tomatoes; drain. Remove core and blossom ends. Cut into quarters. Cook tomatoes in a large saucepot until soft. Press through a sieve or food mill; discard seeds and peels. Place tomato pulp in a large saucepot; simmer until reduced to 3 cups.

To Make Jam: Combine tomato pulp, classic pectin, lemon peel, salt, and lemon juice in a large saucepot. Bring to boil over medium-high heat, stirring occasionally. Add sugar, stirring until dissolved. Return to a rolling boil. Boil hard 1 minute, stirring constantly. Remove from heat. Skim foam if necessary. Ladle hot jam into hot jars, leaving ¼-inch headspace. Adjust two-piece caps. Process 10 minutes in a boiling-water canner.

Rhubarb-Orange Jam

Yield: about 7 half-pints

2 oranges 2½ pounds rhubarb, diced	6 tablespoons Ball Classic Pectin 6 cups sugar

Squeeze juice from oranges. Measure juice, adding water if needed to make 1 cup; set aside. Remove white pith from one-half of orange peel. Cut peel into thin slivers. Combine orange peel, orange juice, and rhubarb in a large saucepot. Simmer covered about 3 minutes, or until rhubarb is tender. Stir in classic pectin. Bring to a boil. Add sugar, stirring until dissolved. Return to a rolling boil. Boil hard 1 minute, stirring constantly. Remove from heat. Skim foam if necessary. Ladle hot jam into hot jars, leaving ¼-inch headspace. Adjust two-piece caps. Process 10 minutes in a boiling-water canner.

Strawberry Jam

Yield: about 4 pints　　　　　　　　　　*No added pectin*

2 quarts strawberries	6 cups sugar

Wash strawberries; drain. Remove stems. Crush strawberries one layer at a time. Combine strawberries and sugar in a large saucepot. Bring slowly to a boil, stirring until sugar dissolves. Cook rapidly to gelling point. As mixture thickens, stir frequently to prevent sticking. Remove from heat. Skim foam if necessary. Ladle hot jam into hot jars, leaving ¼-inch headspace. Adjust two-piece caps. Process 15 minutes in a boiling-water canner.

Strawberry Jam

Yield: about 8 half-pints　　　　　　　　*With added pectin*

2 quarts strawberries 6 tablespoons Ball Classic Pectin	¼ cup lemon juice 7 cups sugar

Wash strawberries; drain. Remove stems. Crush strawberries one layer at a time. Combine strawberries, classic pectin and lemon juice in a large saucepot. Bring to a boil, stirring occasionally. Add sugar, stirring until dissolved. Return to a rolling boil. Boil hard 1 minute, stirring constantly. Remove from heat. Skim foam if necessary. Ladle hot jam into hot jars, leaving ¼-inch headspace. Adjust two-piece caps. Process 10 minutes in a boiling-water canner.

Strawberry-Rhubarb Jam

Yield: about 6 half-pints

2 cups crushed strawberries	6 tablespoons Ball
2 cups chopped rhubarb	Classic Pectin
(about 4 stalks)	¼ cup lemon juice
	5½ cups sugar

Combine strawberries, rhubarb, classic pectin and lemon juice in a large saucepot. Bring to a boil over high heat. Add sugar, stirring until dissolved. Return to a rolling boil. Boil hard 1 minute, stirring constantly. Remove from heat. Skim foam if necessary. Ladle hot jam into hot jars, leaving ¼-inch headspace. Adjust two-piece caps. Process 10 minutes in a boiling-water canner.

Sweet Cherry-Loganberry Jam

Yield: about 6 half-pints

2 cups crushed loganberries	6 tablespoons Ball
(about 1¼ pounds)	Classic Pectin
2 cups chopped and pitted	5 cups sugar
dark sweet cherries	
(about 1 pound)	

Combine loganberries, cherries and classic pectin in a large saucepot. Bring to a boil over high heat. Add sugar, stirring until dissolved. Return to a rolling boil. Boil hard 1 minute, stirring constantly. Remove from heat. Skim foam if necessary. Ladle hot jam into hot jars, leaving ¼-inch headspace. Adjust two-piece caps. Process 10 minutes in a boiling-water canner.

Sweet-Tart Gooseberry Jam

Yield: about 7 half-pints

2½ cups crushed tart	6 tablespoons Ball
gooseberries (about 1 quart)	Classic Pectin
2½ cups crushed sweet	2 tablespoons vinegar
gooseberries (about 1 quart)	6 cups sugar

Combine gooseberries, classic pectin and vinegar in a large saucepot. Bring to a boil over high heat. Add sugar, stirring until dissolved. Return to a rolling boil. Boil hard 1 minute, stirring constantly. Remove from heat. Skim foam if necessary. Ladle hot jam into hot jars, leaving ¼-inch headspace. Adjust two-piece caps. Process 10 minutes in a boiling-water canner.

jellies

Apple Jelly

Yield: about 4 half-pints

4 cups apple juice	2 tablespoons lemon juice
(about 3 pounds)	(optional)
3 cups sugar	

To Prepare Juice: Follow instructions for Juice For Jelly, page 30.

To Make Jelly: Put apple juice in a large saucepot. Add sugar and lemon juice, if desired, stirring until sugar dissolves. Bring to a boil over high heat, stirring constantly. Cook to gelling point or until jelly sheets from a spoon (*see page 29*). Remove from heat. Skim foam if necessary. Ladle hot jelly into hot jars, leaving ¼-inch headspace. Adjust two-piece caps. Process 10 minutes in a boiling-water canner.

    Recipe Variation: Tie whole spices such as cloves, allspice and stick cinnamon in a spice bag. Add spice bag when cooking apples before preparing juice. Remove spice bag before straining juice.

Berry Jelly

Blackberry, Boysenberry, Dewberry, Youngberry
Yield: about 5 half-pints

3½ cups berry juice	2 tablespoons lemon juice
(about 3 quarts)	5 cups sugar
6 tablespoons Ball	
Classic Pectin	

To Prepare Juice: Follow instructions for Juice For Jelly, page 30.

To Make Jelly: Combine fruit juice, classic pectin and lemon juice in a large saucepot. Bring to a boil over high heat. Add sugar, stirring until dissolved. Return to a rolling boil. Boil hard 1 minute, stirring constantly. Remove from heat. Skim foam if necessary. Ladle hot jelly into hot jars, leaving ¼-inch headspace. Adjust two-piece caps. Process 10 minutes in a boiling-water canner.

Blackberry Jelly

Yield: about 8 half-pints

4 cups blackberry juice	7½ cups sugar
(about 3 quarts)	2 pouches Ball Liquid Pectin

To Prepare Juice: Follow instructions for Juice For Jelly, page 30.

To Make Jelly: Put blackberry juice in a large saucepot. Add sugar, stirring until dissolved. Bring to a boil over medium-high heat, stirring constantly. Stir in liquid pectin. Return to a rolling boil. Boil hard 1 minute, stirring constantly. Remove from heat. Skim foam if necessary. Ladle hot jelly into hot jars, leaving ¼-inch headspace. Adjust two-piece caps. Process 10 minutes in a boiling-water canner.

Crab Apple Jelly

Yield: about 6 half-pints

4 cups crab apple juice	4 cups sugar
(about 3 pounds)	

To Prepare Juice: Follow instructions for Juice For Jelly, page 30.

To Make Jelly: Put crab apple juice in a large saucepot. Add sugar, stirring until dissolved. Bring to a boil over high heat, stirring constantly. Cook to gelling point or until jelly sheets from a spoon (*see page 29*). Remove from heat. Skim foam if necessary. Ladle hot jelly into hot jars, leaving ¼-inch headspace. Adjust two-piece caps. Process 10 minutes in a boiling-water canner.

Currant Jelly

Yield: about 8 half-pints

5 cups red currant juice	7 cups sugar
(about 5 pounds)	1 pouch Ball Liquid Pectin

To Prepare Juice: Follow instructions for Juice For Jelly, page 30.

To Make Jelly: Put currant juice in a large saucepot. Add sugar, stirring until dissolved. Bring to a boil over high heat, stirring constantly. Stir in liquid pectin. Return to a rolling boil. Boil hard 1 minute, stirring constantly. Remove from heat. Skim foam if necessary. Ladle hot jelly into hot jars, leaving ¼-inch headspace. Adjust two-piece caps. Process 10 minutes in a boiling-water canner.

Grape Jelly

Yield: about 4 half-pints   *No added pectin*

  4 cups Concord grape juice   3 cups sugar
    (about 3½ pounds)

To Prepare Juice: Follow instructions for Juice For Jelly, page 30. To prevent formation of tartrate crystals in grape jelly, let juice stand in a cool place 12 to 24 hours; strain through a damp jelly bag or several layers of cheesecloth to remove crystals that have formed.

To Make Jelly: Put grape juice in a large saucepot. Add sugar, stirring until dissolved. Boil over high heat, stirring constantly. Cook to gelling point or until jelly sheets from a spoon *(see page 29)*. Remove from heat. Skim foam if necessary. Ladle hot jelly into hot jars, leaving ¼-inch headspace. Adjust two-piece caps. Process 10 minutes in a boiling-water canner.

Grape Jelly

Yield: about 7 half-pints   *With added pectin*

  4 cups Concord grape juice   7 cups sugar
    (about 3½ pounds)   1 pouch Ball Liquid Pectin

To Prepare Juice: Follow recipe instructions for Grape Jelly, no pectin added.

To Make Jelly: Put grape juice in a large saucepot. Add sugar, stirring until dissolved. Bring to a boil over high heat, stirring constantly. Stir in liquid pectin. Return to a rolling boil. Boil hard 1 minute, stirring constantly. Remove from heat. Skim foam if necessary. Ladle hot jelly into hot jars, leaving ¼-inch headspace. Adjust two-piece caps. Process 10 minutes in a boiling-water canner.

Green Pepper Jelly

Yield: about 6 half-pints

  7 sweet green peppers   6 tablespoons Ball
  1 jalapeño pepper   Classic Pectin
 1½ cups cider vinegar, divided   ½ teaspoon salt
 1½ cups apple juice   5 cups sugar
                      Green food coloring (optional)

To Prepare Juice: Wash peppers; remove stems and seeds. Cut peppers into ½-inch pieces. Purée half the peppers and ¾ cup vinegar in a food processor or blender. Purée remaining peppers and vinegar. Combine purée and apple juice in a large bowl. Cover and refrigerate overnight. Strain pureed mixture through a damp jelly bag or several layers of cheesecloth. Measure 4 cups juice. Add additional apple juice to make 4 cups, if needed.

To Make Jelly: Combine juice, classic pectin and salt in a large saucepot. Bring to a boil over high heat, stirring constantly. Add sugar, stirring until dissolved. Return to a rolling boil. Boil hard 1 minute, stirring constantly. Remove from heat. Skim foam if necessary. Stir in a few drops of food coloring, if desired. Ladle hot jelly into hot jars, leaving ¼-inch headspace. Adjust two-piece caps. Process 10 minutes in a boiling-water canner.

    Recipe Variation: Substitute sweet red, orange or yellow peppers and red, orange or yellow food coloring for sweet green peppers and green food coloring.

    Note: When cutting or seeding hot peppers, wear rubber gloves to prevent hands from being burned.

Jalapeño Jelly

Yield: about 5 half-pints

  ¾ pound jalapeño peppers   2 pouches Ball Liquid Pectin
  2 cups cider vinegar, divided   Green food coloring (optional)
  6 cups sugar

Wash peppers; drain. Remove stems and seeds. Purée peppers and 1 cup vinegar in a food processor or blender. Combine purée, 1 cup vinegar and sugar in a large saucepot. Bring to a boil; boil 10 minutes, stirring constantly. Stir in liquid pectin. Return to a rolling boil. Boil hard 1 minute, stirring constantly. Remove from heat. Skim foam if necessary. Stir in a few drops of food coloring, if desired. Ladle hot jelly into hot jars, leaving ¼-inch headspace. Adjust two-piece caps. Process 10 minutes in a boiling-water canner.

    Note: When cutting or seeding hot peppers, wear rubber gloves to prevent hands from being burned.

Mint Jelly

Yield: about 4 half-pints

  1 cup firmly packed   2 tablespoons lemon juice
    mint leaves   3 cups sugar
  1 cup boiling water   Green food coloring (optional)
  4 cups apple juice
    (about 3 pounds)

To Prepare Juice: Follow instructions for Juice For Jelly, page 30.

To Make Jelly: Put mint leaves in a bowl; add boiling water; let stand 1 hour. Strain mint leaves, pressing to extract juice. Measure ½ cup mint extract. Combine mint extract, apple juice, and lemon juice in a large saucepot. Add sugar, stirring until dissolved. Bring to a boil over high heat, stirring constantly. Cook to gelling point or until jelly sheets from a spoon *(see page 29)*. Remove from heat. Skim foam if necessary. Stir in a few drops of food coloring, if desired. Ladle hot jelly into hot jars, leaving ¼-inch headspace. Adjust two-piece caps. Process 10 minutes in a boiling-water canner.

Plum Jelly

Yield: about 8 half-pints

 5½ cups plum juice   6 tablespoons Ball
    (about 5 pounds)   Classic Pectin
                    7½ cups sugar

To Prepare Juice: Follow instructions for Juice For Jelly, page 30.

To Make Jelly: Combine plum juice and classic pectin in a large saucepot. Bring to a boil over high heat, stirring frequently. Add sugar, stirring until dissolved. Return to a rolling boil. Boil hard 1 minute, stirring constantly. Remove from heat. Skim foam if necessary. Ladle hot jelly into hot jars, leaving ¼-inch headspace. Adjust two-piece caps. Process 10 minutes in a boiling-water canner.

Pomegranate Jelly

Yield: about 6 half-pints

 3½ cups pomegranate juice   6 tablespoons Ball
    (about 5 pounds)   Classic Pectin
                    5 cups sugar

To Prepare Juice: Cut pomegranates in half. Extract juice from red seeds with a juice reamer. Strain juice through a damp jelly bag or several layers of cheesecloth. Measure 3½ cups juice.

To Make Jelly: Combine pomegranate juice and classic pectin in a large saucepot. Bring to a boil over medium heat, stirring constantly. Add sugar, stirring until dissolved. Return to a rolling boil. Boil hard 1 minute, stirring constantly. Remove from heat. Skim foam if necessary. Ladle hot jelly into hot jars, leaving ¼-inch headspace. Adjust two-piece caps. Process 10 minutes in a boiling-water canner.

Quick Grape Jelly

Yield: about 5 half-pints

3 cups bottled grape juice, unsweetened	6 tablespoons Ball Classic Pectin
	4½ cups sugar

Combine grape juice and classic pectin in a large saucepot. Bring to a boil over high heat. Add sugar, stirring until dissolved. Return to a boil. Boil hard 1 minute, stirring constantly. Remove from heat. Skim foam if necessary. Ladle hot jelly into hot jars, leaving ¼-inch headspace. Adjust two-piece caps. Process 10 minutes in a boiling-water canner.

Tomato Jelly

Yield: about 4 half-pints

3 pounds tomatoes (about 9 medium)	½ teaspoon salt
6 tablespoons Ball Classic Pectin	2 tablespoons bottled lemon juice
1 tablespoon minced crystallized ginger	½ teaspoon hot pepper sauce
	4 cups sugar

To Prepare Juice: Wash tomatoes; drain. Remove core and blossom ends. Cut into quarters. Simmer tomatoes until they are soft and lose their shape. Strain tomatoes through a damp jelly bag or several layers of cheesecloth. Measure 2 cups tomato juice.

To Make Jelly: Combine tomato juice, classic pectin, ginger, salt, lemon juice and hot pepper sauce in a large saucepot. Bring to a boil, stirring occasionally. Add sugar, stirring until dissolved. Return to a rolling boil. Boil hard 1 minute, stirring constantly. Remove from heat. Skim foam if necessary. Ladle hot jelly into hot jars, leaving ¼-inch headspace. Adjust two-piece caps. Process 10 minutes in a boiling-water canner.

marmalades

Carrot-Pineapple-Orange Marmalade

Yield: about 4 half-pints

2 lemons	1 cup shredded carrots
2 cups chopped orange pulp (about 3 medium)	3 cups sugar
	½ teaspoon allspice
1 cup crushed fresh pineapple, drained	¼ teaspoon nutmeg
	1 pouch Ball Liquid Pectin

Peel lemons, removing just a small portion of the white pith. Slice peel into thin strips; set aside. Squeeze juice from lemons and measure ⅓ cup lemon juice. Combine lemon peel, lemon juice, orange pulp, pineapple and carrots into a large saucepot. Add sugar, allspice and nutmeg, stirring until sugar dissolves. Bring to a boil over medium-high heat. Stir in liquid pectin. Return to a rolling boil. Boil hard 1 minute, stirring constantly. Remove from heat. Skim foam if necessary. Slowly stir marmalade 2 minutes. Ladle hot marmalade into hot jars, leaving ¼-inch headspace. Adjust two-piece caps. Process 10 minutes in a boiling-water canner.

Cherry Marmalade

Yield: about 4 half-pints

1 quart pitted sweet cherries	3½ cups sugar
⅔ cup chopped and seeded orange (about 1 medium)	¼ cup lemon juice

Combine cherries, orange, sugar and lemon juice in a large saucepot, stirring until sugar dissolves. Bring to a boil over high heat, stirring constantly. Cook rapidly almost to gelling point. Remove from heat. Skim foam if necessary. Ladle hot marmalade into hot jars, leaving ¼-inch headspace. Adjust two-piece caps. Process in a boiling-water canner 15 minutes.

Citrus Marmalade

Yield: about 5 half-pints

1½ cups thinly sliced grapefruit peel (about 1 medium)	¾ cup chopped orange pulp (about 1 medium)
½ cup thinly sliced orange peel (about 1 medium)	½ cup thinly sliced and seeded lemon (about 1 medium)
3 quarts water, divided	Sugar
1½ cups chopped grapefruit pulp (about 1 medium)	

Combine fruit peels and 1½ quarts water; boil 5 minutes; drain. Add fruit pulp, sliced lemon and 1½ quarts water; boil 5 minutes. Cover and let stand 12 to 18 hours in a cool place. Cook rapidly until peel is tender. Measure fruit and liquid. Add 1 cup sugar for each cup fruit mixture, stirring until sugar dissolves. Bring to a boil over high heat, stirring constantly. Cook rapidly almost to gelling point. As mixture thickens, stir frequently to prevent sticking. Remove from heat. Skim foam if necessary. Ladle hot marmalade into hot jars, leaving ¼-inch headspace. Adjust two-piece caps. Process 10 minutes in a boiling-water canner.

Grapefruit Marmalade

Yield: about 3 half-pints

⅔ cup thinly sliced grapefruit peel (about 1 medium)	6 cups water, divided
	Sugar
1⅓ cups chopped grapefruit pulp (about 1 medium)	

Cover grapefruit peel with 2 cups water; boil 10 minutes; drain. Add chopped pulp and 1 quart water to drained peel; boil 10 minutes. Cover and let stand 12 to 18 hours in a cool place. Cook rapidly until peel is tender. Measure fruit and liquid. Add 1 cup sugar for each cup fruit mixture, stirring until sugar dissolves. Bring to a boil over high heat, stirring constantly. Cook rapidly almost to gelling point. As mixture thickens, stir frequently to prevent sticking. Remove from heat. Skim foam if necessary. Ladle hot marmalade into hot jars, leaving ¼-inch headspace. Adjust two-piece caps. Process 10 minutes in a boiling-water canner.

Herbed Garden Marmalade

Yield: about 5 half-pints

3 cups chopped, seeded, peeled, cored tomatoes (about 3 pounds)	1 tablespoon minced fresh oregano
2 teaspoons slivered lemon peel	6 tablespoons Ball Classic Pectin
1 clove garlic, minced	¼ cup lemon juice
1 tablespoon minced fresh basil	4½ cups sugar

Put tomatoes in a large saucepot. Cover; simmer 10 minutes. Measure 3 cups cooked tomatoes. Combine tomatoes, lemon peel, garlic, herbs, classic pectin and lemon juice in a large saucepot. Bring to a boil, stirring constantly. Add sugar, stirring until dissolved. Return to a rolling boil. Boil hard one minute, stirring constantly. Remove from heat. Skim foam if necessary. Ladle hot marmalade into hot jars, leaving ¼-inch headspace. Adjust two-piece caps. Process 10 minutes in a boiling-water canner.

Kumquat Marmalade

Yield: about 8 half-pints

2 cups thinly sliced kumquats (about 24)	⅓ cup lemon juice
1½ cups chopped orange pulp (about 2 medium)	1½ quarts water
1½ cups sliced orange peel (about 2 medium)	Sugar

Combine all ingredients, except sugar, in a large saucepot, simmer 5 minutes. Cover and let stand 12 to 18 hours in a cool place. Cook rapidly until peel is tender. Measure fruit and liquid. Add 1 cup sugar for each cup fruit mixture, stirring until sugar dissolves. Bring to a boil over high heat, stirring constantly. Cook rapidly almost to gelling point. As mixture thickens, stir frequently to prevent sticking. Remove from heat. Skim foam if necessary. Ladle hot marmalade into hot jars, leaving ¼-inch headspace. Adjust two-piece caps. Process 10 minutes in a boiling-water canner.

Orange-Lemon Marmalade

Yield: about 6 half-pints

3½ cups chopped orange pulp (about 4 large)	3 cups thinly sliced orange peel (about 4 large)
3½ cups thinly sliced and seeded lemon (about 4 large)	1½ quarts water
	Sugar

Combine orange pulp, sliced lemon, orange peel and water in a large saucepot. Simmer 5 minutes. Cover and let stand 12 to 18 hours in a cool place. Cook rapidly until peel is tender. Measure fruit and liquid. Add 1 cup sugar for each cup fruit mixture, stirring until sugar dissolves. Bring to a boil over high heat, stirring constantly. Cook rapidly almost to gelling point. As mixture thickens, stir frequently to prevent sticking. Remove from heat. Skim foam if necessary. Ladle hot marmalade into hot jars, leaving ¼-inch headspace. Adjust two-piece caps. Process 10 minutes in a boiling-water canner.

Orange Marmalade

Yield: about 7 half-pints

2 cups thinly sliced orange peel (about 10 medium)	1 cup thinly sliced and seeded lemon (about 2 medium)
1 quart chopped orange pulp (about 10 medium)	1½ quarts water
	Sugar

Combine all ingredients, except sugar in a large saucepot; simmer 5 minutes. Cover and let stand 12 to 18 hours in a cool place. Cook rapidly until peel is tender. Measure fruit and liquid. Add 1 cup sugar for each cup fruit mixture, stirring until sugar dissolves. Bring to a boil over high heat, stirring constantly. Cook rapidly almost to gelling point. As mixture thickens, stir frequently to prevent sticking. Remove from heat. Skim foam if necessary. Ladle hot marmalade into hot jars, leaving ¼-inch headspace. Adjust two-piece caps. Process 10 minutes in a boiling-water canner.

Prickly Pear Marmalade

Yield: about 6 half-pints

3 cups chopped and seeded oranges (about 2 large)	1 quart water
1 cup thinly sliced and seeded lemon (about 2 medium)	1 quart chopped, peeled, seeded prickly pears (about 9 medium)
	6 cups sugar

Combine oranges, lemon and water in a large saucepot; simmer 5 minutes. Cover and let stand 12 to 18 hours in a cool place. Cook rapidly until peel is tender. Stir in prickly pears. Add sugar, stirring until dissolved. Bring to a boil over high heat, stirring constantly. Cook rapidly almost to gelling point. As mixture thickens, stir frequently to prevent sticking. Remove from heat. Skim foam if necessary. Ladle hot marmalade into hot jars, leaving ¼-inch headspace. Adjust two-piece caps. Process 15 minutes in a boiling-water canner.

Red Onion Marmalade

Yield: about 5 half-pints

1½ cups thinly sliced, halved, peeled red onions	6 tablespoons Ball Classic Pectin
½ cup finely chopped dried cranberries	2 teaspoons grated orange peel
¼ cup light brown sugar	3 cups bottled unsweetened apple juice
¼ cup cider vinegar	4 cups granulated sugar

Sauté onions, cranberries, brown sugar and cider vinegar in a skillet over medium heat, until onions are transparent. Combine onion mixture, classic pectin, orange peel and apple juice in a large saucepot. Bring to a boil over medium-high heat. Add granulated sugar, stirring until dissolved. Return to a rolling boil. Boil hard 1 minute, stirring constantly. Remove from heat. Skim foam if necessary. Ladle hot marmalade into hot jars, leaving ¼-inch headspace. Adjust two-piece caps. Process 15 minutes in a boiling-water canner.

Strawberry-Lemon Marmalade

Yield: about 7 half-pints

¼ cup thinly sliced lemon peel	6 tablespoons Ball Classic Pectin
4 cups crushed strawberries (about 2 quarts)	1 tablespoon lemon juice
	6 cups sugar

Cover lemon peel with water; boil 5 minutes; drain. Combine lemon peel, strawberries, classic pectin and lemon juice in a large saucepot. Bring slowly to a boil. Add sugar, stirring until dissolved. Bring to a rolling boil. Boil hard 1 minute, stirring constantly. Remove from heat. Skim foam if necessary. Ladle hot marmalade into hot jars, leaving ¼-inch headspace. Adjust two-piece caps. Process 10 minutes in a boiling-water canner.

preserves

Apple Preserves

Yield: about 6 half-pints

6 cups sliced, peeled, cored apples	½ cup thinly sliced and seeded lemon (about 1 medium)
1 cup water	4 cups sugar
1 tablespoon lemon juice	2 teaspoons nutmeg
6 tablespoons Ball Classic Pectin	

Combine apples, water and lemon juice in a large saucepot. Cover; simmer 10 minutes. Stir in classic pectin. Bring to a boil, stirring frequently. Add lemon slices and sugar, stirring until sugar dissolves. Return to a rolling boil. Boil hard 1 minute, stirring frequently. Remove from heat. Skim foam if necessary. Stir in nutmeg. Ladle hot preserves into hot jars, leaving ¼-inch headspace. Adjust two-piece caps. Process 10 minutes in a boiling-water canner.

Apricot Preserves

Yield: about 4 half-pints

5 cups halved, pitted, peeled apricots (about 2 pounds)	4 cups sugar
	¼ cup lemon juice

Combine apricots, sugar and lemon juice in a large saucepot. Cover and let stand 4 to 5 hours in a cool place. Bring slowly to a boil, stirring until sugar dissolves. Cook rapidly almost to gelling point. As mixture thickens, stir frequently to prevent sticking. Remove from heat. Skim foam if necessary. Ladle hot preserves into hot jars, leaving ¼-inch headspace. Adjust two-piece caps. Process 15 minutes in a boiling-water canner.

Bar-le-duc (Currant) Preserves

Yield: about 5 half-pints

2 quarts currants	7 cups sugar, divided
1 cup currant juice	

To Prepare Juice: Follow instructions for Juice For Jelly, page 30.

To Make Preserves: Combine currants and juice in a large saucepot. Stir in 4 cups sugar; cook 5 minutes. Cover and let stand 12 to 18 hours in a cool place. Add remaining sugar. Bring slowly to a boil, stirring until sugar dissolves. Cook rapidly almost to gelling point. As mixture thickens, stir frequently to prevent sticking. Remove from heat. Skim foam if necessary. Ladle hot preserves into hot jars, leaving ¼-inch headspace. Adjust two-piece caps. Process 15 minutes in a boiling-water canner.

Berry Preserves

Blackberry, Black Raspberry, Red Raspberry, Loganberry

Yield: about 4 half-pints

2 pounds berries	4 cups sugar

Combine berries and sugar; let stand until juices begin to flow, about 10 minutes. Bring slowly to a boil, stirring until sugar dissolves. Cook rapidly almost to gelling point. As mixture thickens, stir frequently to prevent sticking. Remove from heat. Skim foam if necessary. Ladle hot preserves into hot jars, leaving ¼-inch headspace. Adjust two-piece caps. Process 15 minutes in a boiling-water canner.

Cherry Preserves

Yield: about 4 half-pints

2 pounds pitted red cherries	4 cups sugar

Drain juice from cherries; set cherries aside. Add sugar to juice (if there is not enough juice to dissolve sugar, add a little water); cook until sugar dissolves, stirring occasionally. Add cherries; cook rapidly until cherries become glossy. Cover and let stand 12 to 18 hours in a cool place. Bring to a boil. Boil hard 1 minute, stirring constantly. Remove from heat. Skim foam if necessary. Ladle hot preserves into hot jars, leaving ¼-inch headspace. Adjust two-piece caps. Process 15 minutes in a boiling-water canner.

Citron Melon Preserves

Yield: about 3 half-pints

1½ quarts prepared citron melon (about 2 pounds)	1 quart water
4 cups sugar, divided	½ cup thinly sliced and seeded lemon (about 1 medium)

To Prepare Melon: The outer part of the citron melon is superior for preserves. The inner part may be used, but should be prepared separately. Cut outer part crosswise into ¾-inch slices; trim off green peel. Cut rind into 1-inch pieces. Remove seeds from inner part; cut into 1-inch pieces. Add 2 cups sugar to water; bring to a boil. Add citron and cook rapidly until tender. Cover and let stand 12 to 18 hours in a cool place.

To Make Preserves: Add remaining sugar and lemon to citron melon mixture. Boil gently until melon is transparent and syrup is thick. Remove from heat. Skim foam if necessary. Ladle hot preserves into hot jars, leaving ¼-inch headspace. Adjust two-piece caps. Process 15 minutes in a boiling-water canner.

Note: If the syrup becomes too thick, add a small amount of boiling water. If syrup is too thin and citron melon is fully cooked, remove citron melon from syrup; set aside. Boil syrup until desired thickness. Return citron melon to syrup and heat throughout.

Cranberry-Apple Preserves

Yield: about 9 half-pints

2 pounds cranberries	3 cups sugar
3 green apples, cored, peeled, chopped	2 cups water
1 orange, seeded and chopped	½ cup honey

Combine all ingredients in a large saucepot. Bring slowly to a boil, stirring until sugar dissolves. Boil gently almost to gelling point. Remove from heat. Skim foam if necessary. Ladle hot preserves into hot jars, leaving ¼-inch headspace. Adjust two-piece caps. Process in a boiling-water canner 15 minutes.

Fig Preserves

Yield: about 6 half-pints

2 quarts figs	1 quart water
2 quarts boiling water	1 lemon, thinly sliced and
2⅔ cups sugar	seeded

Pour boiling water over figs. Let stand 15 minutes. Drain. Rinse figs in cold water; drain. Combine sugar, 1 quart water and lemon slices in a large saucepot. Boil 10 minutes. Skim syrup; remove and discard lemon slices. Dip figs into syrup a few at a time. Cook rapidly until figs are transparent. Remove figs and place in a shallow pan. Boil syrup until thick, pour over figs and let stand 6 to 8 hours. Reheat figs and syrup to boiling. Remove from heat. Skim foam if necessary. Ladle hot preserves into hot jars, leaving ¼-inch headspace. Adjust two-piece caps. Process 10 minutes in a boiling-water canner.

Kiwi Preserves

Yield: about 3 half-pints

4 kiwi, peeled and sliced	¼ cup lime juice
⅛-inch thick	1 pouch Ball Liquid Pectin
3 cups sugar	
¾ cup unsweetened	
pineapple juice	

Combine kiwi, sugar, pineapple juice and lime juice in a large saucepot, stirring until sugar dissolves. Bring to a boil, stirring frequently. Stir in liquid pectin. Return to a rolling boil. Boil hard 1 minute, stirring constantly. Remove from heat. Skim foam if necessary. Ladle hot preserves into hot jars, leaving ¼-inch headspace. Adjust two-piece caps. Process in a boiling-water canner 10 minutes.

Peach Preserves

Yield: about 9 half-pints

4 cups sliced, pitted, peeled	2 tablespoons lemon juice
peaches (about 4 pounds)	7 cups sugar
6 tablespoons Ball	
Classic Pectin	

Combine peaches, classic pectin and lemon juice in a large saucepot. Bring to a boil, stirring gently. Add sugar, stirring until dissolved. Return to a rolling boil. Boil hard 1 minute, stirring constantly. Remove from heat. Skim foam if necessary. Ladle hot preserves into hot jars, leaving ¼-inch headspace. Adjust two-piece caps. Process 10 minutes in a boiling-water canner.

Pear Preserves

Yield: about 5 half-pints

3 cups sugar, divided	½ cup thinly sliced and seeded
3 cups water	lemon (about 1 medium)
6 medium halved or quartered,	
peeled, cored pears	
(about 2 pounds)	

Combine 1½ cups sugar and water in a large saucepot. Cook rapidly 2 minutes. Add pears; boil gently 15 minutes. Add remaining sugar and sliced lemon, stirring until sugar dissolves. Cook rapidly until fruit is transparent. Cover and let stand 12 to 24 hours in a cool place. Remove pears from syrup, set aside. Cook syrup 5 minutes or longer, to thicken. Remove from heat. Skim foam if necessary. Pack pears into hot jars, leaving ¼-inch headspace. Ladle hot syrup over pears, leaving ¼-inch headspace.

Adjust two-piece caps. Process 20 minutes in a boiling-water canner.

Note: If Seckel pears are used, preserve whole with stem intact. Kiefers should be stored in a cool, dry place 3 to 5 weeks before using. A piece of candied ginger may be added to each jar.

Plum Preserves

Yield: about 5 half-pints

5 cups pitted tart plums	4 cups sugar
(about 2½ pounds)	1 cup water

Combine all ingredients in a large saucepot. Bring slowly to a boil, stirring until sugar dissolves. Cook rapidly almost to gelling point. As mixture thickens, stir frequently to prevent sticking. Remove from heat. Skim foam if necessary. Ladle hot preserves into hot jars, leaving ¼-inch headspace. Adjust two-piece caps. Process 15 minutes in a boiling-water canner.

Quince Preserves

Yield: about 4 half-pints

7 cups quartered, peeled,	3 cups sugar
cored quinces	2 quarts water
(about 3 pounds)	

When preparing quinces, discard all gritty parts. Combine sugar and water in a large saucepot. Boil 5 minutes. Add quinces; cook until fruit is transparent and syrup is almost to gelling point. As mixture thickens, stir frequently to prevent sticking. Remove from heat. Skim foam if necessary. Ladle hot preserves into hot jars, leaving ¼-inch headspace. Adjust two-piece caps. Process 15 minutes in a boiling-water canner.

Red Raspberry-Currant Preserves

Yield: about 7 half-pints

3 cups red raspberries	6½ cups sugar
1 cup red currant juice	1 pouch Ball Liquid Pectin
¼ cup raspberry liqueur	

To Prepare Juice: Follow instructions for Juice For Jelly, page 30.

To Make Preserves: Combine raspberries, currant juice and raspberry liqueur in a large saucepot. Bring mixture to a simmer. Add sugar, stirring until dissolved. Bring to a boil. Stir in liquid pectin. Return to a rolling boil. Boil hard 1 minute, stirring constantly. Remove from heat. Skim foam if necessary. Ladle hot preserves into hot jars, leaving ¼-inch headspace. Adjust two-piece caps. Process 10 minutes in a boiling-water canner.

Sour Cherry Preserves

Yield: about 6 half-pints

3 pounds pitted red	6 tablespoons Ball
sour cherries	Classic Pectin
	5 cups sugar

Combine cherries and classic pectin in a large saucepot. Bring to a boil, stirring frequently. Add sugar, stirring until dissolved. Bring to a rolling boil. Boil hard 1 minute, stirring constantly. Remove from heat. Skim foam if necessary. Stir 3 minutes to distribute fruit. Ladle hot preserves into hot jars, leaving ¼-inch headspace. Adjust two-piece caps. Process 15 minutes in a boiling-water canner.

Strawberry Preserves

Yield: about 7 half-pints   *With added pectin*

2 quarts strawberries	¼ cup finely chopped and
6 tablespoons Ball	seeded lemon
Classic Pectin	(about 1 medium)
	¼ cup water
	6½ cups sugar

Combine all ingredients, except sugar, in a large saucepot. Bring to a boil, stirring occasionally. Add sugar, stirring until dissolved. Return to a rolling boil. Boil hard 1 minute, stirring frequently. Remove from heat. Skim foam if necessary. Stir 3 minutes to distribute fruit. Ladle hot preserves into hot jars, leaving ¼-inch headspace. Adjust two-piece caps. Process 15 minutes in a boiling-water canner.

Heirloom Strawberry Preserves

Yield: about 4 half-pints   *No added pectin*

1½ quarts strawberries	⅓ cup lemon juice
5 cups sugar	

Combine strawberries and sugar in a large saucepot. Let stand 3 to 4 hours. Bring slowly to a boil, stirring until sugar dissolves. Add lemon juice. Cook rapidly until strawberries are transparent and syrup is thick. Ladle into a shallow pan. Let stand, uncovered, 12 to 24 hours in a cool place. Stir occasionally to distribute strawberries throughout syrup. Heat strawberries and syrup until hot throughout. Remove from heat. Skim foam if necessary. Ladle hot preserves into hot jars, leaving ¼-inch headspace. Adjust two-piece caps. Process 20 minutes in a boiling-water canner.

Tomato Preserves

Yield: about 6 half-pints

1½ quarts small yellow,	1 (½-inch) piece fresh ginger
green or red tomatoes	4 cups sugar
(about 2 pounds)	1 cup thinly sliced and seeded
1 tablespoon Ball Mixed	lemon (about 2 medium)
Pickling Spice	¾ cup water

Wash and peel tomatoes; drain. Tie spices and fresh ginger in a spice bag. Combine spice bag, sugar, lemon and water in a large saucepot. Simmer 15 minutes. Add tomatoes; cook gently until tomatoes become transparent, stirring frequently to prevent sticking. Remove from heat. Cover and let stand 12 to 18 hours in a cool place. Remove spice bag. Remove tomatoes and lemon from syrup. Boil syrup 3 minutes or longer to thicken. Return tomatoes and lemon to syrup; boil 1 minute. Remove from heat. Skim foam if necessary. Ladle hot preserves into hot jars, leaving ¼-inch headspace. Adjust two-piece caps. Process 20 minutes in a boiling-water canner.

Watermelon Rind Preserves

Yield: about 6 half-pints

1½ quarts prepared	4 cups sugar
watermelon rind	¼ cup lemon juice
4 tablespoons salt	½ cup thinly sliced and seeded
3½ quarts water, divided	lemon (about 1 medium)
1 tablespoon ginger	

To Prepare Rind: Trim green peel and pink flesh from thick watermelon rind. Cut rind into 1-inch pieces. Dissolve salt in 2 quarts water. Pour salted water over rind. Let stand 5 to 6 hours. Drain; rinse; drain again. Cover rind with cold water and let stand 30 minutes. Drain. Sprinkle ginger over rind. Cover with water. Cook until tender. Drain.

To Make Preserves: Combine sugar, lemon juice and 1½ quarts water in a large saucepot. Boil 5 minutes. Add rind. Boil gently until rind is transparent and syrup thickens. Add sliced lemon, cook 5 minutes. Remove from heat. Skim foam if necessary. Ladle hot preserves into hot jars, leaving ¼-inch headspace. Adjust two-piece caps. Process 20 minutes in a boiling-water canner.

Western Special Preserves

Yield: about 5 half-pints

1 cup red currants	2 cups loganberries
1 cup water	2 cups red raspberries
5 cups sugar	2 cups pitted sweet cherries

To Prepare Juice: Crush currants. Combine currants and water in a large saucepot. Cover; simmer currants until soft. Strain mixture through a damp jelly bag or several layers of cheesecloth to extract juice.

To Make Preserves: Add sugar to currant juice, stirring until dissolved. Cook rapidly 5 minutes. Stir in remaining fruit. Cook over medium-high heat almost to gelling point, about 30 minutes. As mixture thickens, stir frequently to prevent sticking. Remove from heat. Skim foam if necessary. Ladle hot preserves into hot jars, leaving ¼-inch headspace. Adjust two-piece caps. Process 15 minutes in a boiling-water canner.

featured prepared recipe

Sunrise Muffins

Yield: about 12 muffins

2 cups all-purpose flour,	1 cup brown sugar, divided
divided	½ cup unsalted butter, divided
1 cup quick cooking	1 egg
rolled oats	1¼ cups milk
1½ teaspoons baking powder	½ cup light raisins
1 teaspoon cinnamon	¼ cup Carrot-Pineapple-Orange
½ teaspoon allspice	Marmalade *(recipe on page 37)*
¾ teaspoon baking soda	1 cup finely chopped walnuts
¼ teaspoon salt	

Combine 1½ cups flour, rolled oats, baking powder, cinnamon, allspice, baking soda and salt in a medium bowl; set aside. Soften ¼ cup butter. Combine softened butter, ½ cup brown sugar and egg; mix well. Add flour mixture and milk alternately to sugar mixture, stirring after each addition. Stir in raisins. Fill greased muffin cups ½ full with batter. Spoon 1 teaspoon of marmalade into center of each muffin. Carefully spoon batter over marmalade to cover; set aside. Combine ½ cup flour, walnuts and ½ cup brown sugar in a small bowl. Cut ¼ cup butter into dry ingredients with a pastry blender just until mixture is uniformly coarse. Sprinkle topping over muffins. Bake at 375°F for 25 minutes or until muffins test done. Cool 5 minutes; remove from pan and cool completely.

canning soft spreads step-by-step

1. Read recipe instructions; assemble equipment and ingredients before starting. Follow guidelines for recipe preparation, jar size, canning method and processing time. Do not make changes in recommended guidelines.

2. Visually examine canning jars for nicks, cracks, uneven rims or sharp edges that may prevent sealing or cause breakage. Examine canning lids to ensure they are free of dents and sealing compound is even and complete. Check bands for proper fit.

3. Wash jars and two-piece caps in hot, soapy water. Rinse well. Dry bands; set aside. Heat jars and lids in a saucepot of simmering water (180°F). DO NOT BOIL LIDS. Allow jars and lids to remain in hot water until ready for use, removing one at a time as needed.

4. Fill boiling-water canner half-full with hot water. Elevate rack in canner. Put canner lid in place. Heat water just to a simmer (180°F). Keep water hot until used for processing.

5. Select fresh strawberries at their peak of quality and flavor. Wash strawberries; dry completely. Remove stems and white under-ripe portions.

6. Crush strawberries, one layer at a time, using a potato masher. Crushed strawberries should be a combination of fruit pulp and fruit juice. Over crushing strawberries may add too much liquid for the recipe to gel. Measure remaining ingredients so they are ready when needed.

7. Combine crushed strawberries with remaining ingredients as instructed by a recipe in this book or on pectin insert. Do not alter ingredient measurements or omit ingredients as this will prevent jam from forming a gel. Use only the type of pectin listed in the recipe.

8. Bring mixture to a rolling boil, one that cannot be stirred down, and cook for the time given in the recipe. Turn off heat. Remove foam using a skimmer or slotted spoon.

9. Remove canning jar from hot water with a jar lifter; set jar on towel. Carefully ladle hot jam into hot jars, leaving ¼ inch headspace.

10. Wipe rim and threads of jar with a clean, damp cloth. Remove lid from hot water using a lid wand. Place lid on jar, centering sealing compound on rim. Screw band down evenly and firmly, just until resistance is met—fingertip tight.

11. As each jar is filled, set it onto the elevated rack in the boiling-water canner. Water in canner should be kept at a simmer (180°F). After all jars are filled and placed onto the rack, lower rack into canner. Water level must cover the two-piece caps on the jars by 1 to 2 inches. Add boiling water, if necessary.

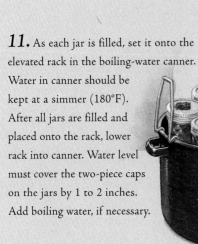

12. Put lid on canner. Bring water to a boil. Start counting processing time after water comes to a rolling boil. Process 10 minutes, at a gentle but steady boil for altitudes at or below 1,000 feet above sea level. For higher altitude areas, refer to Altitude Chart (*see page 5*).

13. When processing time is complete, turn off heat and remove canner lid. Let canner cool 5 minutes before removing jars. Remove jars from canner and set them upright, 1 to 2 inches apart, on a dry towel to cool. Do not retighten bands. Let jars cool 12 to 24 hours.

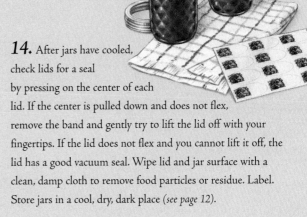

14. After jars have cooled, check lids for a seal by pressing on the center of each lid. If the center is pulled down and does not flex, remove the band and gently try to lift the lid off with your fingertips. If the lid does not flex and you cannot lift it off, the lid has a good vacuum seal. Wipe lid and jar surface with a clean, damp cloth to remove food particles or residue. Label. Store jars in a cool, dry, dark place (*see page 12*).

pickled foods

Chutneys, Pickles & Relishes

Take a break from standard fare. Spread spicy Curried Apple Chutney over a ham steak, crunch into a Sweet Cucumber Pickle, or dress a hot dog with a generous portion of Piccalilli or Green Tomato Relish. From the first to the last savory bite, you'll be amazed at the explosion of flavor in every spoonful.

Pickles, relishes and chutneys are a welcome addition to any gathering. Casual dining sports a sense of elegance with our Antipasto Platter, featuring Pickled Grape Tomatoes, Onion Pickles, and Pickled Mixed Peppers. Add fresh mozzarella, aged salami, and whole mushrooms; then blend the flavors with a drizzle of herb marinade.

Far from the ordinary, Peach Pickles will surprise your guests, with a taste sensation that marries the spicy tang of cloves and ginger with sweet cinnamon and sugar. Your buffet hits just the right note when you include these sweet, spicy, salty and sour offerings, all blended in perfect harmony.

Colorful relishes, pickles and chutneys preserved in decorative Ball Jars: Traditional Style, Quilted Crystal, and Collection Elite are pretty enough to place on the table for serving. In fact, grouped together, they make a gorgeous centerpiece and the perfect parting gift—a delicious memento of the evening's festivities.

The conversation naturally turns to the bountiful spread at hand. Pickled foods present a surprising and striking accent to any meal. And, as your friends and family dive in, the enjoyment you see on their faces translates into deep satisfaction. Along with your homemade treasures, you have also served up a reminder that summer's goodness will come again.

Pictured, Antipasto Platter featuring Pickled Pepper Mix,
Onion Pickles & Pickled Grape Tomatoes.
The Onion Pickles recipe is found on page 56.
Recipes for Pickled Pepper Mix, Pickled Grape
Tomatoes and for the Antipasto Platter
are found on page 57.

getting started

When we speak of pickles, many of us think only of cucumber pickles. But in canning terms, pickling includes any fruit, meat or vegetable prepared by a pickling process. Pickled foods are either fermented in brine (salt) or packed in vinegar to aid preservation. Heat processing is also required to destroy microorganisms that can cause spoilage and inactivate enzymes that may affect flavor, color and texture.

Processing procedures for fermented cucumbers and fresh pack dills are slightly different than the usual boiling-water method. Bring the water to a rolling boil before lowering jars into canner. Start to count the processing time as soon as the filled jars are lowered into the boiling water. Process for the length of time specified by the tested recipe you are following. This method helps to reduce the cooked flavor and a loss of crispness. All other pickles are processed in a boiling-water canner with the processing time beginning when the water comes to a rolling boil.

The boiling-water processing times given for pickled foods in this section are for processing at or below altitudes of 1,000 feet above sea level. For higher altitude areas, adjustments in processing time must be made, refer to Altitude Chart (see page 5).

Pickled foods are generally grouped into five categories:

Brined Pickle

Brined or fermented pickles are made using vegetables, usually cucumbers, that are submerged in a salt water solution to ferment or cure for up to 6 weeks. Lactic acid produced during fermentation helps preserve brined pickles. Dill, garlic and other herbs and spices are often added to the pickling brine for flavoring.

Fresh Pack Pickle

Fresh pack pickles are sometimes brined in a salt water solution for several hours or overnight. After the salt water solution is drained, the cucumbers or vegetables are covered with a boiling hot pickling liquid made of vinegar, spices and herbs.

Relish

Relish is prepared using chopped fruits and/or vegetables cooked in a spicy vinegar solution. Sometimes sugar is added if a sweet relish is desired. Often hot peppers or other spices are added to flavor relish.

Fruit Pickle

Fruit pickles are usually prepared from whole fruits. The fruit is simmered in a spicy, sweet-sour syrup until it becomes tender or transparent.

Chutney And Sauce

Both of these categories are a combination of vegetables and/or fruits, spices and vinegar cooked for long periods to develop flavor and texture. Chutneys are highly spiced and have a sweet-sour blending of flavors. Sauces range from mild to hot.

Ingredients And Preparation

Pickling requires quality ingredients, accurate measurements, daily maintenance and temperature control to achieve satisfactory results. The ingredients and procedures may be right; but, if the correct proportions of sugar, salt, vinegar and spices are not maintained, the quality and safety can be affected.

Fruits And Vegetables

Ideally, fruits and vegetables should be harvested no more than 24 hours before pickling. If preparation is delayed, the produce should be refrigerated until ready for use. Cucumbers, especially, deteriorate rapidly at room temperature.

Select tender vegetables and firm fruit. Unlike other areas of canning, some pickling recipes may specifically call for slightly under-ripe fruits and vegetables for pickling, such as pears, peaches and green tomatoes. Produce should be of the ideal size for the recipe being prepared; and, each fruit or vegetable should be of uniform size.

When making cucumber pickles, use only a pickling-variety cucumber. Other varieties of cucumbers may be good choices for relishes or chutneys, but they often do not make good pickles. Do not use waxed cucumbers since the brine cannot penetrate the wax coating.

Salt

Salt acts as a preservative and adds flavor and crispness to pickles. Use a pure granulated salt for brined and fresh pack pickles. Pure granulated salt like Ball Salt for Pickling and Preserving does not contain iodine or non-caking additives that may cause pickles to darken or brine to become cloudy.

Vinegar

Vinegar gives pickles a tart taste and acts as a preservative. All recipes in this book are developed to be prepared using a high-grade cider or white distilled vinegar of 5 percent (50 grain) acidity. Vinegar of unknown acidity must not be used since its preservative ability is unknown. Cider vinegar imparts a mellow acid flavor while white vinegar gives a sharp pungent acidic taste to pickled foods. Since cider vinegar may discolor produce, use white vinegar when color retention is important. Vinegar must not be diluted unless specified in the recipe. Never decrease the amount of vinegar as the preservative balance will be compromised.

Sugar

Use granulated cane or beet sugar unless the recipe calls for another sweetener. Brown sugar, honey and maple syrup are sometimes called for in a recipe. Sugar substitutes are not recommended unless the manufacturer's specific instructions for pickling are followed.

Spices, Herbs and Crisping Agents

Fresh spices and herbs add immeasurably to the unique flavor of pickles. Each recipe will specify the type of spice or herb to use. Seasoning can be added directly to pickling mixtures; but often, spices and herbs are tied in a spice bag or cheesecloth and held in the solution to impart their flavor, similar to a tea bag. Ball Pickle Crisp is an easy way to add extra crunch to fresh pack pickles and pickled vegetables. Simply measure the granules into each jar following the label instructions. There is no pre-soaking required.

Water

Soft water must be used for making brine. The minerals in hard water will have a negative effect on the quality of pickles. If soft tap water is not available, water can be softened by boiling for 15 minutes and then letting it stand for 24 hours. A scum will likely appear on the top of the water. Remove the scum and ladle water from the container being careful not to disturb any sediment that settled to the bottom. Distilled water can also be used.

Equipment And Utensils

Very little specialized equipment is needed for pickling. Utensils made of zinc, iron, brass, copper, galvanized metal or enamelware with cracks or chips in the enamel should not be used. The metal in these utensils may react with acids or salts and cause undesirable color and taste changes in pickles, making pickles unfit to eat.

For the fresh pack method, which uses vinegar as the pickling ingredient, almost any large container in good condition is suitable. This includes unchipped enamelware, stainless steel, glassware or food-grade plastic.

For fermenting and brining, a crock or stone jar, an unchipped enamel-lined pan, a large glass jar or bowl can be used for small quantities. An enamel, glass or paraffin-lined hardwood keg or barrel can be used for large recipes.

The container must be fitted with an undersized lid. This allows the lid to sit directly on the food and holds the food below the surface of the brine. A glass jar filled with water and closed with a two-piece cap makes a good weight to hold the lid in place and keep cucumbers submerged.

Another method for covering fermenting products consists of placing a food-grade plastic bag filled with a salt brine over the food. The brine for the food-grade bag should be made of 1½ tablespoons salt per 1 quart water. The brine-filled bag seals the surface from exposure to air, prevents the growth of film, yeast or molds and serves as a weight. For extra protection, the brine-filled bag can be placed inside another food-grade plastic bag. Adjust the amount of brine in the plastic bag to provide just enough pressure to keep the fermenting product under the brine.

General Information

Selecting quality cucumbers, accurate measurements of ingredients, daily maintenance of the brine and proper fermentation temperature are all critical factors that must be executed correctly in order to have successful brining results. Carelessness in performing any of these functions increases the possibility of unfit pickles and spoilage.

Select only quality cucumbers that have just reached their peak of flavor and ripeness. Discard cucumbers that are diseased, shriveled, misshapen or float when washed. Fruits and vegetables must be washed thoroughly in cold water. Wash whole before peeling. Use a brush, and scrub under running water or through several rinses. Clinging soil may contain bacteria that are hard to destroy. Remove ¹⁄₁₆-inch from blossom end of cucumbers. It may be the source of enzymes which could soften the cucumbers during fermentation. Stem end does not have to be removed.

Cucumbers take up to 6 weeks to ferment. During fermentation cucumbers must be weighted under the brine at all times. Place the pickling container in a location that will maintain a consistent temperature between 70° and 75°F. As the cucumbers ferment, a scum may form on the top of the brine. Check the pickling container daily. Carefully remove all scum that has accumulated. If left unattended, the scum can reduce the acidity of the brine and cause spoilage. Prior to using brined cucumbers in a pickle recipe, the cucumbers must be desalted.

Brining Cucumbers

1. Weigh cucumbers; keep a record of starting weight. Wash cucumbers and remove ¹⁄₁₆-inch from blossom end. Put cucumbers in a clean pickling container. Make a 10 percent brine by dissolving 1 cup canning salt in 2 quarts water. Pour brine over cucumbers and weight cucumbers under brine.

2. On the second day add 1 cup canning salt for each 5 pounds of cucumbers. This will maintain the 10 percent brine required for fermentation. Add canning salt by placing it on a plate or cloth positioned on top of the cucumbers for even distribution of the salt. Do not pour canning salt directly on the cucumbers.

3. At the end of the first week, add ¼ cup canning salt for each 5 pounds of cucumbers. Repeat adding ¼ cup canning salt for each 5 pounds of cucumbers for the next 4 to 5 weeks.

4. Fermentation resulting in bubble formation or scum should continue for about 4 weeks. Remove scum daily. To determine when fermentation is complete, test for bubbles by tapping container on the side with your hand. Any bubbles rising to the surface indicates the cucumbers are still fermenting. As a second test, cut a cucumber in half to evaluate the coloring. An even consistent color throughout indicates fermentation is complete. If rings or white spots are noticeable, the cucumbers require additional time to ferment.

Desalting Cucumbers

1. Remove cucumbers from brine solution. Measure volume of cucumbers. Submerge cucumbers in hot (180°F) water, using at least 3 times as much water as cucumbers. Let stand about 4 hours, stirring occasionally. Lift cucumbers out of water. Discard water and rinse container. Repeat 2 times.

2. Lift cucumbers from final soak. Prick cucumbers in several places. Pricking will help prevent shriveling when cucumbers are pickled.

3. Put cucumbers in a solution of 1 part water to 3 parts vinegar and let stand for 12 hours. Taste cucumbers to determine if sufficient salt has been removed; if not, let stand 12 hours longer. When desalting is complete, the cucumbers are ready to be used in a pickling recipe.

Note: As an alternative method of desalting, brined cucumbers can be soaked in cold water. Use 3 or 4 times as much water as cucumbers. Change the water every 8 hours, stirring cucumbers occasionally. The salt should be removed within a 24-hour period.

brined pickled vegetables
Brined Dill Pickles

Yield: about 6 quarts

10 pounds 4- to 6-inch cucumbers	1½ cups Ball Salt
¾ cup Ball Mixed Pickling Spice, divided	2 cups vinegar
	2 gallons water
2 to 3 bunches fresh or dried dill, divided	6 cloves garlic (optional)

Wash and drain cucumbers. Place half the mixed pickling spice and one layer of dill in a clean pickling container. Add cucumbers to within 4 inches of top. Combine salt, vinegar and water; ladle over cucumbers. Place a layer of dill and remaining pickling spice over the top. Add garlic, if desired. Weight cucumbers under brine.

Store container in a cool place. Let cucumbers ferment until well flavored with dill and clear throughout. Pickles should be ready to can in about 2 to 3 weeks.

Remove pickles from brine. Strain the brine; bring to a boil in a large saucepot. Pack pickles into hot jars, leaving ½-inch headspace. Ladle hot liquid over pickles, leaving ½-inch headspace. Remove air bubbles.

Adjust two-piece caps. Process 15 minutes in a boiling-water canner.

Recipe Variation: To make Kosher-Style Pickles, pack cucumbers into hot jars, adding 1 bay leaf, 1 clove garlic, 1 piece hot red pepper and ½ teaspoon mustard seed to each jar. Ladle hot liquid over cucumbers. Process as recommended.

You may use desalted, brined cucumbers in this recipe by making a few recipe changes. Reduce salt to ¼ cup. Allow desalted cucumbers to stand in pickling brine for 3 weeks. Drain the brine, heat to boiling and pour over cucumbers once a week during each week of stand time.

Note: When cutting or seeding hot peppers, wear rubber gloves to prevent hands from being burned.

Cucumber Chips

Yield: about 3 pints

6 pounds 4- to 5-inch cucumbers, cut into ¼-inch slices	2 cups granulated sugar
½ cup Ball Salt	2 sticks cinnamon
1 tablespoon turmeric	1 ¼- x 1-inch piece fresh ginger
1 quart plus 3 cups vinegar, divided	1 tablespoon mustard seed
1 quart plus 1 cup water, divided	1 teaspoon whole cloves
	2 cups brown sugar

Put cucumber slices in a large bowl; sprinkle salt over cucumber slices; mix thoroughly. Let stand 3 hours. Drain; rinse and drain thoroughly. Combine turmeric, 3 cups vinegar and 1 quart water in a saucepot; bring to a boil; pour over cucumbers. Let stand until cold; drain. Taste cucumbers; if too salty, rinse thoroughly; drain. Combine granulated sugar, 1 quart vinegar and 1 cup water in a large saucepot. Tie spices in a spice bag; add to pickling liquid. Simmer 15 minutes; pour pickling liquid over cucumbers. Let stand 12 to 24 hours in a cool place. Remove spice bag and pickles; discard spice bag. Combine pickling liquid and brown sugar in a large saucepot; bring to a boil. Pack cucumber slices into hot jars, leaving ½-inch headspace. Ladle hot liquid over cucumbers, leaving ½-inch headspace. Remove air bubbles. Adjust two-piece caps. Process 10 minutes in a boiling-water canner.

Cucumber Chunks

Yield: about 8 pints

5 pounds 3- to 4-inch cucumbers, cut into 1-inch slices	2 quarts plus 1 cup vinegar, divided
1½ cups Ball Salt	4 to 5 cups sugar, divided
4 quarts plus 3 cups water, divided	2 tablespoons Ball Mixed Pickling Spice

Put cucumber slices in a clean pickling container. Dissolve salt in 4 quarts water. Pour over cucumber slices. Weight cucumbers under brine. Cover container and let stand 36 hours in a cool place. Drain; rinse and drain thoroughly. Discard brine. Pour 1 quart vinegar over cucumbers; add water to cover. Simmer 10 minutes. Drain, discarding liquid. Combine 2 cups sugar, 5 cups vinegar and 3 cups water in a large saucepot. Tie spice in a spice bag; add to vinegar mixture. Simmer 10 minutes. Pour pickling liquid over cucumbers; cover and let stand 24 hours. Drain, reserving pickling liquid; add remaining 2 to 3 cups sugar to pickling liquid according to taste; bring to a boil; pour over cucumbers. Cover; let stand 24 hours. Remove spice bag and pickles; discard spice bag. Bring pickling liquid to a boil. Pack pickles into hot jars, leaving ½-inch headspace. Ladle hot liquid over pickles, leaving ½-inch headspace. Remove air bubbles. Adjust two-piece caps. Process 15 minutes in a boiling-water canner.

Cucumber Rings

Yield: about 6 pints

3 pounds brined cucumbers, desalted	3 sticks cinnamon
2 cups water	1½ teaspoons whole cloves
2 cups vinegar, divided	1 ¼- x 1-inch piece fresh ginger
2 cups sugar	1 lemon, sliced thin

Cut cucumbers into ¼-inch slices. Mix water and 1 cup vinegar. Pour over cucumbers and let stand 2 hours. Add remaining vinegar; let stand 2 hours. Drain, reserving pickling liquid. Combine pickling liquid and sugar in a large saucepot. Tie spices in a spice bag. Add spice bag, lemon and cucumbers to pickling liquid. Cook until cucumbers are transparent. Place in a shallow container; let stand overnight to plump slices. Remove and discard spice bag and lemon slices. Drain, reserving pickling liquid. Strain liquid. Bring liquid to a boil in a large saucepot. Pack cucumbers into hot jars, leaving ½-inch headspace. Ladle hot liquid over cucumbers, leaving ½-inch headspace. Remove air bubbles. Adjust two-piece caps. Process 15 minutes in a boiling-water canner.

Note: Brined cucumbers can also be cut into spears or chunks. The yield may vary depending on how the cucumbers are cut.

Cucumber Sandwich Pickles

Yield: about 3 pints

2 pounds 3- to 4-inch cucumbers, cut into ¼-inch slices	1 cup brown sugar
½ cup Ball Salt	1 cup granulated sugar
3 quarts water, divided	½ teaspoon celery seed
5 cups vinegar, divided	½ teaspoon mustard seed
	½ teaspoon turmeric

Put cucumber slices in a clean pickling container. Combine salt and 2 quarts water; pour over cucumbers; let stand 2 to 3 hours. Drain; rinse and drain thoroughly. Discard liquid. Combine 3 cups vinegar and 3 cups water; bring to a boil in a large saucepot. Add cucumbers, simmer about 8 minutes. (Cucumbers should not become soft.) Drain well, discarding liquid. Combine 2 cups vinegar and 1 cup water with remaining ingredients in a large saucepot; simmer 10 minutes. Add drained cucumbers. Bring to a boil. Pack hot pickles and liquid into hot jars, leaving ½-inch headspace. Remove air bubbles. Adjust two-piece caps. Process 10 minutes in a boiling-water canner.

Sauerkraut

Yield: about 12 pints or 6 quarts

20 pounds cabbage	¾ cup Ball Salt

To Ferment: Remove outer leaves and any undesirable portions from firm, mature heads of cabbage; wash and drain. Cut into halves or quarters; remove core. Use a food processor or sharp knife to cut cabbage into thin shreds about 1/16-inch thick. Combine 3 tablespoons salt and 5 pounds shredded cabbage in a large bowl; mixing thoroughly. Let salted cabbage stand for several minutes to wilt slightly; this allows packing without excessive breaking or bruising of the shreds. Pack salted cabbage firmly and evenly into a large, clean pickling container. Use a wooden spoon, tamper or hands to press down firmly until the juice comes to the surface. Repeat shredding, salting and packing of cabbage until the

container is filled to within 3 to 4 inches from the top. If juice does not cover cabbage, add brine. Make brine using 1½ tablespoons salt to 1 quart water; bring brine to a boil; cool. Cover cabbage with muslin or cheesecloth and tuck edges down against the inside of the container. Weight cabbage under brine. Formation of gas bubbles indicates fermentation is taking place. Remove and discard scum formation each day. Store container in a cool place. Fermentation is usually complete in 3 to 6 weeks.

To Can: Bring sauerkraut to a simmer (180°F) in a large saucepot. Do not boil. Pack hot sauerkraut into hot jars, leaving ½-inch headspace. Ladle hot liquid over sauerkraut leaving ½-inch headspace. Remove air bubbles. Adjust two-piece caps. Process pints 15 minutes, quarts 20 minutes, in a boiling-water canner.

Sweet Cucumber Pickles

Yield: about 5 pints

3 pounds brined cucumbers, desalted	1 tablespoon slivered fresh ginger
3⅓ cups sugar	1 tablespoon whole cloves
1 quart vinegar	1 tablespoon whole mace
2 sticks cinnamon	

Combine sugar and vinegar in a large saucepot, stirring until sugar dissolves. Tie spices in a spice bag; add to vinegar mixture. Bring to a boil. Add drained cucumbers; boil 3 minutes. Place in a clean pickling container; let stand for 3 days. Each day drain off liquid, bring to a boil in a large saucepot, then pour over cucumbers. Remove pickles and spice bag after 3 days; discard spice bag. Bring pickling liquid to a boil in a large saucepot. Pack pickles into hot jars, leaving ½-inch headspace. Ladle hot liquid over pickles, leaving ½-inch headspace. Remove air bubbles. Adjust two-piece caps. Process 15 minutes in a boiling-water canner.

Recipe Variation: To make Sour Cucumber Pickles omit all or part of sugar.

Sweet Gherkin Pickles

Yield: about 7 pints

8 pounds 1½- to 2½-inch cucumbers	2 teaspoons celery seed
½ cup Ball Salt, divided	2 teaspoons Ball Mixed Pickling Spice
8 cups sugar, divided	2 sticks cinnamon
6 cups vinegar, divided	½ teaspoon whole allspice
½ teaspoon turmeric	

Wash cucumbers; drain. Combine 6 quarts boiling water and ¼ cup salt; pour over cucumbers. Let stand 6 to 8 hours or overnight. On second day, drain. Combine 6 quarts boiling water and ¼ cup salt; pour over cucumbers. Let stand 6 to 8 hours overnight. On third day, drain. Prick cucumbers in several places. Combine 3 cups sugar, 3 cups vinegar and turmeric in a large saucepot. Tie whole spices in a spice bag; add spice bag to liquid. Bring to a boil. Pour hot liquid over cucumbers; let stand 6 to 8 hours or overnight.. Drain cucumbers, reserving liquid. Add 2 cups sugar and 2 cups vinegar to liquid. Bring to a boil. Pour over cucumbers; let stand 6 to 8 hours overnight. On fourth day, drain, reserving liquid. Add 2 cups sugar and 1 cup vinegar to reserved liquid; bring to a boil. Pour over cucumbers; let stand 6 to 8 hours. Remove spice bag. Drain cucumbers, reserving liquid. Add 1 cup sugar to liquid; bring to a boil. Pack pickles into hot jars, leaving ½-inch headspace. Ladle hot liquid over pickles, leaving ½-inch headspace. Remove air bubbles. Adjust two-piece caps. Process 10 minutes in a boiling-water canner.

Sweet Icicle Pickles

Yield: about 6 pints or 3 quarts

4 pounds 4- to 6-inch cucumbers, cut lengthwise into quarters	1½ tablespoons Ball Mixed Pickling Spice
1 cup Ball Salt	5 cups sugar
2 quarts water	5 cups vinegar

Put cucumber spears in a clean pickling container. Combine salt and water in a saucepan. Bring to a boil. Pour over cucumbers. Weight cucumbers under brine. Cover container; let stand 1 week in a cool place. Drain, discarding brine. Rinse cucumbers thoroughly. Cover cucumbers with boiling water; cover; let stand 24 hours. Drain; discard liquid. Tie mixed pickling spice in a spice bag. Combine spice bag, sugar and vinegar in a large saucepot; bring to a boil. Pour over cucumbers; cover; let stand 24 hours. Drain pickling liquid; bring liquid to a boil. Pour over cucumbers; let stand 24 hours. Reheat pickling liquid once each day for 4 days. Remove spice bag and pickles; discard spice bag. Bring liquid to a boil in a large saucepot. Pack pickles into hot jars, leaving ½-inch headspace. Ladle hot liquid over pickles, leaving ½-inch headspace. Remove air bubbles. Adjust two-piece caps. Process pints and quarts 10 minutes in a boiling-water canner.

fresh pack pickled foods

Allow 4 to 6 weeks for fresh pack pickled foods to cure and develop a satisfactory flavor.

Cucumber & Mixed Vegetable Pickles

Bread And Butter Pickles

Yield: about 7 pints

4 pounds 4- to 6-inch cucumbers, cut into ¼-inch slices	2 tablespoons mustard seed
2 pounds onions, thinly sliced (about 8 small)	2 teaspoons turmeric
	2 teaspoons celery seed
⅓ cup Ball Salt	1 teaspoon ginger
2 cups sugar	1 teaspoon peppercorns
	3 cups vinegar
	Ball Pickle Crisp (optional)

Combine cucumber and onion slices in a large bowl, layering with salt; cover with ice cubes. Let stand 1½ hours. Drain; rinse; drain again. Combine remaining ingredients except Pickle Crisp in a large saucepot; bring to a boil. Add drained cucumbers and onions and return to a boil. Pack hot pickles and liquid into hot jars, leaving ½-inch headspace. Add Pickle Crisp to each jar, if desired. Remove air bubbles. Adjust two-piece caps. Process 10 minutes in a boiling-water canner.

Dill Pickles

Yield: about 7 pints or 3 quarts

8 pounds 4- to 6-inch cucumbers, cut lengthwise into halves	1 quart water
¾ cup sugar	3 tablespoons Ball Mixed Pickling Spice
½ cup Ball Salt	Green or dry dill (1 head per jar)
1 quart vinegar	Ball Pickle Crisp (optional)

Wash cucumbers; drain. Combine sugar, salt, vinegar and water in a large saucepot. Tie spice in a spice bag; add spice bag to vinegar mixture; simmer 15 minutes. Pack cucumbers into hot jars, leaving ½-inch headspace; put one head of dill in each jar. Ladle hot liquid over cucumbers, leaving ½-inch headspace. Add Pickle Crisp to each jar, if desired. Remove air bubbles. Adjust two-piece caps. Process pints and quarts 15 minutes in a boiling-water canner.

Recipe Variation: For Kosher-Style Pickles add 1 bay leaf, 1 clove garlic, 1 piece hot red pepper and ½ teaspoon mustard seed to each jar. Process as recommended.

Note: When cutting or seeding hot peppers, wear rubber gloves to prevent hands from being burned.

End-Of-The-Garden Pickles

Yield: about 5 pints

1 pound zucchini, cut into ¼-inch slices	1 large sweet red pepper, cut into ½-inch strips
1 pound green beans, ends removed	1 cup brown sugar
½ pound carrots, cut into ¼-inch slices (about 3 medium)	1 cup granulated sugar
	2 tablespoons dry mustard
	2 tablespoons mustard seed
½ pound pearl onions, peeled	1½ tablespoons Ball Salt
	1 teaspoon cinnamon
2 large sweet green peppers, cut into ½-inch strips	1 teaspoon ginger
	3 cups cider vinegar
	Ball Pickle Crisp (optional)

Mix vegetables; set aside. Combine sugars, spices and vinegar in a large saucepot; bring mixture to a boil. Add vegetables. Return to a boil. Reduce heat and simmer 15 minutes. Pack hot pickles and liquid into hot jars, leaving ½-inch headspace. Add Pickle Crisp to each jar, if desired. Remove air bubbles. Adjust two-piece caps. Process 15 minutes in a boiling-water canner.

Hamburger Dills

Yield: about 7 pints

4 pounds 4-inch cucumbers	14 heads fresh dill
6 tablespoons Ball Salt	3½ teaspoons mustard seed
4½ cups water	14 peppercorns
4 cups vinegar	Ball Pickle Crisp (optional)

Wash cucumbers; drain. Cut cucumbers into ¼-inch crosswise or lengthwise slices, discarding blossom ends. Combine salt, water and vinegar in a large saucepot; bring to a boil. Pack cucumbers into hot jars, leaving ½-inch headspace. Add 2 heads of dill, ½ teaspoon mustard seed and 2 peppercorns to each jar. Ladle hot liquid over cucumbers, leaving ½-inch headspace. Add Pickle Crisp to each jar, if desired. Remove air bubbles. Adjust two-piece caps. Process 15 minutes in a boiling-water canner.

Hot Pickle Mix

Yield: about 7 pints

1½ quarts ½-inch sliced pickling cucumbers	3 cups cauliflowerets (about 1 small head)
1½ quarts ½-inch sliced long red or green peppers	1 cup peeled pearl onions
	1½ cups Ball Salt
2 medium sweet green peppers, seeded and cut into strips	4 quarts plus 2 cups water, divided
	3 or 4 jalapeño peppers
2 medium sweet red peppers, seeded and cut into strips	¼ cup sugar
	2 tablespoons prepared horseradish
1½ cups sliced carrots (about 3 medium)	2 cloves garlic
	10 cups vinegar
	Ball Pickle Crisp (optional)

Combine vegetables, except jalapeño peppers, in a large bowl. Dissolve salt in 4 quarts water. Pour over vegetables; let stand 1 hour. Cut jalapeño in half; set aside. Combine remaining ingredients except Pickle Crisp in a large saucepot. Simmer 15 minutes; discard garlic. Drain vegetables; rinse thoroughly. Pack vegetables, except jalapeño, into hot jars, leaving ½-inch headspace. Add one piece of jalapeño to each jar. Ladle hot liquid over mixture, leaving ½-inch headspace. Add Pickle Crisp to each jar, if desired. Remove air bubbles. Adjust two-piece caps. Process 10 minutes in a boiling-water canner.

Note: When cutting or seeding hot peppers, wear rubber gloves to prevent hands from being burned.

Mixed Pickles

Yield: about 6 pints

1¼ pounds 3- to 4-inch cucumbers, cut into 1-inch slices	3 cups cauliflowerets (about 1 small head)
	2 hot red peppers, seeded and cut into ½-inch rings
2 cups 1½-inch sliced carrots (about 3 medium)	1 cup Ball Salt
2 cups 1½-inch sliced celery (about 4 stalks)	4 quarts water
	2 cups sugar
2 cups peeled pearl onions	¼ cup mustard seed
2 sweet red peppers, cut into ½-inch strips	2 tablespoons celery seed
	6½ cups vinegar
	Ball Pickle Crisp (optional)

Combine vegetables in a large bowl. Dissolve salt in water. Pour over vegetables; let stand 12 hours. Drain; rinse thoroughly. Combine sugar, spices and vinegar in a large saucepot; boil 3 minutes. Add vegetables; simmer 5 minutes. Pack hot pickles and liquid into hot jars, leaving ½-inch headspace. Add Pickle Crisp to each jar, if desired. Remove air bubbles. Adjust two-piece caps. Process 15 minutes in a boiling-water canner.

Note: When cutting or seeding hot peppers, wear rubber gloves to prevent hands from being burned.

Mustard Pickles

Yield: about 8 pints or 4 quarts

1½ pounds 3- to 4-inch cucumbers, cut into ½-inch slices	2 cups peeled pearl onions
	1 cup Ball Salt
1 quart green tomato wedges (about 6 medium)	4 quarts plus ½ cup water, divided
3 cups cauliflowerets (about 1 small head)	1½ cups sugar
	½ cup flour
3 cups chopped sweet green peppers (about 3 medium)	1 tablespoon turmeric
	½ cup prepared mustard
3 cups chopped sweet red peppers (about 3 medium)	5 cups vinegar
	Ball Pickle Crisp (optional)

Combine vegetables in a large bowl. Dissolve salt in 4 quarts water. Pour over vegetables; let stand 12 hours. Drain; rinse thoroughly. Combine sugar, flour and turmeric in a large saucepot. Gradually add ½ cup water, stirring until smooth. Stir in mustard and vinegar. Cook until sauce coats spoon. Add vegetables; simmer 15 minutes. Pack hot pickles and liquid into hot jars, leaving ½-inch headspace. Add Pickle Crisp to each jar, if desired. Remove air bubbles. Adjust two-piece caps. Process pints and quarts 10 minutes in a boiling-water canner.

Sweet Pickle Spears

Yield: about 10 half-pints

4 pounds 3- to 4-inch cucumbers, cut length-wise into spears	3 tablespoons Ball Salt
	4 teaspoons celery seed
4 cups sugar	4 teaspoons turmeric
3¾ cups vinegar	1½ teaspoons mustard seed
	Ball Pickle Crisp (optional)

Cover cucumbers with boiling water; let stand 2 hours. Drain. Combine remaining ingredients except Pickle Crisp in a large saucepot. Bring to a boil. Pack cucumbers into hot jars, leaving ½-inch headspace. Ladle hot liquid over cucumbers, leaving ½-inch headspace. Add Pickle Crisp to each jar, if desired. Remove air bubbles. Adjust two-piece caps. Process 10 minutes in a boiling-water canner.

chutneys

Curried Apple Chutney

Yield: about 10 pints

2 quarts chopped, peeled, cored apples (about 16 medium)	3 tablespoons mustard seed
	2 tablespoons ginger
	2 teaspoons allspice
2 pounds raisins	2 teaspoons curry powder
4 cups brown sugar	2 teaspoons Ball Salt
1 cup chopped onion	2 hot red peppers, chopped
1 cup chopped sweet red pepper	1 clove garlic, minced
	4 cups vinegar

Combine all ingredients in a large saucepot. Simmer until thick. Stir frequently to prevent sticking. Ladle hot chutney into hot jars, leaving ½-inch headspace. Remove air bubbles. Adjust two-piece caps. Process 10 minutes in a boiling-water canner.

Note: When cutting or seeding hot peppers, wear rubber gloves to prevent hands from being burned.

Nectarine Chutney

Yield: about 3 pints

2 quarts sliced, peeled, pitted nectarines (about 12 large)	2 tablespoons crystallized ginger
	¼ teaspoon cloves
2 teaspoons Ball Salt	¼ teaspoon cinnamon
2½ cups brown sugar	2 cloves garlic, minced
1½ cups red wine vinegar	1 chili pepper, finely chopped
¼ cup Worcestershire sauce	¾ cup lime juice
1 cup finely chopped onion	

Combine nectarines and salt. Let stand 20 minutes. Combine sugar, vinegar and Worcestershire sauce in a large saucepot. Bring mixture to a boil. Stir in nectarines and cook until transparent. Remove nectarines; set aside. Add remaining ingredients to saucepot and cook until onions are tender. Return nectarines to syrup and continue cooking until mixture is thick.

Stir frequently to prevent sticking. Ladle hot chutney into hot jars, leaving ½-inch headspace. Remove air bubbles. Adjust two-piece caps. Process 10 minutes in a boiling-water canner.

Note: When cutting or seeding hot peppers, wear rubber gloves to prevent hands from being burned.

Peach Or Pear Chutney

Yield: about 7 pints

4 quarts finely chopped, peeled, pitted peaches or pears (about 20 medium)	2 tablespoons ginger
	2 teaspoons Ball Salt
	1 clove garlic, minced (optional)
2 to 3 cups brown sugar	1 hot red pepper, finely chopped
1 cup raisins	5 cups vinegar
1 cup chopped onion (about 1 medium)	
¼ cup mustard seed	

Combine all ingredients in a large saucepot. Simmer until thick. Stir frequently to prevent sticking. Ladle hot chutney into hot jars, leaving ½-inch headspace. Remove air bubbles. Adjust two-piece caps. Process 10 minutes in a boiling-water canner.

Recipe Variation: For a milder chutney, remove seeds from hot pepper.

Note: When cutting or seeding hot peppers, wear rubber gloves to prevent hands from being burned.

Plum Chutney

Yield: about 6 pints

4 quarts chopped and pitted plums	2 tablespoons mustard seed
	2 teaspoons ginger
3 cups brown sugar	1 teaspoon Ball Salt
2 cups raisins	3 cups vinegar
1 cup chopped onion	

Combine all ingredients in a large saucepot. Bring mixture to a boil; reduce heat. Simmer until thick. Stir frequently to prevent sticking. Ladle hot chutney into hot jars, leaving ½-inch headspace. Remove air bubbles. Adjust two-piece caps. Process 10 minutes in a boiling-water canner.

Sweet Yellow Tomato Chutney

Yield: about 7 pints

6 pounds yellow tomatoes, cored, peeled, chopped (about 18 medium)	1 cup brown sugar
	¼ cup mustard seed
	1 tablespoon minced fresh ginger
3 pounds Granny Smith apples, cored and chopped (about 10 medium)	1½ teaspoons cinnamon
	1 teaspoon Ball Salt
1 pound onions, chopped (about 2 medium)	3 hot peppers, finely chopped
	2 cloves garlic, minced
1 pound golden raisins	4 cups cider vinegar
1½ cups granulated sugar	

Combine all ingredients in a large saucepot. Simmer until thick. Stir frequently to prevent sticking. Ladle hot chutney into hot jars, leaving ½-inch headspace. Remove air bubbles. Adjust two-piece caps. Process 10 minutes in a boiling-water canner.

Note: When cutting or seeding hot peppers, wear rubber gloves to prevent hands from being burned.

Tomato-Apple Chutney

Yield: about 6 pints

2½ quarts chopped, peeled, cored tomatoes (about 12 large)	1½ cups chopped sweet red peppers (about 2 medium)
1 quart chopped, cored, peeled apples (about 5 medium)	1 cup raisins
3 cups brown sugar	1 hot red pepper, finely chopped
2 cups chopped cucumber (about 1 large)	1 clove garlic, minced
1½ cups chopped onions (about 1½ medium)	1 tablespoon ginger
	1 teaspoon Ball Salt
	1 teaspoon cinnamon
	3 cups vinegar

Combine all ingredients in a large saucepot. Simmer until thick. Stir frequently to prevent sticking. Ladle hot chutney into hot jars, leaving ½-inch headspace. Remove air bubbles. Adjust two-piece caps. Process 15 minutes in a boiling-water canner.

Recipe Variation: For a milder chutney, remove seeds from hot pepper.

Note: When cutting or seeding hot peppers, wear rubber gloves to prevent hands from being burned.

fruit pickles

Fig Pickles

Yield: about 8 pints or 4 quarts

4 quarts firm, ripe figs (about 30 medium)	3 cups vinegar
5 cups sugar, divided	2 sticks cinnamon
2 quarts water	1 tablespoon whole allspice
	1 tablespoon whole cloves

Peel figs. Combine 3 cups sugar and water; cook until sugar dissolves. Add figs and cook slowly 30 minutes. Add 2 cups sugar and vinegar. Tie spices in a spice bag; add to figs. Simmer until figs are transparent. Cover; let stand 12 to 24 hours in a cool place. Remove spice bag. Bring to a simmer. Pack hot figs and liquid into hot jars, leaving ½-inch headspace. Remove air bubbles. Adjust two-piece caps. Process pints and quarts 15 minutes in a boiling-water canner.

Note: If unpeeled figs are preferred, pour boiling water over figs and let stand until cool. Drain. Continue with recipe as instructed.

Peach Pickles

Yield: about 3 quarts

8 pounds small peaches Ball Fruit-Fresh Produce Protector	1 tablespoon grated fresh ginger
4 sticks cinnamon	6 cups sugar
2 tablespoons whole cloves	1 quart vinegar

Peel peaches. Treat with Fruit-Fresh to prevent darkening. Tie spices in a spice bag. Combine spice bag, sugar and vinegar in a large saucepot; boil 5 minutes. Drain peaches. Cook drained peaches in boiling syrup until they can be pierced with a fork, but are not soft. Remove from heat. Cover; let stand 12 to 24 hours in a cool place. Bring to a boil. Remove spice bag. Pack peaches into hot jars, leaving ½-inch headspace. Ladle hot liquid over peaches, leaving ½-inch headspace. Remove air bubbles. Adjust two-piece caps. Process 20 minutes in a boiling-water canner.

Pear Pickles

Yield: about 8 pints or 4 quarts

8 pounds Seckel pears Ball Fruit-Fresh Produce Protector	1 ¼-x 1-inch piece fresh ginger
1 tablespoon Ball Mixed Pickling Spice	4 cups sugar
1 teaspoon whole cloves	½ cup thinly sliced lemon (about ½ medium)
	2½ cups water
	2½ cups vinegar

Peel pears, leaving whole with stem intact. Treat with Fruit-Fresh to prevent darkening. Tie spices in a spice bag. Combine spice bag, sugar, lemon, water and vinegar in a large saucepot; simmer 5 minutes. Add pears one layer at a time, simmer until just tender. Remove pears. Repeat until all pears are cooked. Ladle pickling liquid over pears. Cover; let stand 12 to 18 hours in a cool place. Remove spice bag and pears; discard spice bag. Bring pickling liquid to a boil. Pack pears into hot jars, leaving ½-inch headspace. Ladle hot liquid over pears, leaving ½-inch headspace. Remove air bubbles. Adjust two-piece caps. Process pints and quarts 20 minutes in a boiling-water canner.

Note: Other small, firm, ripe pears may be used. If Kieffer or Sand pears are used, they should be cored, covered with hot water, simmered 10 to 15 minutes and drained before adding to pickling liquid.

Spicy Melon Pickles

Yield: about 7 half-pints

3 cups vinegar	1 teaspoon slivered, whole nutmeg
2 cups water	
2 sticks cinnamon	13 cups 1-inch cantaloupe cubes or balls
2 teaspoons whole cloves	
1 teaspoon whole allspice	4½ cups sugar

Combine vinegar and water in a large saucepot. Tie spices in a spice bag and add to vinegar mixture. Bring to a boil. Reduce heat and simmer 5 minutes. Remove from heat. Add melon; let stand 1½ to 2 hours. Add sugar. Bring to a boil, stirring until sugar dissolves. Reduce heat; simmer until cantaloupe becomes slightly transparent. Pack hot melon into hot jars, leaving ½-inch headspace. Ladle hot pickling liquid over melon, leaving ½-inch headspace. Remove air bubbles. Adjust two-piece caps. Process 10 minutes in a boiling-water canner.

Watermelon Rind Pickles

Yield: about 6 pints

4 quarts 1-inch cubed watermelon rind (white portion only)	1 tablespoon whole allspice
	¼ teaspoon mustard seed
1 cup Ball Salt	7 cups sugar
2 gallons water, divided	½ cup thinly sliced lemon (about 1 medium)
3 sticks cinnamon	
1 tablespoon whole cloves	2 cups vinegar

Cover watermelon rind with salt and 1 gallon water, stirring to dissolve salt. Let stand 12 hours or overnight. Drain; rinse. Cover rind with 1 gallon water in a large saucepot. Cook until tender. Drain; set aside. Tie spices in a spice bag. Combine spice bag, sugar, lemon slices, and vinegar in a large saucepot. Bring to a boil. Reduce heat and simmer 10 minutes. Add rind, simmer until rind is transparent. Remove spice bag. Pack hot rind and liquid into hot jars, leaving ½-inch headspace. Remove air bubbles. Adjust two-piece caps. Process 10 minutes in a boiling-water canner.

relishes

Artichoke Relish

Yield: about 10 half-pints

- 2 pounds Jerusalem artichokes
- 1 cup plus ¼ teaspoon Ball Salt, divided
- 4 quarts water
- 2 cups ground sweet red or green peppers (about 3 medium)
- 2 cups ground onions (about 3 medium)
- 3⅓ cups sugar
- 1 quart vinegar
- 2 tablespoons mustard seed
- 1 tablespoon turmeric
- Ball Pickle Crisp (optional)

Wash artichokes well and trim as needed. Dissolve 1 cup salt in water. Add artichokes; let stand overnight. Drain; rinse and dry. Using coarse blade of food processor or food grinder, grind artichokes. Combine artichokes, peppers and onions; set aside. Dissolve sugar in vinegar in a large saucepot. Bring to a boil. Add vegetables, ¼ teaspoon salt and spices. Bring mixture to a boil. Pack hot relish into hot jars, leaving ½-inch headspace. Add Pickle Crisp to each jar, if desired. Remove air bubbles. Adjust two-piece caps. Process 10 minutes in a boiling-water canner.

Beet Or Red Relish

Yield: about 10 half-pints

- 1 quart chopped cooked beets (about 12 medium)
- 1 quart chopped cabbage (about 1 small head)
- 1½ cups sugar
- 1 cup chopped onion (about 1 medium)
- 1 cup chopped sweet red peppers (about 2 small)
- 1 tablespoon prepared horseradish
- 1 tablespoon Ball Salt
- 3 cups vinegar
- Ball Pickle Crisp (optional)

Combine all ingredients in a large saucepot. Simmer 10 minutes. Bring to a boil. Pack hot relish into hot jars, leaving ½-inch headspace. Add Pickle Crisp to each jar, if desired. Remove air bubbles. Adjust two-piece caps. Process 15 minutes in a boiling-water canner.

Chow-Chow Relish

Yield: about 4 pints

- 1 quart chopped cabbage (about 1 small head)
- 3 cups cauliflowerets (about 1 medium head)
- 2 cups chopped green tomatoes (about 4 medium)
- 2 cups chopped onions (about 2 medium)
- 2 cups chopped sweet green peppers (about 4 small)
- 1 cup chopped sweet red peppers (about 2 small)
- 3 tablespoons Ball Salt
- 1½ cups sugar
- 2 teaspoons celery seed
- 2 teaspoons dry mustard
- 1 teaspoon mustard seed
- 1 teaspoon turmeric
- ½ teaspoon ginger
- 2½ cups vinegar
- Ball Pickle Crisp (optional)

Combine vegetables; sprinkle with salt. Let stand 4 to 6 hours. Drain well. Rinse and drain. Combine sugar, spices and vinegar in a large saucepot. Simmer 10 minutes. Add vegetables; simmer 10 minutes. Bring to a boil. Pack hot relish into hot jars, leaving ½-inch headspace. Add Pickle Crisp to each jar, if desired. Remove air bubbles. Adjust two-piece caps. Process 10 minutes in a boiling-water canner.

Corn Relish

Yield: about 6 pints

- 2 quarts cut cooked corn (about 18 ears)
- 1 quart chopped cabbage (about 1 small head)
- 1 cup chopped onion (about 1 medium)
- 1 cup chopped sweet green peppers (about 2 small)
- 1 cup chopped sweet red peppers (about 2 small)
- 1 to 2 cups sugar
- 2 tablespoons dry mustard
- 1 tablespoon celery seed
- 1 tablespoon mustard seed
- 1 tablespoon Ball Salt
- 1 tablespoon turmeric
- 1 quart vinegar
- 1 cup water
- Ball Pickle Crisp (optional)

Combine all ingredients in a large saucepot. Bring to a boil; reduce heat and simmer 20 minutes. Pack hot relish into hot jars, leaving ½-inch headspace. Add Pickle Crisp to each jar, if desired. Remove air bubbles. Adjust two-piece caps. Process 15 minutes in a boiling-water canner.

Recipe Variation: To make corn relish without cabbage, substitute 1 cup chopped celery for cabbage. Add 1 clove garlic, minced. Follow directions in recipe.

Cucumber Relish

Yield: about 6 pints

- 2 quarts chopped cucumbers (about 8 medium)
- 2 cups chopped sweet green peppers (about 4 small)
- 2 cups chopped sweet red peppers (about 4 small)
- 1 cup chopped onion (about 1 medium)
- 1 tablespoon turmeric
- ½ cup Ball Salt
- 4 quarts cold water, divided
- 1½ cups brown sugar
- 1 quart vinegar
- 2 sticks cinnamon
- 1 tablespoon mustard seed
- 2 teaspoons whole allspice
- 2 teaspoons whole cloves
- Ball Pickle Crisp (optional)

Combine vegetables in a large bowl; sprinkle with turmeric. Dissolve salt in 2 quarts cold water and pour over vegetables; let stand 3 to 4 hours. Drain; cover vegetables with 2 quarts cold water and let stand 1 hour. Drain thoroughly. Combine sugar and vinegar in a large saucepot. Tie spices in a spice bag; add to sugar mixture. Bring to a boil; pour over vegetables. Cover; let stand 12 to 18 hours. Bring vegetables to a boil; reduce heat and simmer until hot throughout. Remove spice bag. Pack hot relish into hot jars, leaving ½-inch headspace. Add Pickle Crisp to each jar, if desired. Remove air bubbles. Adjust two-piece caps. Process 10 minutes in a boiling-water canner.

Dill Relish

Yield: about 7 pints

- 8 pounds pickling cucumbers
- ½ cup Ball Salt
- 2 teaspoons turmeric
- 1 quart water
- 1 pound yellow onions
- ⅓ cup sugar
- 2 tablespoons dill seed
- 1 quart white wine vinegar
- Ball Pickle Crisp (optional)

Wash cucumbers; drain. Finely chop cucumbers in a food processor or food grinder. Place chopped cucumbers in a bowl and sprinkle with salt and turmeric. Pour water over cucumbers; let stand 2 hours. Peel and finely chop onions. Drain cucumbers. Rinse under cold water; drain. Combine cucumbers, onions, sugar, dill seed and white wine vinegar in a large saucepot; bring to a boil. Reduce heat and simmer 10 minutes. Ladle hot relish into hot jars, leaving ½-inch headspace. Add Pickle Crisp to each jar, if desired. Remove air bubbles. Adjust two-piece caps. Process 15 minutes in a boiling-water canner.

Dixie Relish

Yield: about 7 half-pints

1 quart chopped cabbage (about one small head)	½ cup Ball Salt
2 cups chopped onions (about 2 medium)	2 quarts cold water
2 cups chopped sweet green peppers (about 4 small)	¾ cup sugar
	3 tablespoons mustard seed
	2 tablespoons celery seed
2 cups chopped sweet red peppers (about 4 small)	1 quart vinegar
	Ball Pickle Crisp (optional)

Combine vegetables in a large bowl. Dissolve salt in water and pour over vegetables; let stand 1 hour. Drain. If too salty, rinse and drain again. Combine vegetables, sugar, spices and vinegar in a large saucepot. Simmer 20 minutes. Bring to a boil. Pack hot relish into hot jars, leaving ½-inch headspace. Add Pickle Crisp to each jar, if desired. Remove air bubbles. Adjust two-piece caps. Process 15 minutes in a boiling-water canner.

Pepper-Onion Relish

Yield: about 6 pints

2 quarts chopped sweet green peppers (about 10 medium)	2 hot red peppers, finely chopped
	4 teaspoons Ball Mixed Pickling Spice
2 quarts chopped sweet red peppers (about 10 medium)	1½ cups sugar
	4 teaspoons Ball Salt
1½ cups chopped onions (about 1½ medium)	3½ cups vinegar
	Ball Pickle Crisp (optional)

Combine vegetables in a large bowl. Cover vegetables with boiling water; let stand 5 minutes. Drain; cover again with boiling water and let stand 10 minutes. Drain. Tie mixed pickling spice in a spice bag. Combine spice bag, sugar, salt and vinegar in a large saucepot. Simmer 15 minutes. Add drained vegetables; simmer 10 minutes. Remove spice bag. Bring to a boil. Pack hot relish into hot jars, leaving ½-inch headspace. Add Pickle Crisp to each jar, if desired. Remove air bubbles. Adjust two-piece caps. Process 15 minutes in a boiling-water canner.

Note: When cutting or seeding hot peppers, wear rubber gloves to prevent hands from being burned.

Piccalilli Or Green Tomato Relish

Yield: about 7 pints

4 quarts chopped, cored green tomatoes (about 32 medium)	½ cup Ball Salt
	1½ cups brown sugar
	2 tablespoons mustard seed
2 quarts chopped cabbage (about 1 large head)	1 tablespoon celery seed
	1 tablespoon prepared horseradish
2 cups chopped sweet green peppers (about 4 small)	4½ cups vinegar
1 cup chopped onion (about 1 medium)	Ball Pickle Crisp (optional)

Combine vegetables in a large bowl. Sprinkle salt over vegetables and mix thoroughly; let stand 3 to 4 hours. Drain; rinse and drain thoroughly. Combine sugar, spices, horseradish and vinegar in a large saucepot. Simmer 15 minutes. Add vegetables and bring to a boil. Pack hot relish into hot jars, leaving ½-inch headspace. Add Pickle Crisp to each jar, if desired. Remove air bubbles. Adjust two-piece caps. Process 10 minutes in a boiling-water canner.

Sweet Pickle Relish

Yield: about 8 half-pints

1 quart chopped cucumbers (about 4 medium)	¼ cup Ball Salt
	3½ cups sugar
2 cups chopped onions (about 2 medium)	1 tablespoon celery seed
	1 tablespoon mustard seed
1 cup chopped sweet green pepper (about 1 medium)	2 cups cider vinegar
	Ball Pickle Crisp (optional)
1 cup chopped sweet red pepper (about 1 medium)	

Combine cucumbers, onions, green and red peppers in a large bowl; sprinkle with salt and cover with cold water. Let stand 2 hours. Drain; rinse and drain thoroughly. Combine sugar, spices and vinegar in a large saucepot. Bring to a boil. Add drained vegetables; simmer 10 minutes. Pack hot relish into hot jars, leaving ½-inch headspace. Add Pickle Crisp to each jar, if desired. Remove air bubbles. Adjust two-piece caps. Process 10 minutes in a boiling-water canner.

Zucchini Relish

Yield: about 4 half-pints

2 cups chopped zucchini (about 3 medium)	2 tablespoons Ball Salt
	1¾ cups sugar
1 cup chopped onion (about 1 medium)	2 teaspoons celery seed
	1 teaspoon mustard seed
½ cup chopped sweet green pepper (about 1 small)	1 cup cider vinegar
	Ball Pickle Crisp (optional)
½ cup chopped sweet red pepper (about 1 small)	

Combine zucchini, onion, green and red peppers; sprinkle with salt; cover with cold water. Let stand 2 hours. Drain; rinse and drain thoroughly. Combine remaining ingredients in a large saucepot. Bring to a boil. Add vegetables; simmer 10 minutes. Pack hot relish into hot jars, leaving ½-inch headspace. Add Pickle Crisp to each jar, if desired. Remove air bubbles. Adjust two-piece caps. Process 10 minutes in a boiling-water canner.

sauces

Barbecue Sauce

Yield: about 8 half-pints or 4 pints

4 quarts chopped, peeled, cored tomatoes (about 24 large)	1 teaspoon peppercorns
	1 cup brown sugar
2 cups chopped celery (about 3 stalks)	2 cloves garlic, minced
	1 tablespoon dry mustard
2 cups chopped onions (about 2 medium)	1 tablespoon paprika
	1 tablespoon Ball Salt
1½ cups chopped sweet green or sweet red peppers (about 2 medium)	1 teaspoon hot pepper sauce
	⅛ teaspoon cayenne pepper
2 hot red peppers, finely chopped	1 cup vinegar

Combine tomatoes, celery, onions and peppers in a large saucepot. Cook until vegetables are soft. Purée using a food processor or food mill. Simmer purée until reduced by one-half. Tie peppercorns in a spice bag; add spice bag and remaining ingredients to tomato sauce. Simmer until sauce is the consistency of ketchup. As sauce thickens, stir frequently to prevent

sticking. Remove spice bag. Ladle hot sauce into hot jars, leaving ½-inch headspace. Adjust two-piece caps. Process half-pints and pints 20 minutes in a boiling-water canner.

Note: When cutting or seeding hot peppers, wear rubber gloves to prevent hands from being burned.

Chili Sauce

Yield: about 6 pints

4 quarts chopped, peeled, cored tomatoes (about 24 large)	1 cup sugar
2 cups chopped onions (about 2 medium)	3 tablespoons Ball Salt
	3 tablespoons Ball Mixed Pickling Spice
2 cups chopped sweet red peppers (about 4 medium)	1 tablespoon celery seed
1 hot red pepper, finely chopped	1 tablespoon mustard seed
	2½ cups vinegar

Combine tomatoes, onions, peppers, sugar and salt in a large saucepot. Simmer 45 minutes. Tie whole spices in a spice bag. Add spice bag to tomato mixture. Simmer until reduced by one-half. As mixture thickens, stir frequently to prevent sticking. Add vinegar and simmer to desired thickness. Remove spice bag. Ladle hot sauce into hot jars, leaving ½-inch headspace. Adjust two-piece caps. Process 15 minutes in a boiling-water canner.

Note: When cutting or seeding hot peppers, wear rubber gloves to prevent hands from being burned.

Red Hot Sauce

Yield: about 4 half-pints

2 quarts chopped, peeled, cored tomatoes (about 12 large)	1 quart vinegar, divided
	1 cup sugar
	1 tablespoon Ball Salt
1½ cups chopped and seeded hot red peppers (about 24)	2 tablespoons Ball Mixed Pickling Spice

Combine tomatoes, peppers and 2 cups vinegar in a large saucepot. Cook until tomatoes are soft. Purée using a food processor or food mill. Add sugar and salt. Tie mixed pickling spice in a spice bag and add to tomato mixture. Simmer until thick. As mixture thickens, stir frequently to prevent sticking. Add remaining 2 cups vinegar. Simmer to desired thickness. Ladle hot sauce into hot jars, leaving ½-inch headspace. Adjust two-piece caps. Process 15 minutes in a boiling-water canner.

Note: When cutting or seeding hot peppers, wear rubber gloves to prevent hands from being burned.

Taco Sauce

Yield: about 6 half-pints

3 cups tomato paste	½ teaspoon hot pepper sauce
2 tablespoons chili powder	5 cups water
1 tablespoon Ball Salt	1 cup cider vinegar
1 teaspoon cayenne pepper	½ cup corn syrup

Combine all ingredients in a large saucepot. Bring to a boil. Reduce heat and simmer until thick. As mixture thickens, stir frequently to prevent sticking. Ladle hot sauce into hot jars, leaving ½-inch headspace. Adjust two-piece caps. Process 30 minutes in a boiling-water canner.

Tomato Ketchup

Yield: about 3 pints

4 quarts chopped, peeled, cored tomatoes (about 24 large)	1 teaspoon whole allspice
	1 teaspoon mustard seed
1 cup chopped onion (about 1 medium)	1 stick cinnamon
	1 cup sugar
½ cup chopped sweet red pepper (about ½ medium)	1 tablespoon Ball Salt
	1 tablespoon paprika
1½ teaspoons celery seed	1½ cups vinegar

Combine tomatoes, onion and pepper in a large saucepot. Cook until tomatoes are tender. Purée using a food processor or food mill. Cook purée rapidly until thick and reduced by one-half. Tie whole spices in a spice bag. Add spice bag, sugar, salt, paprika and vinegar to tomato mixture; simmer until thick. As mixture thickens, stir frequently to prevent sticking. Remove spice bag. Ladle hot ketchup into hot jars, leaving ½-inch headspace. Adjust two-piece caps. Process 10 minutes in a boiling-water canner.

Victoria Or Rhubarb Sauce

Yield: about 4 pints

2 quarts chopped rhubarb (about 12 stalks)	½ cup vinegar
	1 teaspoon allspice
1½ cups chopped raisins	1 teaspoon cinnamon
½ cup chopped onion (about ½ medium)	1 teaspoon ginger
	1 teaspoon Ball Salt
3½ cups brown sugar	

Combine rhubarb, raisins, onion, sugar and vinegar in a large saucepot. Simmer until thick. As mixture thickens, stir frequently to prevent sticking. Add spices; cook 5 minutes longer. Ladle hot sauce into hot jars, leaving ½-inch headspace. Adjust two-piece caps. Process 15 minutes in a boiling-water canner.

other pickled vegetables

Beet Pickles

Yield: about 6 pints or 3 quarts

3 quarts beets (about 24 small)	1 tablespoon whole allspice
	1½ teaspoons salt
2 cups sugar	3½ cups vinegar
2 sticks cinnamon	1½ cups water
	Ball Pickle Crisp (optional)

Wash beets; drain. Cook beets; peel. Combine all ingredients except beets and Pickle Crisp in a large saucepot. Bring mixture to a boil; reduce heat. Simmer 15 minutes. Remove cinnamon sticks. Pack beets into hot jars, leaving ½-inch headspace. Add Pickle Crisp to each jar, if desired. Ladle hot liquid over beets, leaving ½-inch headspace. Remove air bubbles. Adjust two-piece caps. Process pints and quarts 30 minutes in a boiling-water canner.

Dilled Green Tomatoes

Yield: about 6 pints

5 pounds small, firm green tomatoes	6 or 7 cloves garlic
¼ cup Ball Salt	6 or 7 heads fresh dill or ¼ cup dill seeds
3½ cups vinegar	6 or 7 bay leaves
3½ cups water	Ball Pickle Crisp (optional)

Wash tomatoes; drain. Core tomatoes; cut into halves or quarters. Combine salt, vinegar and water in a large saucepot. Bring to a boil. Pack tomatoes into hot jars, leaving ½-inch headspace. Add 1 clove garlic, 1 head of dill (or 2 teaspoons dill seeds) and 1 bay leaf to each jar. Add Pickle Crisp to each jar, if desired. Ladle hot liquid over tomatoes, leaving ½-inch headspace. Remove air bubbles. Adjust two-piece caps. Process 15 minutes in a boiling-water canner.

Dilly Beans

Yield: about 4 pints or 2 quarts

2 pounds green beans	1 teaspoon cayenne pepper, divided
¼ cup Ball Salt	4 cloves garlic
2½ cups vinegar	4 heads dill
2½ cups water	Ball Pickle Crisp (optional)

Trim ends off green beans. Combine salt, vinegar and water in a large saucepot. Bring to a boil. Pack beans lengthwise into hot jars, leaving ½-inch headspace. Add ¼ teaspoon cayenne pepper, 1 clove garlic and 1 head dill to each pint jar. Add ½ teaspoon cayenne pepper, 2 cloves garlic and 2 heads dill to each quart jar. Add Pickle Crisp to each jar, if desired. Ladle hot liquid over beans, leaving ½-inch headspace. Remove air bubbles. Adjust two-piece caps. Process pints and quarts 10 minutes in a boiling-water canner.

Hot Peppers

Yield: about 5 pints

1½ pounds banana peppers	6 cups vinegar
1 pound jalapeño peppers	2 cups water
¼ pound serrano peppers	3 cloves garlic, crushed
	Ball Pickle Crisp (optional)

Leave peppers whole or cut into 1-inch pieces. Mix peppers together. Combine vinegar, water and garlic in a large saucepot. Bring mixture to a boil; reduce heat and simmer 5 minutes. Discard garlic. Pack peppers into hot jars, leaving ½-inch headspace. Add Pickle Crisp to each jar, if desired. Ladle hot liquid over peppers, leaving ½-inch headspace. Remove air bubbles. Adjust two-piece caps. Process 10 minutes in a boiling-water canner.

Note: When cutting or seeding hot peppers, wear rubber gloves to prevent hands from being burned.

Okra Pickles

Yield: about 4 pints

3½ pounds small okra pods	3 cups vinegar
⅓ cup Ball Salt	4 cloves garlic
2 teaspoons dill seed	2 small hot red peppers, cut in half
3 cups water	Ball Pickle Crisp (optional)

Trim stems of okra, being careful not to cut pods; set aside. Combine salt, dill seed, water and vinegar in a large saucepot. Bring to a boil. Pack okra into hot jars, leaving ½-inch headspace. Put 1 clove garlic and one-half pepper in each jar. Add Pickle Crisp to each jar, if desired. Ladle hot liquid over okra, leaving

½-inch headspace. Remove air bubbles. Adjust two-piece caps. Process 15 minutes in a boiling-water canner.

Note: When cutting or seeding hot peppers, wear rubber gloves to prevent hands from being burned.

Onion Pickles

Yield: about 14 half-pints or 7 pints

4 quarts peeled pearl onions	2½ tablespoons prepared horseradish
1 cup Ball Salt	2 quarts vinegar
2 cups sugar	7 small hot red peppers
¼ cup mustard seed	7 bay leaves
	Ball Pickle Crisp (optional)

Sprinkle onions with salt; add cold water to cover. Let stand 12 to 18 hours. Drain; rinse and drain thoroughly. Combine sugar, mustard seed, horseradish and vinegar in a large saucepot. Simmer 15 minutes. Pack onions into hot jars, leaving ½-inch headspace. Cut two small slits in hot red peppers. Add ½ pepper and ½ bay leaf to each half-pint jar. Add 1 pepper and 1 bay leaf to each pint jar. Add Pickle Crisp to each jar, if desired. Ladle hot liquid over onions, leaving ½-inch headspace. Remove air bubbles. Adjust two-piece caps. Process half-pints and pints 10 minutes in a boiling-water canner.

Recipe Variation: For Sour Onion Pickles omit all or part of sugar and bay leaves.

Note: When cutting or seeding hot peppers, wear rubber gloves to prevent hands from being burned.

Pickled Cauliflower

Yield: about 5 pints

3 quarts cauliflowerets (about 2 large heads)	2 tablespoons mustard seed
1½ cups peeled pearl onions	1 tablespoon celery seed
¼ cup Ball Salt	1 teaspoon turmeric
2 cups sugar	1 quart vinegar
	1 hot red pepper (optional)
	Ball Pickle Crisp (optional)

Combine cauliflowerets, onions and salt. Cover with ice; let stand 2 to 3 hours. Drain; rinse and drain thoroughly. Combine sugar, mustard seed, celery seed, turmeric and vinegar in a large saucepot. Cut two small slits in hot red pepper. Add pepper to vinegar, if desired. Bring to a boil. Add cauliflowerets and onions; return to a boil. Reduce heat and simmer 5 minutes. Discard hot red pepper. Pack hot vegetables and liquid into hot jars, leaving ½-inch headspace. Add Pickle Crisp to each jar, if desired. Remove air bubbles. Adjust two-piece caps. Process 10 minutes in a boiling-water canner.

Note: When cutting or seeding hot peppers, wear rubber gloves to prevent hands from being burned.

Pickled Garlic

Yield: about 6 half-pints

6 cups peeled cloves garlic	1 teaspoon Ball Salt
1 cup sugar	3 cups vinegar
	Ball Pickle Crisp (optional)

Blanch garlic in boiling water for 1 minute. Drain. Combine sugar, salt and vinegar in a large saucepot. Bring to a boil. Pack hot garlic into hot jars, leaving ½-inch headspace. Add Pickle Crisp to each jar, if desired. Ladle hot liquid over garlic, leaving ½-inch headspace. Remove air bubbles. Adjust two-piece caps. Process 10 minutes in a boiling-water canner.

Pickled Grape Tomatoes

Yield: about 4 pints

2 quarts grape tomatoes	1 quart water
1 teaspoon Ball Salt	4 cloves garlic, peeled
1 cup white wine vinegar	4 sprigs fresh rosemary
1 cup white vinegar	Ball Pickle Crisp (optional)

Wash grape tomatoes; drain. Combine salt, white wine vinegar, white vinegar and water in a medium saucepan and bring to a boil. Reduce heat and simmer 10 minutes. Pack grape tomatoes into hot jars, leaving ½-inch headspace. Add 1 clove garlic and 1 sprig rosemary to each jar. Add Pickle Crisp to each jar, if desired. Ladle hot liquid over tomatoes, leaving ½-inch headspace. Remove air bubbles. Adjust two-piece caps. Process 10 minutes in a boiling-water canner.

Note: Prick tomatoes to help prevent skin from cracking.

Pickled Pepper Mix

Yield: about 12 half-pints or 6 pints

3 quarts long red, green or yellow peppers (Hungarian, Banana or other varieties)	3 tablespoons sugar
	1½ teaspoons prepared horseradish
1 cup Ball Salt	2 cloves garlic
3½ quarts water, divided	1½ quarts vinegar
	Ball Pickle Crisp (optional)

Cut two small slits in each pepper. Dissolve salt in 3 quarts water. Pour over peppers and let stand 12 to 18 hours in a cool place. Drain; rinse and drain thoroughly. Combine 2 cups water and remaining ingredients in a large saucepot. Simmer 15 minutes. Discard garlic. Bring pickling liquid to a boil. Pack peppers into hot jars, leaving ½-inch headspace. Add Pickle Crisp to each jar, if desired. Ladle hot liquid over peppers, leaving ½-inch headspace. Remove air bubbles. Adjust two-piece caps. Process half-pints and pints 10 minutes in a boiling-water canner.

Note: When cutting or seeding hot peppers, wear rubber gloves to prevent hands from being burned.

Spiced Red Cabbage

Yield: about 5 quarts

12 pounds red cabbage (about 3 large heads)	2 quarts red wine vinegar
	¼ cup whole cloves
½ cup Ball Salt	¼ cup whole allspice
1 cup brown sugar	¼ cup peppercorns
½ cup mustard seed	¼ cup celery seed
¼ cup mace	2 sticks cinnamon
	Ball Pickle Crisp (optional)

Remove outer leaves of cabbage; core and shred. Layer cabbage and salt in a large bowl. Cover; let stand 24 hours. Rinse. Drain thoroughly on paper towel-lined trays, about 6 hours. Combine sugar, mustard seed, mace and vinegar in a large saucepot. Tie whole spices in a spice bag; add spice bag to vinegar. Boil 5 minutes. Remove spice bag. Pack cabbage into hot jars, leaving ½-inch headspace. Add Pickle Crisp to each jar, if desired. Ladle hot liquid over cabbage, leaving ½-inch headspace. Remove air bubbles. Adjust two-piece caps. Process 20 minutes in a boiling-water canner.

Vinegared Red Onions

Yield: about 6 half-pints

3 pounds red onions	1 clove garlic
4 cups red wine vinegar	Ball Pickle Crisp (optional)

Peel onions. Slice onions ¼-inch thick; separate slices into rings. Bring vinegar and garlic to a boil; reduce heat and simmer 5 minutes. Add onion rings to vinegar. Simmer, covered, 5 minutes. Discard garlic. Pack hot onions into hot jars, leaving ½-inch headspace. Add Pickle Crisp to each jar, if desired. Ladle hot pickling liquid over onions, leaving ½-inch headspace. Remove air bubbles. Adjust two-piece caps. Process 10 minutes in a boiling-water canner.

Zucchini Pickles

Yield: about 4 half-pints

2 pounds zucchini, sliced (about 8 small)	2 teaspoons mustard seed
	1 teaspoon celery salt
⅓ pound onion, quartered and sliced (about 1 small)	1 teaspoon turmeric
	3 cups vinegar
¼ cup Ball Salt	Ball Pickle Crisp (optional)
2 cups sugar	

Combine zucchini and onion; sprinkle with salt; add cold water to cover. Let stand 2 hours. Drain; rinse and drain thoroughly. Combine remaining ingredients in a large saucepot. Bring to a boil. Pour vinegar mixture over zucchini and onion. Let stand 2 hours. Bring all ingredients to a boil; reduce heat and simmer 5 minutes. Pack hot vegetables and liquid into hot jars, leaving ½-inch headspace. Add Pickle Crisp to each jar, if desired. Remove air bubbles. Adjust two-piece caps. Process 15 minutes in a boiling-water canner.

featured prepared recipe

Antipasto Platter

Makes 6 servings

Pickled Grape Tomatoes in Herb Marinade

1 pint jar Pickled Grape Tomatoes *(recipe on page 57)*	½ teaspoon minced fresh thyme
½ cup extra-virgin olive oil	¼ teaspoon kosher salt
½ teaspoon minced fresh rosemary	¼ teaspoon fresh cracked pepper
½ teaspoon minced fresh oregano	

Drain pickled grape tomatoes, reserving pickling liquid. Combine pickling liquid, olive oil, herbs and spices in a small bowl. Add pickled grape tomatoes stirring to coat evenly with marinade. Refrigerate overnight.

For Platter

6 ounces small whole portabella mushrooms	8 ounces black or Italian olives
¼ cup extra-virgin olive oil	6 ounces artichoke hearts
1½ pounds assorted Italian cured meats: prosciutto, salami, and bresaola	2 tablespoons capers
	½ pound asparagus, steamed
½ cantaloupe, peeled and cut into thin wedges	1 half-pint jar Onion Pickles *(recipe on page 56)*
1 pound fresh mozzarella bocconicini	1 pint jar Pickled Pepper Mix *(recipe on page 57)*

To Assemble Antipasto Platter: Bring marinated pickled grape tomatoes to room temperatuer. Lightly sauté mushrooms in ¼ cup olive oil. Cool. Wrap prosciutto around cantaloupe wedges and place on platter. Roll or fold salami and bresaola then arrange on platter. Place olives, artichoke hearts, mushrooms and asparagus on platter. Use half of marinade for tomatoes to drizzle over vegetables. Add mozzarella bocconicini. Garnish with capers. Serve marinated Pickled Grape Tomatoes, Onion Pickles, and Pickled Pepper Mix with antipasto platter.

low-acid foods

Meats, Seafoods & Vegetables

The crisp late afternoon air reminds you that this might be the last barbecue of the season. You gather with friends for great food and fellowship, enjoying the bounty you preserved at the peak of freshness earlier in the season.

Compliments to the chef are doubly satisfying because you have canned these gems yourself. A juicy melt-in-your-mouth grilled Flank Steak with Honey Glazed Red Onions takes center stage. On a plate bursting with flavor, crisp vegetables of bright yellows, reds and greens present a visual treat, served as hearty side dishes. And what barbeque would be complete without your famous Boston Baked Beans, rich with molasses and brown sugar that play opposite dry mustard, onions and salt pork. Yummm!

The volleyball game commences. Frisbees fly high. Children frolic on the swing set. Guests gather in clusters for impromptu and long overdue conversations. But you notice people often meander back to the food table to sample just a little more. On this brisk fall day and through the winter months, how rewarding to know that the secret of bringing new flavors to your table is the wholesome goodness of food you preserved when the days were long and warm.

Pictured, Flank Steak with
Honey Glazed Red Onions
Recipe for canned
Red Onions—With Honey on page 68.
Recipe for Flank Steak with
Honey Glazed Red Onions found on page 69.

getting started

Vegetables, meats, poultry, seafoods and combination recipes, such as soups and stews may be easily and safely canned at home. These foods are classified as low-acid, meaning they have a pH level greater than 4.6 on the acidity-alkalinity scale (*see page 4*). Because these foods have little natural acid that help guard against bacterial growth, it is necessary to process low-acid foods using a pressure canner.

Ensuring that spoilage microorganisms are destroyed when canning low-acid foods is achieved by following a tested home canning recipe that provides the correct processing method, processing time and temperature. Low-acid foods MUST be processed in a pressure canner at 240°F (at or below 1,000 feet above sea level). The steps for preparing recipes and filling jars are the same as for high-acid foods.

All recipes for low-acid foods in this book are based on processing at 10 pounds pressure using a weighted gauge canner and processing at or below 1,000 feet above sea level. When using a dial-gauge canner or processing at altitudes higher than 1,000 feet above sea level, an adjustment in the pounds pressure must be made, refer to Altitude Chart (*see page 5*).

Ingredients And Preparation

General instructions for canning low-acid foods at the beginning of this book must be followed for canning meats, poultry, seafoods and combination recipes. Special preparation instructions for a specific food type are outlined below and in the individual recipes.

Meats

The flavor and texture of canned meats depend upon the breed, feed and manner of handling the meat at the time of slaughter, and immediately thereafter. If you slaughter your own meat, contact your county Cooperative Extension Service for complete information on slaughtering, chilling and aging the meat.

To prepare the meat, cut meat into pieces suitable for cooking or canning. Cut slices across the grain about 1-inch thick. Then cut with the grain into jar-size pieces. For stew, cut into uniform cubes. Trim away gristle, bruised spots and fat. Too much fat is likely to cause the meat to develop a strong flavor and may also contribute to seal failure.

Do not let meat stand in water. However, strong-flavored game should be soaked in salt water before canning. Soak game 1 hour in a salt brine made of 1 tablespoon salt for each quart of water. Prepare, pack and process according to the tested recipes in this book.

Poultry

One- or two-year old fowl is best for canning. Begin separating poultry into parts by cutting skin between legs and body. Bend legs until hip joints snap. Slip knife under ends of shoulder blades and cut up to wings. Cut back and breast apart. Wash and dry. Do not salt. Chill 6 to 12 hours before canning.

Seafoods

Prepare freshly caught fish as for cooking. Leave backbone in small fish; debone large fish. Fish should be soaked in salt water before canning. Fish must not be canned in jars larger than pint sized. Because seafood is very low in acidity, heat penetration in larger jars may be inadequate for destroying bacterial spores.

Combination Recipes

Ingredients should be cut into uniform pieces for even heat penetration during processing. For recipes containing vegetables and meat, the length of processing time used must be adequate for the vegetable or meat requiring the longest processing. Combination recipes that contain some low-acid and some high-acid ingredients and have a pH higher than 4.6 must be processed as a low-acid product using a pressure canner, refer to Pressure Method (*see page 4*).

Equipment And Utensils

Standard kitchen equipment is basically all you will need to prepare vegetables, meats, poultry, seafoods and other low-acid foods for home canning. Time-saving equipment like a food processor and meat grinder help make quick work of chopping, grinding and dicing.

meats

Broth For Canning Meat

Remove meat from cooking pan. Add 1 cup boiling water or broth for each 1 to 2 tablespoons fat in the pan. Boil 2 to 3 minutes. Do not add a thickening agent such as flour or cornstarch before canning.

Chopped Meat

Beef, Lamb, Mutton, Pork, Veal, Venison

Grind fresh meat in a food processor or meat grinder. Sear meat in a hot skillet. Add 1 to 1½ cups boiling water, broth or tomato juice for each quart of chopped meat. Add ½ teaspoon salt to each pint jar, 1 teaspoon salt to each quart jar, if desired. Pack hot meat and liquid into hot jars, leaving 1-inch headspace. Remove air bubbles. Adjust two-piece caps. Process pints 1 hour and 15 minutes, quarts 1 hour and 30 minutes, at 10 pounds pressure in a pressure canner.

To Serve: Use canned chopped meat for casseroles, baked hash or stuffing sweet green peppers.

Pork Sausage

Grind fresh pork in a food processor or meat grinder. Season pork with salt, black pepper, cayenne pepper, thyme, oregano and basil in any combination, if desired. Shape ground pork into patties or 3- to 4-inch links. Cook until lightly browned. Drain. Pack hot sausage into hot jars, leaving 1-inch headspace. Ladle hot broth over sausage, leaving 1-inch headspace. Remove air bubbles. Adjust two-piece caps. Process pints 1 hour and 15 minutes, quarts 1 hour and 30 minutes, at 10 pounds pressure in a pressure canner.

Note: Do not use sage to season sausage as it may become bitter.

Pork Tenderloin

Raw Pack: Slice pork tenderloin crosswise into ½- to 1-inch slices. Add ½ teaspoon salt to each pint jar, 1 teaspoon salt to each quart jar, if desired. Pack tenderloin into hot jars, leaving 1-inch headspace. Ladle hot water or broth over tenderloin, leaving 1-inch headspace. Remove air bubbles. Adjust two-piece caps. Process pints 1 hour and 15 minutes, quarts 1 hour and 30 minutes, at 10 pounds pressure in a pressure canner.

Hot Pack: Cook whole pork tenderloin until a third to half done. Slice pork tenderloin crosswise into ½- to 1-inch slices. Add ½ teaspoon salt to each pint jar, 1 teaspoon salt to each quart jar, if desired. Pack hot tenderloin into hot jars, leaving 1-inch headspace. Ladle hot water or broth over tenderloin, leaving 1-inch headspace. Remove air bubbles. Adjust two-piece caps. Process pints 1 hour and 15 minutes, quarts 1 hour and 30 minutes, at 10 pounds pressure in a pressure canner.

Roast

Beef, Lamb, Mutton, Pork, Veal, Venison

Cut meat into jar-length strips ½- to 1-inch thick. Bake or roast meat until well browned but not done. Meat may also be browned in a small amount of fat. Add ½ teaspoon salt to each pint jar, 1 teaspoon salt to each quart jar, if desired. Pack hot meat into hot jars, leaving 1-inch headspace. Ladle hot broth over meat, leaving 1-inch headspace. Remove air bubbles. Adjust two-piece caps. Process pints 1 hour and 15 minutes, quarts 1 hour and 30 minutes, at 10 pounds pressure in a pressure canner.

Spareribs

Crack ribs evenly. Cook until about half done. Remove bones. Cut meat into squares. Add ½ teaspoon salt to each pint jar, 1 teaspoon salt to each quart jar, if desired. Pack hot ribs into hot jars, leaving 1-inch headspace. Ladle hot barbecue sauce *(see page 54)* or broth over meat, leaving 1-inch headspace. Remove air bubbles. Adjust two-piece caps. Process pints 1 hour and 15 minutes, quarts 1 hour and 30 minutes, at 10 pounds pressure in a pressure canner.

Steaks And Chops

Beef, Lamb, Mutton, Pork, Veal, Venison

Raw Pack: Cut meat into 1-inch slices. Remove large bones. Add ½ teaspoon salt to each pint jar, 1 teaspoon salt to each quart jar, if desired. Pack meat into hot jars, leaving 1-inch headspace. Ladle hot broth over meat, leaving 1-inch headspace. Remove air bubbles. Adjust two-piece caps. Process pints 1 hour and 15 minutes, quarts 1 hour and 30 minutes, at 10 pounds pressure in a pressure canner.

Hot Pack: Cut meat into 1-inch slices. Remove large bones. Quickly brown meat in a small amount of fat. Add ½ teaspoon salt to each pint jar, 1 teaspoon salt to each quart jar, if desired. Pack hot meat into hot jars, leaving 1-inch headspace. Ladle hot broth over meat, leaving 1-inch headspace. Remove air bubbles. Adjust two-piece caps. Process pints 1 hour and 15 minutes, quarts 1 hour and 30 minutes, at 10 pounds pressure in a pressure canner.

Stew Meat

Use beef or other meat suitable for stewing. Cut into 1½- to 2-inch cubes. Remove fat and gristle. Simmer meat in water to cover until hot throughout. Add ½ teaspoon salt to each pint jar, 1 teaspoon salt to each quart jar, if desired. Pack hot meat into hot jars, leaving 1-inch headspace. Ladle hot cooking liquid over meat, leaving 1-inch headspace. Remove air bubbles. Adjust two-piece caps. Process pints 1 hour and 15 minutes, quarts 1 hour and 30 minutes, at 10 pounds pressure in a pressure canner.

Rabbit And Squirrel

Soak fresh game meat for 1 hour in salt brine made by dissolving 1 tablespoon salt for each quart water. Rinse.

Raw Pack: Separate rabbit or squirrel at joints. Bones may be left in or removed. Pack meat into hot jars, leaving 1-inch headspace. Ladle hot water or broth over meat, leaving 1-inch headspace. Remove air bubbles. Adjust two-piece caps. For boned meat process pints 1 hour and 15 minutes, quarts 1 hour and 30 minutes, at 10 pounds pressure in a pressure canner. For bone-in meat process pints 1 hour and 5 minutes, quarts 1 hour and 15 minutes, at 10 pounds pressure in a pressure canner.

Hot Pack: Boil, steam or bake rabbit or squirrel until about two-thirds done. Separate at joints. Bones may be left in or removed. Pack meat into hot jars, leaving 1-inch headspace. Ladle hot water or broth over meat, leaving 1-inch headspace. Adjust two-piece caps. For boned meat process pints 1 hour and 15 minutes, quarts 1 hour and 30 minutes, at 10 pounds pressure in a pressure canner. For bone-in meat process pints 1 hour and 5 minutes, quarts 1 hour and 15 minutes, at 10 pounds pressure in a pressure canner.

Chicken, Duck, Goose, Turkey, Game Birds

Raw Pack: Separate poultry or game bird at joints. Bones may be left in or removed. Pack meat into hot jars, leaving 1-inch headspace. Ladle hot water or broth over meat, leaving 1-inch headspace. Remove air bubbles. Adjust two-piece caps. For boned meat process pints 1 hour and 15 minutes, quarts 1 hour and 30 minutes, at 10 pounds pressure in a pressure canner. For bone-in meat process pints 1 hour and 5 minutes, quarts 1 hour and 15 minutes, at 10 pounds pressure in a pressure canner.

Hot Pack: Boil, steam or bake poultry or game bird until about ⅔ done. Separate at joints. Bones may be left in or removed. Pack meat into hot jars, leaving 1-inch headspace. Ladle hot water or broth over meat, leaving 1-inch headspace. Remove air bubbles. Adjust two-piece caps. For boned meat process pints 1 hour and 15 minutes, quarts 1 hour and 30 minutes, at 10 pounds pressure in a pressure canner. For bone-in meat process pints 1 hour and 5 minutes, quarts 1 hour and 15 minutes, at 10 pounds pressure in a pressure canner.

seafoods

Clams

Keep clams alive, moist and chilled until ready to can. Scrub clams. Steam and open shells; remove meat. (If shell does not open, discard clam.) Reserve juice. Drop clam meat into salt water brine made by dissolving ½ cup salt in 1 gallon water. Drain. Wash thoroughly. Add 2 tablespoons bottled lemon juice to 1 gallon boiling water. Add clam meat; boil 2 minutes. Drain. Only process in half-pints or pints. Pack hot clam meat into hot jars, leaving 1-inch headspace. Ladle reserved hot juice over clams. If there is not enough juice to cover clams, add boiling water, leaving 1-inch headspace. Remove air bubbles. Adjust two-piece caps. Process half-pints 1 hour, pints 1 hour and 10 minutes, at 10 pounds pressure in a pressure canner.

Crab Meat

King, Dungeness

Keep crabs alive, moist and chilled until ready to can. Wash crabs through several changes of cold water. Combine ¼ cup bottled lemon juice, 2 tablespoons salt and 1 gallon water in a large saucepot; bring to a boil. Add crabs; boil 20 minutes. Drain cooked crabs. Cool in cold water. Drain. Remove back shell. Remove meat from body and claws. Place crab meat in brine of 2 tablespoons salt, 2 cups bottled lemon juice or 4 cups vinegar and 1 gallon cold water. Soak crab meat 2 minutes. Drain. Squeeze excess liquid from meat. Only process in half-pints and pints. Pack 6 ounces crab meat into hot half-pint jars, or 12 ounces crab meat into hot pint jars, leaving 1-inch headspace. Add 2 tablespoons bottled lemon juice to each half-pint jar, 4 tablespoons bottled lemon juice to each pint jar. Ladle hot water over meat, leaving 1-inch headspace. Remove air bubbles. Adjust two-piece caps. Process half-pints and pints 1 hour and 20 minutes at 10 pounds pressure in a pressure canner.

Fish

All varieties, including Salmon and Shad. For Tuna, see Tuna recipe.

Clean fish within 2 hours after it is caught. Keep cleaned fish chilled until ready to can. Dissolve 1 cup salt in 1 gallon water to make brine. Cut fish into jar-length pieces. Soak fish in brine for 1 hour. Drain for 10 minutes. Only process in half-pints or pints. Pack fish into hot jars, skin side next to glass, leaving 1-inch headspace. Adjust two-piece caps. Process half-pints and pints 1 hour and 40 minutes at 10 pounds pressure in a pressure canner.

Oysters

Keep oysters alive and chilled until ready to can. Wash shells. Bake oysters at 400°F for 5 to 7 minutes. Quickly cool in ice water. Drain. Remove oyster meat from shells. Wash meat in salted water made with ½ cup salt and 1 gallon water. Drain. Only process in half-pints or pints. Pack oysters into hot jars, leaving 1-inch headspace. Ladle hot water over oysters, leaving 1-inch headspace. Remove air bubbles. Adjust two-piece caps. Process half-pints and pints 1 hour and 15 minutes at 10 pounds pressure in a pressure canner.

Shrimp

Remove heads immediately after shrimp is caught. Wash shrimp and drain. Keep shrimp chilled until ready to can. Prepare a brine of 1 cup salt, 1 cup vinegar and 1 gallon water. Bring brine to a boil in a large saucepot. Boil shrimp in brine for 10 minutes. Transfer shrimp to cold water. Drain. Peel and remove sand vein. Rinse in cold water. Prepare canning brine using 1 to 3 tablespoons salt and 1 gallon water. Bring brine to a boil in a large saucepot. Only process in half-pints or pints. Pack shrimp into hot jars, leaving 1-inch headspace. Ladle hot brine over shrimp, leaving 1-inch headspace. Remove air bubbles. Adjust two-piece caps. Process half-pints and pints 45 minutes at 10 pounds pressure in a pressure canner.

Tuna

Raw Pack: Fillet raw tuna. Remove skin; lightly scrape surface to remove blood vessels and any discolored flesh. Cut fish into quarters; remove all bones; discard dark flesh. Cut quarters crosswise into jar-length pieces.

Only process in half-pints or pints. Pack fish into hot jars, leaving 1-inch headspace. Add ½ teaspoon salt to each half-pint jar, 1 teaspoon salt to each pint jar. Ladle hot water over tuna, leaving 1-inch headspace. Remove air bubbles. Adjust two-piece caps. Process half-pints and pints 1 hour and 40 minutes at 10 pounds pressure in a pressure canner.

Hot Pack: Place cleaned tuna on a rack in a large baking pan. Bake at 350°F for 1 hour or until done. The internal temperature of the tuna must be 165° to 175°F. Refrigerate overnight. Remove skin and lightly scrape surface to remove blood vessels and any discolored flesh. Cut fish into quarters, removing all bones. Discard all dark flesh. Cut quarters crosswise into jar-length pieces. Only process in half-pints or pints. Pack fish into hot jars, leaving 1-inch headspace. Add ½ teaspoon salt and 1 tablespoon vegetable oil or water to each half-pint jar. Add 1 teaspoon salt and 2 tablespoons vegetable oil or water to each pint jar. Remove air bubbles. Adjust two-piece caps. Process half-pints and pints 1 hour and 40 minutes at 10 pounds pressure in a pressure canner.

Note: Crystals of magnesium ammonium phosphate may form in canned tuna. There is no way to prevent crystals from forming in home canned tuna. They usually dissolve when the tuna is heated. If the crystals do not dissolve, they are safe to eat.

entrées, soups & stocks

Bean Soup

Yield: about 5 pints or 2 quarts

2 cups dried navy beans (about 1 pound)	½ hot red pepper, finely chopped
1 ham hock or ¼ pound salt pork	Salt and pepper to taste
½ cup chopped onion (about ½ medium)	

Put beans in a large saucepot; add water to cover by 2 inches. Bring beans to a boil; boil 2 minutes. Remove from heat and let beans soak 1 hour. Drain. Cover beans with water by 2 inches. Add meat, onion and pepper; bring to a boil. Cover; simmer 2 hours. Remove ham hock and dice meat. Return meat to soup. Discard bone. Season with salt and pepper to taste. Ladle hot soup into hot jars, leaving 1-inch headspace. Adjust two-piece caps. Process pints 1 hour and 15 minutes, quarts 1 hour and 30 minutes, at 10 pounds pressure in a pressure canner.

Note: When cutting or seeding hot peppers, wear rubber gloves to prevent hands from being burned.

Beef In Wine Sauce

Yield: about 3 pints or 1 quart

2 pounds round steak, cut into 1-inch cubes	½ cup water
1 tablespoon oil	½ cup red cooking wine
1 cup shredded apple (about 1 large)	1 teaspoon salt
1 cup shredded carrot (about ½ large)	2 cloves garlic, minced
¾ cup sliced onion (about ½ large)	2 beef bouillon cubes
	2 bay leaves
	½ teaspoon browning and seasoning sauce

Brown meat in oil in a large saucepot. Add apple, carrot, onion, ½ cup water, wine, salt, garlic, bouillon cubes and bay leaves. Simmer 1 hour. Remove bay leaves. Add browning and seasoning sauce. Pack hot beef and

sauce into hot jars, leaving 1-inch headspace. Remove air bubbles. Adjust two-piece caps. Process pints 1 hour and 15 minutes, quarts 1 hour and 30 minutes, at 10 pounds pressure in a pressure canner.

To Serve: Stir 2 teaspoons cornstarch into each pint or 1 tablespoon plus 1 teaspoon into each quart and cook until mixture thickens.

Note: Do not add cornstarch before canning.

Beef Stew With Vegetables

Yield: about 14 pints or 7 quarts

4 to 5 pounds beef stew meat	3 cups chopped celery
1 tablespoon oil	(about 5 stalks)
3 quarts cubed and	3 cups chopped onions
peeled potatoes	(about 4 small)
(about 12 medium)	1½ tablespoons salt
2 quarts sliced carrots	1 teaspoon thyme
(about 16 small)	½ teaspoon pepper

Cut meat into 1½-inch cubes; brown in oil. Combine meat, vegetables and seasonings in a large saucepot. Cover with boiling water. Bring stew to a boil. Ladle hot stew into hot jars, leaving 1-inch headspace. Remove air bubbles. Adjust two-piece caps. Process pints 1 hour and 15 minutes, quarts 1 hour and 30 minutes, at 10 pounds pressure in a pressure canner.

Beef Stock

Yield: about 4 pints or 2 quarts

4 pounds meaty beef bones	1 stalk celery, sliced
2 quarts water	1 bay leaf
1 medium onion,	Salt and pepper to taste
finely chopped	Beef bouillon cubes or
1 carrot, sliced	granules (optional)

Bring beef bones and water to a boil over high heat in a large saucepot. Reduce heat; skim foam. Add onion, carrot, celery, and bay leaf. Cover; simmer 2 to 3 hours. If more flavor is desired, simmer longer or add beef bouillon cubes or granules to stock. Remove beef bones from stock. Strain stock through a sieve or several layers of cheesecloth. Allow stock to cool until fat solidifies; skim off fat. Bring stock to a boil in a large saucepot. Season with salt and pepper to taste. Ladle hot stock into hot jars, leaving 1-inch headspace. Adjust two-piece caps. Process pints 20 minutes, quarts 25 minutes, at 10 pounds pressure in a pressure canner.

Chicken Soup

Yield: about 8 pints or 4 quarts

4 quarts chicken stock	1 cup diced onion
3 cups diced chicken	(about 1 medium)
(about one 3 pound chicken)	Salt and pepper to taste
1½ cups diced celery	3 chicken bouillon cubes
(about 2 stalks)	(optional)
1½ cups sliced carrots	

Combine chicken stock, chicken, celery, carrots and onion in a large saucepot. Bring mixture to a boil. Reduce heat; simmer 30 minutes. Season with salt and pepper to taste. Add bouillon cubes, if desired. Cook until bouillon cubes are dissolved. Ladle hot soup into hot jars, leaving 1-inch headspace. Adjust two-piece caps. Process pints 1 hour and 15 minutes, quarts 1 hour and 30 minutes, at 10 pounds pressure in a pressure canner.

Chicken Stock

Yield: about 8 pints or 4 quarts

1 (3 to 4 pound) chicken,	2 medium onions, quartered
cut into pieces	10 peppercorns
4 quarts water	2 bay leaves
2 stalks celery	1 tablespoon salt

Combine chicken and water in a large saucepot. Bring to a boil. Add remaining ingredients. Reduce heat; simmer 2 hours or until chicken is tender. Remove from heat; skim off foam. Remove chicken from stock, reserving chicken for another use. Strain stock through a sieve or several layers of cheesecloth. Allow stock to cool until fat solidifies; skim off fat. Bring stock to a boil in a large saucepot. Ladle hot stock into hot jars, leaving 1-inch headspace. Adjust two-piece caps. Process pints 20 minutes, quarts 25 minutes, at 10 pounds pressure in a pressure canner.

Chili

Yield: about 6 pints or 3 quarts

5 pounds ground beef	½ cup chili powder
2 cups chopped onions	1½ tablespoons salt
(about 2 medium)	1 hot red pepper,
1 clove garlic, minced	finely chopped
6 cups canned tomatoes	1 teaspoon cumin seed
and juice	

Brown meat in a large saucepot. Drain off excess fat. Add onions and garlic; cook slowly until onions are tender. Add remaining ingredients and simmer 20 minutes. Skim off excess fat, if necessary, before canning. Ladle hot chili into hot jars, leaving 1-inch headspace. Remove air bubbles. Adjust two-piece caps. Process pints 1 hour and 15 minutes, quarts 1 hour and 30 minutes, at 10 pounds pressure in a pressure canner.

To Serve: Add cooked or canned pinto or kidney beans; heat and serve.

Note: When cutting or seeding hot peppers, wear rubber gloves to prevent hands from being burned.

Clam Chowder Base

Yield: about 20 half-pints or 10 pints

½ pound diced salt pork	2 quarts diced and peeled
1 cup chopped onion	potatoes (about 8 medium)
(about 1 medium)	2 quarts boiling water
3 to 4 quarts cleaned	Salt and pepper to taste
chopped clams with juice	

Cook salt pork until light brown in a large saucepot. Drain off excess fat. Add onion and cook until onion is tender but not brown. Add clams with juice, potatoes and water. Boil 10 minutes. Season with salt and pepper to taste. Only process in half-pints or pints. Ladle hot chowder base into hot jars, leaving 1-inch headspace. Adjust two-piece caps. Process half-pints and pints 1 hour and 40 minutes at 10 pounds pressure in a pressure canner.

Recipe Variation: For Manhattan Chowder, add the following ingredients, removing bay leaf before canning.

2 cups cooked tomatoes	½ bay leaf
½ cup chopped celery	½ teaspoon thyme
(about ½ stalk)	

To Serve: For New England Chowder, add 2 tablespoons butter and 2 cups milk to each pint of clam chowder base before heating for serving. Reduce butter and milk by half for half-pints.

Note: Do not add butter and milk before canning.

Creole Sauce

Yield: about 4 pints or 2 quarts

3 quarts chopped, peeled, cored tomatoes (about 18 medium)	1 clove garlic, minced
	1 hot red pepper, finely chopped
2 cups chopped onions (about 2 medium)	1 tablespoon chopped parsley
1 cup chopped sweet red peppers (about 2 medium)	1 tablespoon sugar
	2 teaspoons salt
½ cup chopped celery	½ teaspoon marjoram
	¼ teaspoon chili powder

Combine all ingredients in a large saucepot. Cook slowly until thick. As sauce thickens, stir frequently to prevent sticking. Ladle hot sauce into hot jars, leaving 1-inch headspace. Adjust two-piece caps. Process pints 25 minutes, quarts 30 minutes, at 10 pounds pressure in a pressure canner.

Note: When cutting or seeding hot peppers, wear rubber gloves to prevent hands from being burned.

Goulash

Yield: about 4 pints or 2 quarts

4 pounds boned beef chuck roast	3 bay leaves
1 tablespoon salt	2 teaspoons caraway seeds
3 tablespoons paprika	6 stalks celery, cut in half
2 teaspoons dry mustard	4 large carrots, cut in half
⅓ cup oil	3 medium onions, cut in half
20 peppercorns	1 cup water
	⅓ cup vinegar

Cut beef chuck roast into 1-inch cubes. Combine salt, paprika and dry mustard. Roll meat in spice mixture. Brown slowly in hot oil in a large saucepot. Sprinkle excess spice mixture over meat. Tie whole spices in a spice bag. Add spice bag and remaining ingredients to beef mixture. Cover; simmer until almost tender. Remove spice bag and vegetables; discard. Pack hot meat and sauce into hot jars, leaving 1-inch headspace. Remove air bubbles. Adjust two-piece caps. Process pints 1 hour and 15 minutes, quarts 1 hour and 30 minutes, at 10 pounds pressure in a pressure canner.

Green Tomato Mincemeat

Yield: about 10 pints or 5 quarts

2 quarts chopped and cored green tomatoes (about 20 small)	1 pound raisins
	⅔ cup chopped orange pulp (about 1 medium)
1 tablespoon salt	3 tablespoons grated orange peel (about 1 medium)
2½ quarts chopped, peeled, cored apples (about 12 medium)	2 teaspoons cinnamon
	1 teaspoon nutmeg
3½ cups brown sugar	1 teaspoon cloves
1½ cups chopped suet (about 6 ounces)	½ teaspoon ginger
	½ cup vinegar

Put green tomatoes in a large bowl. Sprinkle tomatoes with salt; let stand 1 hour. Rinse and drain. Cover tomatoes with boiling water; let stand 5 minutes. Drain. Combine all ingredients in a large saucepot. Bring to a boil; reduce heat and simmer 15 minutes. Ladle hot mincemeat into hot jars, leaving 1-inch headspace. Remove air bubbles. Adjust two-piece caps. Process pints and quarts 1 hour and 30 minutes at 10 pounds pressure in a pressure canner.

Madeira Pear Mincemeat

Yield: about 8 pints or 4 quarts

2 quarts coarsely chopped and cored pears	2 cups chopped sweet yellow pepper
1 cup golden raisins	1 cup chopped yellow onion
1 cup dried cherries	¼ cup minced crystallized ginger
1 cup sugar	1 tablespoon grated fresh ginger
1 cup water	
1 cup Madeira	2 teaspoons allspice
1 quart sliced zucchini	1 teaspoon salt
1 quart sliced yellow squash	2 cups diced mushrooms

Combine pears, raisins, dried cherries, sugar, water and Madeira in a large saucepot. Let stand 1 hour. Add remaining ingredients. Bring to a boil; reduce heat and simmer 15 minutes. Ladle hot mincemeat into hot jars, leaving 1-inch headspace. Remove air bubbles. Adjust two-piece caps. Process pints and quarts 25 minutes at 10 pounds pressure in a pressure canner.

Meat Sauce

Yield: about 6 pints or 3 quarts

5 pounds ground beef	2 tablespoons brown sugar
2 cups chopped onions (about 2 medium)	2 tablespoons minced parsley
	1½ tablespoons salt
1 cup chopped green peppers (about 2 medium)	1 tablespoon oregano
	½ teaspoon pepper
9 cups cooked or canned tomatoes and juice	½ teaspoon ginger
	½ teaspoon allspice
2⅔ cups tomato paste (about 24 ounces)	2 tablespoons vinegar

Brown beef in a large saucepot. Drain off excess fat. Add onions and green peppers and cook slowly until tender. Add remaining ingredients; simmer until as thick as desired. Skim off excess fat, if necessary. Ladle hot sauce into hot jars, leaving 1-inch headspace. Adjust two-piece caps. Process pints 1 hour, quarts 1 hour and 15 minutes, at 10 pounds pressure in a pressure canner.

Mincemeat—Traditional

Yield: about 12 pints or 6 quarts

5 cups cooked ground beef (about 2 pounds)	1 (8-ounce) package candied citron, chopped
1 quart ground suet (about 1 pound)	4½ cups brown sugar
	1 tablespoon salt
3 pounds raisins, mixture of light and dark	1 tablespoon cinnamon
	1 tablespoon allspice
2 pounds dried currants	2 teaspoons nutmeg
3 quarts chopped, peeled, cored, tart apples (about 12 medium)	1 teaspoon cloves
	¼ teaspoon ginger
⅓ cup finely chopped orange peel (about 1 large)	1 quart sweet apple cider or white grape juice
1½ cups chopped orange pulp (about 2 large)	¼ cup lemon juice

Combine all ingredients in a large saucepot; simmer 30 minutes. As mixture thickens, stir frequently to prevent sticking. Pack hot mincemeat into hot jars, leaving 1-inch headspace. Remove air bubbles. Adjust two-piece caps. Process pints and quarts 1 hour and 30 minutes at 10 pounds pressure in a pressure canner.

Seasoned Ground Beef

Yield: about 5 pints or 2 quarts

4 pounds lean ground beef	2 cups tomato juice
1½ cups chopped onions (about 2 medium)	1½ cups beef broth
2 cloves garlic, minced	1 teaspoon seasoned salt
	½ teaspoon pepper

Brown meat. Drain off excess fat. Add onions and garlic; cook slowly until onions are tender. Add remaining ingredients and simmer 15 minutes or until hot throughout. Skim off excess fat, if necessary. Pack hot meat and sauce into hot jars, leaving 1-inch headspace. Adjust two-piece caps. Process pints 1 hour and 15 minutes, quarts 1 hour and 30 minutes, at 10 pounds pressure in a pressure canner.

Spiced Tomato Soup

Yield: about 4 pints

4 quarts chopped, peeled, cored tomatoes	1 cup sliced carrots
3½ cups chopped onions	7 bay leaves
2½ cups chopped celery	1 tablespoon whole cloves
2 cups chopped sweet red peppers	1 clove garlic
	1 cup brown sugar
	2 teaspoons salt

Combine tomatoes, onions, celery, peppers, carrots, bay leaves, cloves and garlic in a large saucepot. Simmer until vegetables are tender. Purée in a food processor or food mill. Return purée to saucepot. Add sugar and salt. Cook over medium heat 15 minutes. Ladle hot soup into hot jars, leaving 1-inch headspace. Adjust two-piece caps. Process pints 20 minutes at 10 pounds pressure in a pressure canner.

Southwestern Vegetable Soup

Yield: about 9 pints or 4 quarts

6 cups whole kernel corn, uncooked	¾ cup chopped and seeded long green pepper
1 quart chopped, peeled, cored tomatoes	¼ cup chopped and seeded hot pepper
2 cups chopped, cored, husked tomatillos	3 tablespoons minced cilantro
1 cup sliced carrots	2 teaspoons chili powder
1 cup chopped onion	1 teaspoon cayenne pepper
1 cup chopped sweet red pepper	1 teaspoon black pepper
	1 teaspoon salt
1 cup chopped sweet green pepper	6 cups tomato juice
	1 cup water
	4 teaspoons hot pepper sauce

Combine all ingredients in a large saucepot. Bring to a boil. Reduce heat and simmer 15 minutes. Ladle hot soup into hot jars, leaving 1-inch headspace. Adjust two-piece caps. Process pints 55 minutes, quarts 1 hour and 25 minutes, at 10 pounds pressure in a pressure canner.

Note: When cutting or seeding hot peppers, wear rubber gloves to prevent hands from being burned.

Split Pea Soup

Yield: about 5 pints or 2 quarts

1 (16-ounce) package dried split peas	1 cup diced, cooked ham
2 quarts water	1 bay leaf
1½ cups sliced carrots (about 3 medium)	¼ teaspoon allspice
	Salt and pepper to taste
1 cup chopped onion (about 1 medium)	

Combine dried peas and water in a large saucepot. Bring to a boil; reduce heat. Cover, simmer about 1 hour or until peas are soft. If a smooth soup is desired, purée in a food processor or food mill. Return purée to saucepot. Add remaining ingredients and simmer 30 minutes. If mixture is too thick, add boiling water. Ladle hot soup into hot jars, leaving 1-inch headspace. Adjust two-piece caps. Process pints 1 hour and 15 minutes, quarts 1 hour and 30 minutes, at 10 pounds pressure in a pressure canner.

Ten Bean Soup

Yield: about 6 quarts

½ cup dried black beans	¼ cup dried chick peas
½ cup dried kidney beans	¼ cup dried lentils
½ cup dried navy beans	1½ cups diced ham (optional)
½ cup dried pinto beans	½ cup cut fresh green beans
½ cup dried Great Northern beans	2 bay leaves
	1 tablespoon tarragon
¼ cup dried blackeye peas	1 tablespoon summer savory
¼ cup dried split peas	Salt and pepper to taste

Put dried beans in a large saucepot; add water to cover by 2 inches. Bring dried beans to a boil; boil 2 minutes. Remove from heat and let beans soak 1 hour. Drain. Cover beans with water by 2 inches in a large saucepot. Add ham, if desired. Stir in green beans, bay leaves, tarragon and summer savory. Bring to a boil. Cover, boil 30 minutes. Salt and pepper to taste. Remove bay leaves. Ladle hot soup into hot jars, leaving 1-inch headspace. Remove air bubbles. Adjust two-piece caps. Process 1 hour and 30 minutes at 10 pounds pressure in a pressure canner.

Vegetable Soup

Yield: about 14 pints or 7 quarts

2 quarts chopped, peeled, cored tomatoes (about 12 large)	1 quart whole kernel corn, uncooked
	2 cups 1-inch sliced celery (about 4 stalks)
1½ quarts cubed and peeled potatoes (about 6 medium)	2 cups chopped onions (about 2 medium)
1½ quarts ¾-inch sliced carrots (about 12 medium)	1½ quarts water
1 quart lima beans	Salt and pepper to taste

Combine all vegetables in a large saucepot. Add water; simmer 15 minutes. Season with salt and pepper to taste. Ladle hot soup into hot jars, leaving 1-inch headspace. Remove air bubbles. Adjust two-piece caps. Process pints 55 minutes, quarts 1 hour and 25 minutes, at 10 pounds pressure in a pressure canner.

Vegetable Stock

Yield: about 8 pints or 4 quarts

1 pound carrots, cut into 1-inch pieces	2 medium tomatoes, seeded and diced
6 stalks celery, cut into 1-inch pieces	2 medium turnips, diced
3 medium onions, quartered	3 cloves garlic, crushed
2 sweet red peppers, cut into 1-inch pieces	3 bay leaves
	1 teaspoon crushed thyme
	8 peppercorns
	7 quarts water

Combine all ingredients in a large saucepot. Bring to a boil; reduce heat. Cover, simmer 2 hours. Uncover and continue cooking 2 hours. Strain stock through several layers of cheesecloth. Discard vegetables and seasonings. Ladle hot stock into hot jars, leaving 1-inch headspace. Adjust two-piece caps. Process pints 30 minutes, quarts 35 minutes, at 10 pounds pressure in a pressure canner.

vegetables

Asparagus

3½ pounds asparagus per quart	Salt (optional) Water

Raw Pack: Wash asparagus; drain. Remove tough ends and scales. Wash again. Pack asparagus as tightly as possible without crushing into hot jars, leaving 1-inch headspace. Add ½ teaspoon salt to each pint jar, 1 teaspoon salt to each quart jar, if desired. Ladle boiling water over asparagus, leaving 1-inch headspace. Remove air bubbles. Adjust two-piece caps. Process pints 30 minutes, quarts 40 minutes, at 10 pounds pressure in a pressure canner.

Hot Pack: Wash asparagus; drain. Remove tough ends and scales. Wash again. Cut asparagus into 1-inch pieces. Boil 3 minutes. Pack hot asparagus into hot jars, leaving 1-inch headspace. Add ½ teaspoon salt to each pint jar, 1 teaspoon salt to each quart jar, if desired. Ladle boiling water over asparagus, leaving 1-inch headspace. Remove air bubbles. Adjust two-piece caps. Process pints 30 minutes, quarts 40 minutes, at 10 pounds pressure in a pressure canner.

Beans—Boston Baked

Yield: about 6 pints or 3 quarts

1 quart dried navy beans (about 2 pounds)	⅔ cup brown sugar
½ pound salt pork, cut into pieces	2 teaspoons salt
3 large onions, sliced	2 teaspoons dry mustard
	⅔ cup molasses

Put beans in a large saucepot; add water to cover by 2 inches. Bring beans to a boil; boil 2 minutes. Remove from heat and let beans soak 1 hour. Drain. Cover beans with water by 2 inches in a large saucepot. Bring beans to a boil; reduce heat. Cover; simmer until skins begin to crack. Drain, reserving liquid. Pour beans into a baking dish or bean pot. Add pork and onions. Combine remaining ingredients and 4 cups reserved bean liquid (add water to make 4 cups, if necessary). Ladle sauce over beans. Cover; bake at 350°F for about 3½ hours. Add water, if necessary, as beans should be "soupy." Pack hot beans and sauce into hot jars, leaving 1-inch headspace. Remove air bubbles. Adjust two-piece caps. Process pints 1 hour and 20 minutes, quarts 1 hour and 35 minutes, at 10 pounds pressure in a pressure canner.

Beans Or Peas—Dried

Kidney, Navy, Pinto, Etc.

¾ pounds dried beans or peas per quart	Salt (optional) Water

Put beans or peas in a large saucepot; add water to cover by 2 inches. Bring beans or peas to a boil; boil 2 minutes. Remove from heat and let beans or peas soak 1 hour. Drain. Cover beans or peas with cold water by 2 inches in a large saucepot. Bring to a boil; boil 30 minutes, stirring frequently. Pack hot beans or peas into hot jars, leaving 1-inch headspace. Add ½ teaspoon salt to each pint jar, 1 teaspoon salt to each quart jar, if desired. Ladle hot cooking liquid or boiling water over beans or peas, leaving 1-inch headspace. Remove air bubbles. Adjust two-piece caps. Process pints 1 hour and 15 minutes, quarts 1 hour and 30 minutes, at 10 pounds pressure in a pressure canner.

Beans—Green, Snap And Wax

Green, Hull, Italian, Purple, Snap and Wax

1½ to 2½ pounds beans per quart	Salt (optional) Water

Raw Pack: Wash beans; drain. Remove string, trim ends and break or cut freshly gathered beans into 2-inch pieces. Pack beans tightly into hot jars, leaving 1-inch headspace. Add ½ teaspoon salt to each pint jar, 1 teaspoon salt to each quart jar, if desired. Ladle boiling water over beans, leaving 1-inch headspace. Remove air bubbles. Adjust two-piece caps. Process pints 20 minutes, quarts 25 minutes, at 10 pounds pressure in a pressure canner.

Hot Pack: See pages 70-71 for Canning Green Beans Step-By-Step. Wash beans; drain. Remove string, trim ends and break or cut freshly gathered beans into 2-inch pieces. Blanch in boiling water 5 minutes. Pack hot beans into hot jars, leaving 1-inch headspace. Add ½ teaspoon salt to each pint jar, 1 teaspoon salt to each quart jar, if desired. Ladle boiling water over beans, leaving 1-inch headspace. Remove air bubbles. Adjust two-piece caps. Process pints 20 minutes, quarts 25 minutes, at 10 pounds pressure in a pressure canner.

Note: The processing time given applies only to young, tender pods.

Beans—Lima And Butter

3 to 5 pounds beans per quart	Salt (optional) Water

Raw Pack: Wash beans; drain. Shell beans. Wash again. Pack beans loosely into hot jars, leaving 1-inch headspace. Do not press or shake down. Add ½ teaspoon salt to each pint jar, 1 teaspoon salt to each quart jar, if desired. Ladle boiling water over beans, leaving 1-inch headspace. Remove air bubbles. Adjust two-piece caps. Process pints 40 minutes, quarts 50 minutes, at 10 pounds pressure in a pressure canner.

Hot Pack: Wash beans; drain. Shell beans. Wash again. Blanch in boiling water 3 minutes. Pack hot beans into hot jars, leaving 1-inch headspace. Add ½ teaspoon salt to each pint jar, 1 teaspoon salt to each quart jar, if desired. Ladle boiling water over beans, leaving 1-inch headspace. Remove air bubbles. Adjust two-piece caps. Process pints 40 minutes, quarts 50 minutes, at 10 pounds pressure in a pressure canner.

Beans—With Pork And Tomato Sauce

Yield: about 6 pints or 3 quarts

1 quart dried navy beans (about 2 pounds)	3 tablespoons sugar
¼ pound salt pork, cut in pieces	2 teaspoons salt
1 cup chopped onion (about 1 medium)	¼ teaspoon cloves
	¼ teaspoon allspice
	1 quart tomato juice

Put beans in a large saucepot; add water to cover by 2 inches. Bring to a boil; boil 2 minutes. Remove from heat and let beans soak 1 hour. Drain. Cover beans with boiling water by 2 inches in a large saucepot. Boil 3 minutes. Remove from heat and let stand 10 minutes; drain. Combine onion, sugar, salt, spices and tomato juice; heat to boiling. Pack 1 cup beans into hot jars; top with a piece of pork; fill jar ¾ full with beans. Ladle hot tomato sauce over beans, leaving 1-inch headspace. Remove air bubbles. Adjust two-piece caps. Process pints 1 hour and 5 minutes, quarts 1 hour and 15 minutes, at 10 pounds pressure in a pressure canner.

Beets

2 to 3½ pounds red beets per quart, 1- to 2-inch diameter	Salt (optional) Water

Wash beets; drain. Leave 2 inches of stem and tap root on beets. Boil until skins slip off. Remove skins; trim. Slice, dice or leave beets whole. Pack beets into hot jars, leaving 1-inch headspace. Add ½ teaspoon salt to each pint jar, 1 teaspoon salt to each quart jar, if desired. Ladle boiling water over beets, leaving 1-inch headspace. Remove air bubbles. Adjust two-piece caps. Process pints 30 minutes, quarts 35 minutes, at 10 pounds pressure in a pressure canner.

Carrots

2 to 3 pounds carrots per quart, 1- to 1½-inch diameter	Salt (optional) Water

Raw Pack: Wash carrots; drain. Peel carrots. Wash again. Slice, dice or leave carrots whole. Pack carrots tightly into hot jars, leaving 1-inch headspace. Add ½ teaspoon salt to each pint jar, 1 teaspoon salt to each quart jar, if desired. Ladle boiling water over carrots, leaving 1-inch headspace. Remove air bubbles. Adjust two-piece caps. Process pints 25 minutes, quarts 30 minutes, at 10 pounds pressure in a pressure canner.

Hot Pack: Wash carrots; drain. Peel carrots. Wash again. Slice, dice or leave carrots whole. Cover carrots with water; bring to a boil. Reduce heat; simmer 5 minutes. Pack hot carrots into hot jars, leaving 1-inch headspace. Add ½ teaspoon salt to each pint jar, 1 teaspoon salt to each quart jar, if desired. Ladle boiling water over carrots, leaving 1-inch headspace. Remove air bubbles. Adjust two-piece caps. Process pints 25 minutes, quarts 30 minutes, at 10 pounds pressure in a pressure canner.

Corn—Cream Style

1 to 1½ pounds ears of corn per pint	Salt (optional) Water

Husk corn; remove silk. Wash. Cut kernels from cob, leaving tip ends. Scrape cob to extract pulp and milk. Measure kernels, pulp and milk together. Add ½ teaspoon salt and 1¼ cups boiling water to each pint of cut corn. Boil 3 minutes. Only process in pints. Ladle hot corn and liquid into hot jars, leaving 1-inch headspace. Remove air bubbles. Adjust two-piece caps. Process pints 1 hour and 25 minutes at 10 pounds pressure in a pressure canner.

Corn—Whole Kernel

3 to 6 pounds ears of corn per quart	Salt (optional) Water

Raw Pack: Husk corn; remove silk. Wash. Cut kernels from cob. Do not scrape cob. Pack corn loosely into hot jars, leaving 1-inch headspace. Do not shake or press down. Add ½ teaspoon salt to each pint jar, 1 teaspoon salt to each quart jar, if desired. Ladle boiling water over corn, leaving 1-inch headspace. Remove air bubbles. Adjust two-piece caps. Process pints 55 minutes, quarts 1 hour and 25 minutes, at 10 pounds pressure in a pressure canner.

Hot Pack: Husk corn; remove silk. Wash. Cut kernels from cob. Do not scrape cob. Measure. Add ½ teaspoon salt and 1 cup boiling water to each pint of cut corn, 1 teaspoon salt and 2 cups boiling water to each quart of cut corn. Bring to a boil; reduce heat and simmer 5 minutes. Ladle hot corn and liquid into hot jars, leaving 1-inch headspace. Remove air bubbles. Adjust two-piece caps. Process pints 55 minutes, quarts 1 hour and 25 minutes, at 10 pounds pressure in a pressure canner.

Note: The sugar content in young ears of corn and sweet varieties of corn may cause browning.

Greens

Beet, Chard, Kale, Mustard, Poke, Spinach and Turnip

2 to 6 pounds greens per quart	Salt (optional) Water

Wash greens thoroughly in several changes of water. Discard large, tough stems. Heat greens until wilted in just enough water to prevent sticking. To hasten wilting and prevent overcooking, turn greens over when steam begins to rise around the edges of the pan. Cut through greens several times with a sharp knife before packing. Pack hot greens into hot jars, leaving 1-inch headspace. Add ½ teaspoon salt to each pint jar, 1 teaspoon salt to each quart jar, if desired. Ladle boiling water over greens, leaving 1-inch headspace. Remove air bubbles. Adjust two-piece caps. Process pints 1 hour and 10 minutes, quarts 1 hour and 30 minutes, at 10 pounds pressure in a pressure canner.

Mixed Vegetables

Yield: about 7 quarts

7 cups sliced carrots	6 cups cubed zucchini
7 cups corn	1 cup chopped
7 cups lima beans	sweet red pepper

Combine vegetables in a large saucepan; add water to cover. Boil vegetables 5 minutes. Pack hot vegetables and liquid into hot jars, leaving 1-inch headspace. Remove air bubbles. Adjust two-piece caps. Process pints 1 hour and 15 minutes, quarts 1 hour and 30 minutes, at 10 pounds pressure in a pressure canner.

Mushrooms

Cultivated mushrooms

2 pounds mushrooms per pint	Salt (optional) Water

Clean dirt from mushrooms with a soft brush. Rinse under cold water. Trim stem ends. Leave small mushrooms whole; cut large mushrooms in half. Put mushrooms in a saucepot, adding water to cover. Bring to a boil; boil 5 minutes. Only process in half-pints or pints. Pack hot mushrooms into hot jars, leaving 1-inch headspace. Add ¼ teaspoon salt to each half-pint jar, ½ teaspoon salt to each pint jar, if desired. Ladle boiling water over mushrooms, leaving 1-inch headspace. Remove air bubbles. Adjust two-piece caps. Process half-pints and pints 45 minutes at 10 pounds pressure in a pressure canner.

Note: Do not can wild mushrooms.

Okra

1½ to 2 pounds okra per quart	Salt (optional) Water

Wash and drain okra. Remove stem and blossom ends without cutting into pod. Leave whole or slice. Cover okra with cold water in a large saucepot; boil 2 minutes. Pack hot okra into hot jars, leaving 1-inch headspace. Add ½ teaspoon salt to each pint jar, 1 teaspoon salt to each quart jar, if desired. Ladle boiling water over okra, leaving 1-inch headspace. Remove air bubbles. Adjust two-piece caps. Process pints 25 minutes, quarts 40 minutes, at 10 pounds pressure in a pressure canner.

Parsnips, Rutabagas Or Turnips

1½ to 2 pounds vegetables per quart	Salt (optional) Water

Wash vegetable; drain. Prepare vegetable as for cooking, cutting to desired size. Cover vegetable with cold water in a large saucepot; boil 3 minutes. Pack hot vegetable into hot jars, leaving 1-inch headspace. Add ½ teaspoon salt to each pint jar, 1 teaspoon salt to each quart jar, if desired. Ladle boiling water over vegetable, leaving 1-inch headspace. Remove air bubbles. Adjust two-piece caps. Process pints 30 minutes, quarts 35 minutes, at 10 pounds pressure in a pressure canner.

Note: Rutabagas usually discolor when canned and also develops a strong flavor.

Peas—Blackeye, Crowder And Field

2 to 2¼ pounds pea pods per quart	Salt (optional) Water

Raw Pack: Wash peas; drain. Shell peas. Wash again. Pack peas loosely into hot jars, leaving 1-inch headspace. Do not shake or press down. Add ½ teaspoon salt to each pint jar, 1 teaspoon salt to each quart jar, if desired. Ladle boiling water over peas, leaving 1-inch headspace. Remove air bubbles. Adjust two-piece caps. Process pints 40 minutes, quarts 50 minutes, at 10 pounds pressure in a pressure canner.

Hot Pack: Wash peas; drain. Shell peas. Wash again. Cover peas with water in a large saucepot; boil 3 minutes. Ladle hot peas and liquid into hot jars, leaving 1-inch headspace. Add ½ teaspoon salt to each pint jar, 1 teaspoon salt to each quart jar, if desired. Remove air bubbles. Adjust two-piece caps. Process pints 40 minutes, quarts 50 minutes, at 10 pounds pressure in a pressure canner.

Peas—Green Or "English"

3 to 6 pounds pea pods per quart	Salt (optional) Water

Raw Pack: Wash peas; drain. Shell peas. Wash again. Pack peas loosely into hot jars, leaving 1-inch headspace. Do not shake or press down. Add ½ teaspoon salt to each pint jar, 1 teaspoon salt to each quart jar, if desired. Ladle boiling water over peas, leaving 1-inch headspace. Remove air bubbles. Adjust two-piece caps. Process pints and quarts 40 minutes at 10 pounds pressure in a pressure canner.

Hot Pack: Wash peas; drain. Shell peas. Wash again. Boil small peas (less than ¼") 3 minutes; boil medium peas (¼" to ⅓") 5 minutes in a large saucepot; drain. Rinse peas in hot water; drain again. Pack hot peas into hot jars, leaving 1-inch headspace. Add ½ teaspoon salt to each pint jar, 1 teaspoon salt to each quart jar, if desired. Ladle boiling water over peas, leaving 1-inch headspace. Remove air bubbles. Adjust two-piece caps. Process pints and quarts 40 minutes at 10 pounds pressure in a pressure canner.

Peppers—Green

1 pound sweet peppers per pint Salt	Vinegar Water

Wash sweet peppers; drain. Remove stem and seeds. Cut peppers into quarters. Cover peppers with water in a large saucepot; boil 3 minutes. Only process in half-pints or pints. Pack hot peppers into hot jars, leaving 1-inch headspace. Add ¼ teaspoon salt and ½ tablespoon vinegar to each half-pint jar. Add ½ teaspoon salt and 1 tablespoon vinegar to each pint jar. Ladle boiling water over peppers, leaving 1-inch headspace. Remove air bubbles. Adjust two-piece caps. Process half-pints and pints 35 minutes at 10 pounds pressure in a pressure canner.

Potatoes—Sweet

2 to 3 pounds sweet potatoes per quart	Water

Wash sweet potatoes; drain. Boil or steam potatoes until peel can be easily removed. Peel potatoes and cut into quarters. Pack hot potatoes into hot jars, leaving 1-inch headspace. Ladle boiling water, medium or light syrup (*see page 16*) over potatoes, leaving 1-inch headspace. Remove air bubbles. Adjust two-piece caps. Process pints 1 hour and 5 minutes, quarts 1 hour and 30 minutes, at 10 pounds pressure in a pressure canner.

Potatoes—White Or Irish

2 to 3 pounds white potatoes per quart	Salt (optional) Water

Wash white potatoes; drain. Peel potatoes. Wash again. Leave small potatoes whole; cut large potatoes into quarters. Cover potatoes with water in a large saucepot; boil 10 minutes. Pack hot potatoes into hot jars, leaving 1-inch headspace. Add ½ teaspoon salt to each pint jar, 1 teaspoon salt to each quart jar, if desired. Ladle boiling water over potatoes, leaving 1-inch headspace. Remove air bubbles. Adjust two-piece caps. Process pints 35 minutes, quarts 40 minutes, at 10 pounds pressure in a pressure canner.

Red Onions — With Honey

Yield: about 4 pints

2½ quarts thick sliced, peeled red onions (about 15 large) 1 tablespoon salt	1 cup honey 1½ cups water ½ cup white wine

Put red onions in a bowl and sprinkle with salt. Combine remaining ingredients in a saucepan. Bring mixture to a boil over medium heat. Reduce heat. Simmer sauce until reduced by half, about 30 minutes. As sauce thickens stir frequently to prevent sticking. Pack red onions into hot jars, leaving 1-inch headspace. Ladle hot sauce over onions, leaving 1-inch headspace. Remove air bubbles. Adjust two-piece caps. Process pints 15 minutes at 10 pounds pressure in a pressure canner.

Succotash

Boil ears of corn 5 minutes in a large saucepot. Cut kernels from cob. Boil green beans or lima beans 3 minutes in a large saucepot. Using an equal measure of corn and green beans or lima beans, combine vegetables. Pack hot vegetables into hot jars, leaving 1-inch headspace. Add ½ teaspoon salt to each pint jar, 1 teaspoon salt to each quart jar, if desired. Ladle boiling water over vegetables, leaving 1-inch headspace. Remove air bubbles. Adjust two-piece caps. Process pints 1 hour, quarts 1 hour and 25 minutes, at 10 pounds pressure in a pressure canner.

tomatoes

Tomatoes–Packed In Water

Whole, Halved Or Quartered

2½ to 3½ pounds tomatoes per quart	Ball Citric Acid or bottled lemon juice
	Salt (optional)

Raw Pack: Prepare tomatoes *(see steps 5-7, page 24).* Add ¼ teaspoon citric acid or 1 tablespoon bottled lemon juice to each pint jar, ½ teaspoon citric acid or 2 tablespoons bottled lemon juice to each quart jar. Pack tomatoes into hot jars, leaving 1-inch headspace. Ladle hot water over tomatoes, leaving 1-inch headspace. Add ½ teaspoon salt to each pint jar, 1 teaspoon salt to each quart jar, if desired. Remove air bubbles. Adjust two-piece caps. Process pints and quarts 10 minutes at 10 pounds pressure in a pressure canner.

Hot Pack: Prepare tomatoes *(see steps 5-7, page 24).* Place tomatoes in a large saucepot; add enough water to cover tomatoes. Boil gently 5 minutes, stirring to prevent sticking. Add ¼ teaspoon citric acid or 1 tablespoon bottled lemon juice to each pint jar, ½ teaspoon citric acid or 2 tablespoons bottled lemon juice to each quart jar. Pack hot tomatoes into hot jars, leaving 1-inch headspace. Ladle hot cooking liquid over tomatoes, leaving 1-inch headspace. Add ½ teaspoon salt to each pint jar, 1 teaspoon salt to each quart jar, if desired. Remove air bubbles. Adjust two-piece caps. Process pints and quarts 10 minutes at 10 pounds pressure in a pressure canner.

Tomatoes–Packed In Own Juice

Whole, Halved Or Quartered

2½ to 3½ pounds tomatoes per quart	Ball Citric Acid or bottled lemon juice
	Salt (optional)

Prepare tomatoes *(see steps 5-7, page 24).* Add ¼ teaspoon citric acid or 1 tablespoon bottled lemon juice to each pint jar, ½ teaspoon citric acid or 2 tablespoons bottled lemon juice to each quart jar. Pack tomatoes into hot jars, pressing gently on tomatoes until the natural juice fills the spaces between tomatoes, leaving 1-inch headspace. Add ½ teaspoon salt to each pint, 1 teaspoon salt to each quart jar, if desired. Remove air bubbles. Adjust two-piece caps. Process pints and quarts 25 minutes at 10 pounds pressure in a pressure canner.

Tomatoes And Celery

Use equal measures of chopped, peeled, cored tomatoes and sliced celery. Cook tomatoes and celery 15 minutes in a large saucepot. Add ¼ teaspoon citric acid or 1 tablespoon bottled lemon juice to each pint jar, ½ teaspoon citric acid or 2 tablespoons bottled lemon juice to each quart jar. Pack hot vegetables into hot jars, leaving 1-inch headspace. Add ½ teaspoon salt to each pint, 1 teaspoon salt to each quart, if desired. Ladle boiling water over vegetables, leaving 1-inch headspace. Remove air bubbles. Adjust two-piece caps. Process pints 30 minutes, quarts 35 minutes, at 10 pounds pressure in a pressure canner.

Tomatoes With Okra

Use equal measures of chopped, peeled, cored tomatoes and sliced okra. Cook tomatoes 15 minutes in a large saucepot. Add okra. Cook 5 minutes. Add ¼ teaspoon citric acid or 1 tablespoon bottled lemon juice to each pint jar, ½ teaspoon citric acid or 2 tablespoons bottled lemon juice to each quart jar. Ladle hot vegetables into hot jars, leaving 1-inch headspace. Add ½ teaspoon salt to each pint jar, 1 teaspoon salt to each quart jar, if desired. Remove air bubbles. Adjust two-piece caps. Process pints 30 minutes, quarts 35 minutes, at 10 pounds pressure in a pressure canner.

Stewed Tomatoes

Yield: about 7 pints or 3 quarts

4 quarts chopped, peeled, cored tomatoes (about 24 large)	¼ cup chopped green pepper (about ¼ medium)
1 cup chopped celery (about 1 stalk)	1 tablespoon sugar
	2 teaspoons salt
½ cup chopped onion (about ½ medium)	Ball Citric Acid or bottled lemon juice

Combine all ingredients in a large saucepot. Cover; cook 10 minutes, stirring to prevent sticking. Add ¼ teaspoon citric acid or 1 tablespoon bottled lemon juice to each pint jar, ½ teaspoon citric acid or 2 tablespoons bottled lemon juice to each quart jar. Ladle hot vegetables into hot jars, leaving 1-inch headspace. Remove air bubbles. Adjust two-piece caps. Process pints 15 minutes, quarts 20 minutes, at 10 pounds pressure in a pressure canner.

featured prepared recipe

Flank Steak with Honey Glazed Red Onions

Makes about 6 servings

1 pint jar Red Onions with Honey *(recipe on page 68)*	1 cup tomato puree
	½ cup chili sauce
2 tablespoons extra-virgin olive oil	Juice of 1 lime
	2 pounds flank steak
2 tablespoons minced garlic	1 tablespoon kosher salt
1 tablespoon coriander seeds	2 teaspoons coarsely ground black pepper
2 teaspoons paprika	

Drain onions, reserving liquid. Heat olive oil in sauté pan; cook garlic in olive oil just until translucent. Add coriander seeds and continue cooking until seeds are lightly toasted. Stir in paprika, tomato puree, chili sauce and lime juice; simmer 10 minutes. Add red onions and continue cooking about 5 minutes. Keep honey glazed red onions warm. Meanwhile rub both sides of flank steak with salt and pepper. Grill steak at 400°F about 4 minutes on each side for medium-rare or longer for desired doneness. Baste steak with honey glaze; cook 5 minutes. Turn steak over; baste with honey glaze and continue cooking 5 minutes or until sauce begins to form a crust. Remove steak from grill and let rest 10 minutes before slicing. Cut slices about ¼-inch thick across the grain. Serve immediately with remaining honey glazed red onions.

canning green beans step-by-step

1. Read recipe instructions; assemble equipment and ingredients before starting. Follow guidelines for recipe preparation, jar size, canning method and processing time. Do not make changes in recommended guidelines.

2. Visually examine canning jars for nicks, cracks, uneven rims or sharp edges that may prevent sealing or cause breakage. Examine canning lids to ensure they are free of dents and sealing compound is even and complete. Check bands for proper fit.

3. Wash jars and two-piece caps in hot, soapy water. Rinse well. Dry bands; set aside. Heat jars and lids in a saucepot of simmering water (180°F). DO NOT BOIL LIDS. Allow jars and lids to remain in hot water until ready for use, removing one at a time as needed.

4. Select fresh green beans which are young, tender and crisp. Wash beans in several changes of water; lift beans out of water and drain.

5. Remove strings and trim ends. Cut or break beans into uniform pieces. Prepare only enough for one canner load.

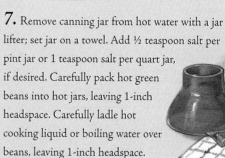

6. Cover beans with boiling water; boil 5 minutes. Remove beans from cooking water.

7. Remove canning jar from hot water with a jar lifter; set jar on a towel. Add ½ teaspoon salt per pint jar or 1 teaspoon salt per quart jar, if desired. Carefully pack hot green beans into hot jars, leaving 1-inch headspace. Carefully ladle hot cooking liquid or boiling water over beans, leaving 1-inch headspace.

8. Slide a nonmetallic spatula between green beans and jar; press back gently on beans to release trapped air bubbles. Repeat procedure 2 to 3 times around inside of jar.

9. Wipe rim and threads of jar with a clean, damp cloth. Remove lid from hot water using a lid wand. Place lid on jar, centering sealing compound on rim. Screw band down evenly and firmly, just until resistance is met— fingertip tight.

12. Bring pressure to 10 pounds for altitudes at or below 1,000 feet above sea level. When using a dial gauge, or for higher altitude areas, refer to Altitude Chart (*see page 5*). Keep pressure steady during entire processing period. Process pints 20 minutes, quarts 25 minutes. When processing is complete, turn off heat.

13. Let canner return to zero pressure naturally. Remove gauge or open petcock. Let canner cool 10 minutes before opening lid. Unfasten lid; raise canner lid toward you, allowing steam to escape in opposite direction. Lift off lid. Let canner cool 10 minutes before removing jars. Remove jars from canner and set them upright, 1 to 2 inches apart, on a dry towel to cool. Do not retighten bands. Let jars cool 12 to 24 hours.

10. As each jar is filled, set it onto the rack in the pressure canner. The canner should contain 2 to 3 inches of hot water; keep water at a simmer (180°F) until all filled jars are placed in the canner. Check the water level; add boiling water, if necessary.

14. After jars have cooled, check lids for a seal by pressing on the center of each lid. If the center is pulled down and does not flex, remove the band and gently try to lift the lid off with your fingertips. If the lid does not flex and you cannot lift it off, the lid has a good vacuum seal. Wipe off lid and jar surface with a clean, damp cloth to remove food particles or residue. Label. Store jars in a cool, dry, dark place (*see page 12*).

11. Put lid onto canner and turn to lock lid in place. Adjust heat; bring water to a boil. Leave vent open until steam has escaped steadily from vent for 10 minutes. Put weight on vent.

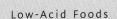

special diet

Low-Sugar & Low-Salt Recipes

A mid-day respite from the norm. The table is set with flowers and fine china. The choicest recipe for an elegant luncheon? Mango Salad with Praline Glazed Salmon. The sweet taste of ripe mango, papaya and grapes juxtaposed with ginger, scallions and spices complements a thick salmon steak glazed with praline syrup. Get ready to hear the oohhs and aahhs. It's a gourmet dish that's as impressive visually as it is gastronomically.

Low-sugar and low-salt recipes are not just for those with dietary restrictions. These delicious recipes are for everyone interested in healthy eating. Quick and flavorful meals like this are a snap when you begin with carefully preserved foods right from your pantry's shelf.

Satisfy your sweet cravings with low-sugar Pineapple-Apricot Conserve or Peach-Pineapple Spread atop a freshly baked scone. Or serve low-salt chervil and thyme Herbed Peas or Green Beans with Lemon Peel to make a plain meal extraordinary. You will marvel at the true essence and vibrant flavors of foods captured in this very natural way.

Today, people are more concerned about good nutrition and healthy eating than ever before. Preserving your own food is the best way to start. Step-by-step, you control the ingredients, the quality and the flavor. About the only thing you can't control is the absolute delight that is found in each and every bite.

Pictured, Mango Salad and Praline Glazed Salmon.
Recipe for Mango Relish found on page 76.
Recipe for Praline Syrup found on page 84.
Recipes for Mango Salad & Praline
Glazed Salmon found on page 77.

getting started

Whether the result of a need to meet special dietary requirements or a desire to make healthy eating choices, individuals today want control over the quality of foods they eat. An alternative to the high price of commercially prepared specialty foods is home canning. This section includes recipes for canning low-sugar, low-salt and preservative-free foods.

Canning Fruits Without Sugar

Prepare fruit for canning as instructed in the individual recipe found in this section and in the High-Acid Foods section (see page 14). Water or unsweetened fruit juice may be used in place of a sugar syrup. Use only the Hot Pack method when canning fruit without sugar. Figs require added lemon juice or citric acid and rhubarb requires sugar; therefore, use only recipes in the High-Acid Foods section for these fruits.

There are a variety of non-sugar sweeteners available to replace sugar in canning recipes, including soft spreads. Each has unique properties and usage recommendations. Select the type best suited for the specific recipe to be prepared. Non-sugar sweeteners that are sensitive to heat or long term storage should be added just before serving canned fruits. Follow the manufacturer's instructions for measuring non-sugar sweeteners.

Unsweetened fruit juices, spices, herbs and citrus peel can be used to enhance the flavor of fruits canned without sugar. Try your own combination of spices or mild herbs to create a unique and flavorful taste.

Canning Low-Acid Foods Without Salt

The amount of salt called for in canning meats and vegetables is too small to help prevent spoilage; the salt is there only for seasoning. Follow recipes for canning low-acid vegetables, meats and poultry, but omit salt. Do not omit salt from seafood recipes.

Vegetables are made more flavorful by adding spices and herbs in place of salt. A small amount of lemon juice or orange juice, a tiny piece of citrus peel or a sliver of pimiento are also simple ways to enhance vegetables.

General Information

Canning methods covered under Learning About Canning (see pages 2-13) apply to the canning recipes in this section. It will be helpful to review the general information for these methods before preparing recipes. Refer to the specific section of the book for the type of recipe you are preparing if additional information is needed. Half-pint and pint jars are usually the best size to use when canning special diet foods for one person. Use only the jar size indicated in the recipe.

fruits & tomatoes

Apricots In Pineapple Juice

2 to 2½ pounds apricots per quart
Unsweetened pineapple juice
Ball Fruit-Fresh Produce Protector

Wash and blanch apricots; remove peel. Cut apricots into halves and pit. Treat with Fruit-Fresh to prevent darkening. Drain; rinse and drain again. Cook apricots in water one layer at a time until hot throughout. Heat pineapple juice just to a boil. Pack hot apricots, cavity side down, into hot jars, leaving ½-inch headspace. Ladle hot juice over apricots, leaving ½-inch headspace. Remove air bubbles. Adjust two-piece caps. Process pints 20 minutes, quarts 25 minutes, in a boiling-water canner.

Basil-Garlic Tomato Sauce

Yield: about 7 pints

20 pounds tomatoes	1 tablespoon olive oil
1 cup chopped onion	¼ cup finely minced, fresh basil
8 cloves garlic, minced	Ball Citric Acid or bottled lemon juice

Wash tomatoes; drain. Remove core and blossom ends. Cut into quarters; set aside. Sauté onion and garlic in olive oil until transparent. Add tomatoes; simmer 20 minutes, stirring occasionally. Purée tomato mixture using a food processor or food mill. Strain purée to remove seeds and peel. Combine tomato purée and basil in a large saucepot. Cook over medium-high heat until volume is reduced by one-half, stirring to prevent sticking. Add ¼ teaspoon citric acid or 1 tablespoon bottled lemon juice to each pint jar. Ladle hot sauce into hot jars, leaving ½-inch headspace. Adjust two-piece caps. Process 35 minutes in a boiling-water canner.

Cinnamon Pears In Apple Juice

1 to 1½ pounds pears per pint	Stick cinnamon
	Unsweetened apple juice
Ball Fruit-Fresh Produce Protector	

Wash pears; drain. Cut into halves, core and peel. Treat with Fruit-Fresh to prevent darkening. Drain; rinse and drain again. Cook pears in water one layer at a time until hot throughout. Heat apple juice just to a boil. Pack hot pears, cavity side down, into hot jars, leaving ½-inch headspace. Place 1 cinnamon stick in each jar. Ladle hot juice over pears, leaving ½-inch headspace. Remove air bubbles. Adjust two-piece caps. Process pints 20 minutes in a boiling-water canner.

Grapes, Pineapple And Peaches In White Grape Juice

½ pineapple per quart (about 2 pounds)	½ pound peaches per quart
½ pound grapes per quart	Ball Fruit-Fresh Produce Protector
	Unsweetened white grape juice

Peel and core pineapple. Cut pineapple into 1-inch chunks. Wash grapes; drain. Stem grapes. Wash and blanch peaches. Peel peaches; cut in half and pit. Slice peaches. Treat with Fruit-Fresh to prevent darkening. Drain; rinse and drain again. Cook fruit together in a small amount of water until hot throughout. Heat white grape juice just to a boil. Pack hot fruit into hot jars, leaving ½-inch headspace. Ladle hot juice over fruit, leaving ½-inch headspace. Remove air bubbles. Adjust two-piece caps. Process pints 20 minutes, quarts 25 minutes, in a boiling-water canner.

Italian Tomato Sauce

Yield: about 7 pints or 3 quarts

4 quarts chopped, seeded, peeled, cored tomatoes (about 24 large)	1 tablespoon basil
	1 tablespoon oregano
1 cup chopped celery (about 2 stalks)	1 tablespoon minced parsley
½ cup chopped onion (about ½ medium)	2 teaspoons crushed red pepper (optional)
¼ cup chopped green pepper (about ¼ medium)	Ball Citric Acid or bottled lemon juice

Combine all ingredients in a large saucepot. Cover and cook 10 minutes, stirring occasionally to prevent sticking. Add ¼ teaspoon citric acid or 1 tablespoon bottled lemon juice to each pint jar, ½ teaspoon citric acid or 2 tablespoons

bottled lemon juice to each quart jar. Ladle hot sauce into hot jars, leaving 1-inch headspace. Remove air bubbles. Adjust two-piece caps. Process pints 20 minutes, quarts 25 minutes, at 10 pounds pressure in a pressure canner.

Peaches In Apple Juice

2 to 3 pounds peaches per quart	Ball Fruit-Fresh Produce Protector Unsweetened apple juice

Wash and blanch peaches. Peel peaches; cut in half and pit. Treat with Fruit-Fresh to prevent darkening. Drain; rinse and drain again. Cook peaches in water one layer at a time until hot throughout. Heat apple juice just to a boil. Pack hot peaches, cavity side down, into hot jars, leaving ½-inch headspace. Ladle hot juice over peaches, leaving ½-inch headspace. Remove air bubbles. Adjust two-piece caps. Process pints 20 minutes, quarts 25 minutes, in a boiling-water canner.

Pears And Nectarines In White Grape Juice

1 to 1½ pounds pears per quart	Ball Fruit-Fresh Produce Protector Unsweetened white grape juice
1 to 1½ pounds nectarines per quart	

Wash pears and nectarines; drain. Cut pears and nectarines into halves; core, pit and peel. Treat with Fruit-Fresh to prevent darkening. Drain; rinse and drain again. Cook pears and nectarines in water one layer at a time until hot throughout. Heat white grape juice just to a boil. Pack hot fruit, cavity side down, into hot jars, leaving ½-inch headspace. Ladle hot juice over fruit, leaving ½-inch headspace. Remove air bubbles. Adjust two-piece caps. Process pints 20 minutes, quarts 25 minutes in a boiling-water canner.

Puréed Fruits

Apples, Apricots, Peaches, Pears, etc.

For Sauces: Follow recipe for Applesauce (*see page 17*). Pack in half-pints or pints. Remove air bubbles. Adjust two-piece caps and process as recommended.

For Puréed Fruits: Follow recipe for Fruit Purée (*see page 22*). Pack in half-pints or pints. Remove air bubbles. Adjust two-piece caps and process as recommended.

Note: Sugar may be omitted from sauce and purée.

Spiced Pineapple In Pineapple Juice

1 fresh pineapple per quart (about 5 pounds)	Stick cinnamon Unsweetened pineapple juice

Peel and core pineapple. Cut pineapple into 1-inch chunks or ½-inch slices. Cook pineapple in water until hot throughout. Heat pineapple juice just to a boil. Pack hot pineapple into hot jars, leaving ½-inch headspace. Add 1 cinnamon stick to each jar. Ladle hot juice over pineapple, leaving ½-inch headspace. Remove air bubbles. Adjust two-piece caps. Process pints 15 minutes, quarts 20 minutes, in a boiling-water canner.

soft spreads

Apple Jelly

Yield: about 4 half-pints

4 pounds apples	3 tablespoons Ball Low or
4 cups water	No-Sugar Needed Pectin

To Prepare Juice: Wash apples; drain. Remove stems and blossom ends; do not peel or core. Coarsely chop fruit. Combine apples and water in a large saucepot. Cover; simmer fruit until soft. Strain juice through a damp jelly bag or several layers of cheesecloth. Measure 4 cups juice.

To Make Jelly: Combine apple juice and low or no-sugar needed pectin in a large saucepot, stirring to dissolve pectin. Bring to a boil, stirring constantly. Add sweetener, if desired. Boil 1 minute, stirring constantly. If gel starts to form before 1 minute boil is complete, remove from heat. Ladle hot jelly into hot jars, leaving ¼-inch headspace. Remove air bubbles. Adjust two-piece caps. Process 10 minutes in a boiling-water canner.

Apple-Cinnamon Conserve

Yield: about 6 half-pints

4 cups unsweetened applesauce	1 cup chopped dried apples
1 (20-ounce) can unsweetened, crushed pineapple, drained	¾ cup raisins
	½ teaspoon cinnamon
	2 tablespoons lemon juice

Combine all ingredients in a large saucepot. Simmer until thick, stirring frequently to prevent sticking. Ladle hot conserve into hot jars, leaving ¼-inch headspace. Remove air bubbles. Adjust two-piece caps. Process 10 minutes in a boiling-water canner.

Berry-Cherry Jam

Yield: about 6 half-pints

1 quart strawberries	1 cup water
½ pint sweet cherries	3 tablespoons Ball Low or
½ pint blackberries	No-Sugar Needed Pectin

Wash strawberries, cherries and blackberries; drain. Stem and crush strawberries. Pit and crush cherries. Combine strawberries, cherries, blackberries, water and low or no-sugar needed pectin in a large saucepot, stirring to dissolve pectin. Bring to a boil, stirring constantly. Add sweetener, if desired. Boil 1 minute, stirring constantly. If gel starts to form before 1 minute boil is complete, remove from heat. Ladle hot jam into hot jars, leaving ¼-inch headspace. Remove air bubbles. Adjust two-piece caps. Process 10 minutes in a boiling-water canner.

Grape Jelly

Yield: about 4 half-pints

3 pounds grapes	3 tablespoons Ball Low or
1 cup water	No-Sugar Needed Pectin

To Prepare Juice: Wash grapes; drain. Stem grapes; crush. Combine grapes and water in a large saucepot. Cover; simmer 10 minutes. Strain juice through a damp jelly bag or several layers of cheesecloth. Measure 4 cups juice.

To Make Jelly: Combine grape juice and low or no-sugar needed pectin in a large saucepot, stirring to dissolve pectin. Bring to a boil, stirring constantly. Add sweetener, if desired. Boil 1 minute, stirring constantly. If gel starts to form before 1 minute boil is complete, remove from heat. Ladle hot jelly into hot jars, leaving ¼-inch headspace. Remove air bubbles. Adjust two-piece caps. Process 10 minutes in a boiling-water canner.

Peach Jam

Yield: about 6 half-pints

5 cups finely chopped, peeled, pitted peaches	2 tablespoons lemon juice
1 cup unsweetened white grape juice	3 tablespoons Ball Low or No-Sugar Needed Pectin

Combine peaches, white grape juice, lemon juice and low or no-sugar needed pectin in a large saucepot, stirring to dissolve pectin. Bring to a boil, stirring constantly. Add sweetener, if desired. Boil 1 minute, stirring constantly. If gel starts to form before 1 minute boil is complete, remove from heat. Ladle hot jam into hot jars, leaving ¼-inch headspace. Remove air bubbles. Adjust two-piece caps. Process 10 minutes in a boiling-water canner.

Peach-Pineapple Spread

Yield: about 6 half-pints

2 cups dried peaches	⅔ cup chopped orange pulp (about 1 medium)
3½ cups sugar	
1½ cups unsweetened, crushed pineapple	2 tablespoons lemon juice

Combine peaches and just enough water to cover in a medium saucepot. Simmer peaches in water until peaches are tender. Coarsely crush peaches in a food processor or with a potato masher. Combine crushed peaches with remaining ingredients. Cook over medium-high heat until thick, stirring frequently. Ladle hot spread into hot jars, leaving ¼-inch headspace. Remove air bubbles. Adjust two-piece caps. Process 10 minutes in a boiling-water canner.

Pineapple-Apricot Conserve

Yield: about 5 half-pints

2 cups dried apricots	1 cup golden raisins
2 cups water	1 teaspoon ginger
4 cups unsweetened, crushed pineapple, drained	4 teaspoons lemon juice

Combine apricots and water in a medium saucepot. Boil until tender. Purée apricots in a food processor or a food mill. Combine apricot purée with remaining ingredients. Simmer until thick, stirring frequently. Ladle hot conserve into hot jars, leaving ¼-inch headspace. Remove air bubbles. Adjust two-piece caps. Process 10 minutes in a boiling-water canner.

Raspberry Jam

Yield: about 6 half-pints

2½ quarts red raspberries	3 tablespoons Ball Low or No-Sugar Needed Pectin
1 cup water	

Wash red raspberries; drain. Crush red raspberries; measure 5 cups. Combine red raspberries with low or no-sugar pectin in a large saucepot, stirring to dissolve pectin. Bring to a boil, stirring constantly. Add sweetener, if desired. Boil 1 minute, stirring constantly. If gel starts to form before 1 minute boil is complete, remove from heat. Ladle hot jam into hot jars, leaving ¼-inch headspace. Remove air bubbles. Adjust two-piece caps. Process 10 minutes in a boiling-water canner.

Strawberry Jam

Yield: about 6 half-pints

2 quarts strawberries	3 tablespoons Ball Low or No-Sugar Needed Pectin
1 cup water	

Wash strawberries; drain. Stem and crush strawberries; measure 5 cups. Combine strawberries, water and low or no-sugar needed pectin in a large saucepot, stirring to dissolve pectin. Bring to a boil, stirring constantly. Add sweetener, if desired. Boil 1 minute, stirring constantly. If gel starts to form before 1 minute boil is complete, remove from heat. Ladle hot jam into hot jars, leaving ¼-inch headspace. Remove air bubbles. Adjust two-piece caps. Process 10 minutes in a boiling-water canner.

pickled foods

Chili Sauce

Yield: about 6 half-pints

3 quarts chopped, peeled, cored tomatoes (about 18 medium)	2 teaspoons Ball Salt
	¾ teaspoon cinnamon
2 cups chopped green peppers (about 2 medium)	¾ teaspoon cloves
	2 cups vinegar
2 cups chopped onions (about 2 medium)	Non-sugar sweetener to taste (optional)

Combine all ingredients, except non-sugar sweetener, in a large saucepot. Bring mixture to a boil. Reduce heat and simmer to desired thickness. As mixture thickens, stir frequently to prevent sticking. Stir in non-sugar sweetener, if desired. Ladle hot sauce into hot jars, leaving ½-inch headspace. Adjust two-piece caps. Process 15 minutes in a boiling-water canner.

Mango Relish

Yield: about 4 pints

4 cups ½-inch cubed, peeled under ripe mango (about 4 medium)	3 tablespoons minced crystallized ginger
	2 teaspoons coriander seed, toasted
3 cups ½-inch cubed, peeled under ripe papaya (about 1 large)	1 teaspoon mixed peppercorns
	1 cup white grape juice
2 cups green seedless grapes	1 cup white wine vinegar
¼ cup sliced green onions	

Combine all ingredients in a medium saucepan. Bring mixture to a boil; reduce heat and simmer 10 minutes. Ladle hot relish into hot jars, leaving ½-inch headspace. Remove air bubbles. Adjust two-piece caps. Process 15 minutes in a boiling-water canner.

Reduced-Salt Dill Pickles

Yield: about 6 pints

4 pounds 3- to 5-inch cucumbers	2 tablespoons Ball Mixed Pickling Spice
3 cups sugar	Green or dry dill (1 head per jar)
2 tablespoons Ball Salt	
6 cups vinegar	

Wash cucumbers; drain. Cut cucumbers into ¼-inch slices, discarding stem and blossom ends. Combine sugar, salt and vinegar in a large saucepot. Tie spices in a spice bag; add spice bag to vinegar mixture. Bring to a boil. Reduce heat and simmer 15 minutes; keep hot. Remove spice bag.

Pack cucumbers into hot jars, leaving ½-inch headspace; put one head of dill in each jar. Ladle hot liquid over cucumbers, leaving ½-inch headspace. Remove air bubbles. Adjust two-piece caps. Process 15 minutes in a boiling-water canner.

Reduced-Salt Sweet Pickles

Yield: about 4 pints

4 pounds 3- to 4-inch cucumbers	5⅔ cups vinegar, divided
1 tablespoon Ball Salt	1 tablespoon whole allspice
3½ cups sugar, divided	1 tablespoon celery seed
	2 teaspoons mustard seed

Wash cucumbers; drain. Cut cucumbers into ¼-inch slices, discarding stem and blossom ends. Combine salt, ½ cup sugar and 4 cups vinegar in a large saucepot. Bring to a boil. Reduce heat and add cucumbers. Simmer cucumbers 5 minutes, or until color changes. Drain; keep cucumbers hot. Combine 3 cups sugar, 1⅔ cups vinegar, whole allspice, celery seed and mustard seed. Bring to a boil. Reduce heat and simmer 15 minutes; keep hot. Pack cucumbers into hot jars, leaving ½-inch headspace. Ladle hot liquid over cucumbers, leaving ½-inch headspace. Remove air bubbles. Adjust two-piece caps. Process 10 minutes in a boiling-water canner.

meats & vegetables

Chopped Beef, Lamb, Pork, Veal

Trim fresh, raw meat free of fat, gristle and heavy connective tissue. Chop meat; measure. Cook meat in a skillet until seared. Stir in 1 to 1½ cups boiling water for each quart of meat measured. Pack hot meat and liquid into hot jars, leaving 1-inch headspace. Remove air bubbles. Adjust two-piece caps. Process half-pints 1 hour and 15 minutes, pints 1 hour and 30 minutes, at 10 pounds pressure in a pressure canner.

Corn And Red Peppers With Basil

Yield: about 5 pints

15 pounds ears of corn	Basil
1 pound sweet red peppers (about 3 medium)	

Cut corn from cob. Cut red peppers into strips. Pack corn loosely into hot jars, leaving 1-inch headspace. Add 3 to 4 strips of red pepper and ½ teaspoon basil to each jar. Ladle boiling water over corn, leaving 1-inch headspace. Remove air bubbles. Adjust two-piece caps. Process 55 minutes at 10 pounds pressure in a pressure canner.

Glazed Carrots

Yield: about 6 pints or 3 quarts

6½ to 7 pounds carrots	2 cups water
2 cups brown sugar	1 cup orange juice

Wash and peel carrots. Wash again. Cut carrots into 3-inch pieces. Slice thicker ends in half lengthwise. Combine brown sugar, water and orange juice in a saucepot. Cook over medium heat, stirring until sugar dissolves. Keep syrup hot. Pack carrots tightly into hot jars, leaving 1-inch headspace. Ladle hot syrup over carrots, leaving 1-inch headspace. Remove air bubbles. Adjust two-piece caps. Process pints and quarts 30 minutes at 10 pounds pressure in a pressure canner.

Green Beans With Lemon Peel

Yield: about 10 pints or 5 quarts

7½ to 12½ pounds green beans	1 lemon

Wash beans; drain. Trim ends and break or cut beans into 1-inch pieces. Cut peel from lemon; remove white pith. Cut lemon peel into narrow strips. Put beans in a large saucepot and add water just to cover. Boil beans 5 minutes. Pack hot beans into hot jars, leaving 1-inch headspace. Add 1 to 2 pieces of lemon peel to each jar. Ladle boiling water over beans, leaving 1-inch headspace. Remove air bubbles. Adjust two-piece caps. Process pints 20 minutes, quarts 25 minutes, at 10 pounds pressure in a pressure canner.

Herbed Peas

1½ to 3 pounds peas per pint	Chervil
	Thyme

Wash peas; drain. Shell peas. Wash again. Boil small peas (less than ¼") 3 minutes; medium peas (¼" to ⅓") 5 minutes. Drain; rinse in hot water; drain again. Pack hot peas into hot jars, leaving 1-inch headspace. Add ¼ teaspoon chervil and ¼ teaspoon thyme to each pint jar, ½ teaspoon chervil and ½ teaspoon thyme to each quart jar. Ladle boiling water over peas, leaving 1-inch headspace. Remove air bubbles. Adjust two-piece caps. Process pints and quarts 40 minutes at 10 pounds pressure in a pressure canner.

featured prepared recipe

Mango Salad And Praline Glazed Salmon

Makes 4 servings

Mango Salad

1 pint jar Mango Relish (recipe on page 76)	4 cups Frisée
	¼ cup sunflower seed oil

To Prepare Salad: Drain Mango Relish, reserving liquid. Place Frisée on serving platter; top with mango relish; set aside. Whisk together sunflower seed oil and reserved liquid; drizzle over salad.

Praline Glazed Salmon

1 (8-ounce) jar Praline Syrup (recipe on page 84)	¼ teaspoon salt
2 tablespoons lemon juice	¼ teaspoon lemon-pepper
4 (5- to 6-ounce) salmon fillets, skin removed	

To Prepare Salmon: Combine Praline Syrup and lemon juice in a small saucepan. Cook over medium-high heat until reduced by half. Grill salmon about 4 minutes, basting occasionally with syrup of praline glaze. Turn salmon over and sprinkle with salt and lemon-pepper. Continue grilling about 3 minutes, basting occasionally with syrup of praline glaze. Spoon pecans over salmon and continue grilling about 2 minutes. Salmon is done if it just flakes when tested with a fork. Place on serving platter with Mango Salad. Serve immediately.

something extra

Sweet & Savory Condiments, Gourmet Spreads & Salsas

Can meals be casual, quick, easy—and still be a gourmet delight? Indeed they can, with our Something Extra recipes that serve up delicious dishes and lasting memories. The foundation of these gourmet feasts are the sweet spreads, hot and spicy salsas, flavorful syrups and delicately herbed sauces you preserved at season's peak.

Consider, for example, hearty Linguine with Roasted Roma Sauce and Spinach—each mouthful bursting with the flavor of succulent garden tomatoes that become the base for this dish. Roasted Roma Tomatoes are turned into a meal with just a hint of garlic, rich cream, tender spinach and a sprinkling of shaved parmesan cheese. Couple that with a crusty Italian baguette and a fresh Romaine salad, and the party is on.

Perfect as gifts, a homemade treasure from your pantry is a personal yet practical way to add a little flair to the everyday. Tie a ribbon on a jar of Champagne Blush or Cranberry Wine Jelly, jazz up an event with Pineapple-Chile Salsa, or bring Blueberry Syrup to drizzle atop waffles at a Saturday brunch.

When everyday meals are transformed into memorable repasts, something extraordinary happens. Laughter rings out as families linger at the table, sharing the adventures of the day. Friends toast the chef with accolades that elevate this meal above the ordinary. And you experience a sense of satisfaction and pride, knowing you are giving family and friends the fruits of your labor that say you care.

Pictured, Linguine with Roasted Roma Sauce & Spinach.
Recipe for canned Roasted Roma Tomatoes found on page 82.
Linguine with Roasted Roma Sauce & Spinach
recipe found on page 87.

getting started

Although the holiday season comes to mind for gift-giving, many of these recipes are best prepared throughout the year when fruits and vegetables are at their peak of ripeness and flavor. Because they are heat processed, the finished jars can be stored until given as gifts.

Follow the general guidelines in Learning About Canning (see pages 2-13) at the beginning of this book for information on recommended processing methods and jar, lid and band use. Specific information about preparing ingredients and cooking recipes is available in the preceding sections under High-Acid Foods, Soft Spreads and Pickled Foods (see pages 16; 28 and 44).

sweet spreads
Apple-Maple Jam

Yield: about 8 half-pints

3 quarts chopped, peeled, cored apples (about 6 pounds)	½ teaspoon allspice
	½ teaspoon nutmeg
	¼ teaspoon cloves
6 cups sugar	1 cup maple syrup
1 teaspoon cinnamon	

Combine all ingredients in a large saucepot. Bring slowly to a boil. Cook rapidly to gelling point. As mixture thickens, stir frequently to prevent sticking. Remove from heat. Skim foam if necessary. Ladle hot jam into hot jars, leaving ¼-inch headspace. Adjust two-piece caps. Process 10 minutes in a boiling-water canner.

Chablis Jelly

Yield: about 5 half-pints

3½ cups Chablis	6 tablespoons Ball Classic Pectin
½ cup lemon juice	4½ cups sugar

Combine wine and lemon juice in a large saucepot; stir in classic pectin. Bring to a boil, stirring frequently. Add sugar, stirring until dissolved. Return to a rolling boil. Boil hard 1 minute, stirring constantly. Remove from heat. Skim foam if necessary. Ladle hot jelly into hot jars, leaving ¼-inch headspace. Adjust two-piece caps. Process 10 minutes in a boiling-water canner.

Champagne Blush Jelly

Yield: about 6 half-pints

3 cups bottled raspberry juice	6 tablespoons Ball Classic Pectin
¼ cup lemon juice	4 cups sugar
	1¼ cups Champagne

Combine raspberry juice and lemon juice in a large saucepot; stir in classic pectin. Bring to a boil, stirring frequently. Add sugar, stirring until dissolved. Return to a rolling boil. Boil hard 1 minute, stirring constantly. Remove from heat. Stir in Champagne. Skim foam if necessary. Ladle hot jelly into hot jars, leaving ¼-inch headspace. Adjust two-piece caps. Process 10 minutes in a boiling-water canner.

Cherry-Almond Jam

Yield: about 6 half-pints

3 (12-ounce) bags frozen sweet cherries, thawed and drained	¾ cup almond liqueur
	3 tablespoons lemon juice
	4½ cups sugar
6 tablespoons Ball Classic Pectin	

Finely chop cherries. Combine cherries, classic pectin, almond liqueur and lemon juice in a large saucepot. Bring to a boil, stirring frequently. Add sugar, stirring until dissolved. Return to a rolling boil. Boil hard 1 minute, stirring constantly. Remove from heat. Skim foam if necessary. Ladle hot jam into hot jars, leaving ¼-inch headspace. Adjust two-piece caps. Process 10 minutes in a boiling-water canner.

Cinnamon Anise Jelly

Yield: about 3 half-pints

2 cups apple juice	3½ cups sugar
2 cinnamon sticks	1 pouch Ball Liquid Pectin
1 teaspoon anise seed	

Put apple juice in a large saucepot. Tie spices in a spice bag. Add spice bag to apple juice; simmer 10 minutes. Add sugar, stirring until dissolved. Bring to a boil, stirring frequently. Stir in liquid pectin. Return to a rolling boil. Boil hard 1 minute, stirring constantly. Remove from heat. Remove spice bag. Skim foam if necessary. Ladle hot jelly into hot jars, leaving ¼-inch headspace. Adjust two-piece caps. Process 10 minutes in a boiling-water canner.

Note: To prepare juice, see page 30.

Cranberry-Cider Jelly

Yield: about 6 half-pints

3 cups apple cider	1 teaspoon lemon juice
1 cup cranberry juice cocktail	6 tablespoons Ball Classic Pectin
	5 cups sugar

Combine apple cider, cranberry juice cocktail and lemon juice in a large saucepot. Stir in classic pectin. Bring to a rolling boil, stirring frequently. Add sugar, stirring until dissolved. Return to a rolling boil. Boil hard 1 minute, stirring constantly. Remove from heat. Skim foam if necessary. Ladle hot jelly into hot jars, leaving ¼-inch headspace. Adjust two-piece caps. Process 10 minutes in a boiling-water canner.

Cranberry Wine Jelly

Yield: about 4 half-pints

2 cups cranberry juice cocktail	1 pouch Ball Liquid Pectin
3½ cups sugar	¼ cup Burgundy wine

Combine cranberry juice cocktail and sugar in a large saucepot, stirring until sugar dissolves. Bring to a boil, stirring frequently. Stir in liquid pectin. Return to a rolling boil. Boil hard 1 minute, stirring constantly. Remove from heat. Stir in wine. Skim foam if necessary. Ladle hot jelly into hot jars, leaving ¼-inch headspace. Adjust two-piece caps. Process 10 minutes in a boiling-water canner.

Garlic Jelly

Yield: about 5 half-pints

¼ pound garlic	5 cups sugar
2 cups vinegar, divided	1 pouch Ball Liquid Pectin

Roast garlic under a broiler or on a grill at 425°F for 10 to 15 minutes. Cool. Peel garlic. Purée garlic and ½ cup vinegar in a food processor or blender. Combine garlic, 1½ cups vinegar and sugar in a large saucepot, stirring until sugar dissolves. Bring to a boil, stirring constantly. Stir in liquid pectin. Return to a rolling boil. Boil hard 1 minute, stirring constantly. Remove from heat. Skim foam if necessary. Ladle hot jelly into hot jars, leaving ¼-inch headspace. Adjust two-piece caps. Process 10 minutes in a boiling-water canner.

Plum-Orange Jam

Yield: about 6 half-pints

5 cups chopped and pitted plums (about 3½ pounds)	6 tablespoons Ball Classic Pectin
1 tablespoon grated orange peel	5½ cups sugar
	¼ cup orange liqueur

Combine plums, orange peel and classic pectin in a large saucepot. Bring to a boil, stirring frequently. Add sugar, stirring until dissolved. Return to a rolling boil. Boil hard 1 minute, stirring constantly. Remove from heat. Stir in orange liqueur. Skim foam if necessary. Ladle hot jam into hot jars, leaving ¼-inch headspace. Adjust two-piece caps. Process 10 minutes in a boiling-water canner.

Strawberry-Kiwi Jam

Yield: about 6 half-pints

3 cups crushed strawberries	6 tablespoons Ball Classic Pectin
3 kiwi, peeled and diced	1 tablespoon lemon juice
1 tablespoon minced crystallized ginger	5 cups sugar

Combine strawberries, kiwi, ginger, classic pectin and lemon juice in a large saucepot. Bring to a boil, stirring frequently. Add sugar, stirring until dissolved. Return to a rolling boil. Boil hard 1 minute, stirring constantly. Remove from heat. Skim foam if necessary. Ladle hot jam into hot jars, leaving ¼-inch headspace. Adjust two-piece caps. Process 10 minutes in a boiling-water canner.

Tangerine Jelly

Yield: about 5 half-pints

6 cups chopped tangerine pulp (about 3½ pounds)	1 cup water
1 cup chopped lemon pulp (about 2 medium)	6 tablespoons Ball Classic Pectin
½ cup thinly sliced tangerine peel (about 3 medium)	5 cups sugar

To Prepare Juice: Combine tangerine pulp, lemon pulp, tangerine peel and water in a large saucepot. Cover; simmer 10 minutes, stirring occasionally. Strain juice through a damp jelly bag or several layers of cheesecloth. Measure 4 cups juice.

To Make Jelly: Combine juice and classic pectin in a large saucepot. Bring to a boil over high heat. Add sugar, stirring until dissolved. Return to a rolling boil. Boil hard 1 minute, stirring constantly. Remove from heat. Skim foam if necessary. Ladle hot jelly into hot jars, leaving ¼-inch headspace. Adjust two-piece caps. Process 10 minutes in a boiling-water canner.

hot & savory

Fiesta Salsa

Yield: about 4 pints

7 cups chopped, seeded, peeled, cored tomatoes	½ cup chopped jalapeño peppers
2 cups chopped, seeded, peeled cucumbers	¼ cup minced cilantro
2 cups chopped and seeded banana peppers	3 cloves garlic, minced
1 cup sliced green onion	1 tablespoon minced fresh marjoram
½ cup chopped, peeled, roasted Anaheim peppers	1 teaspoon salt
	½ cup cider vinegar
	2 tablespoons lime juice

Combine all ingredients in a large saucepot. Bring mixture to a boil. Reduce heat and simmer 10 minutes. Ladle hot salsa into hot jars, leaving ½-inch headspace. Adjust two-piece caps. Process 15 minutes in a boiling-water canner.

Note: When cutting or seeding hot peppers, wear rubber gloves to prevent hands from being burned.

Jalapeño Salsa

Yield: about 3 pints

3 cups chopped, seeded, peeled, cored tomatoes	2 tablespoons minced cilantro
3 cups chopped jalapeño peppers	2 teaspoons oregano
1 cup chopped onion	1½ teaspoons salt
6 cloves garlic, minced	½ teaspoon cumin
	1 cup cider vinegar

Combine all ingredients in a large saucepot. Bring mixture to a boil. Reduce heat and simmer 10 minutes. Ladle hot salsa into hot jars, leaving ½-inch headspace. Adjust two-piece caps. Process 15 minutes in a boiling-water canner.

Note: When cutting or seeding hot peppers, wear rubber gloves to prevent hands from being burned. If a less hot salsa is desired, seed jalapeño peppers before chopping.

Pineapple-Chile Salsa

Yield: about 6 half-pints

4 cups cubed, seeded, peeled papaya	2 tablespoons minced green onions
2 cups cubed, cored, peeled pineapple	2 tablespoons minced cilantro
1 cup golden raisins	2 tablespoons brown sugar
½ cup chopped Anaheim peppers	1 cup lemon juice
	½ cup lime juice
	½ cup pineapple juice

Combine all ingredients in a large saucepot. Bring to a boil. Reduce heat and simmer 10 minutes. Ladle hot salsa into hot jars, leaving ½-inch headspace. Adjust two-piece caps. Process 15 minutes in a boiling-water canner.

Roasted Red Pepper Spread

Yield: about 5 half-pints

6 pounds sweet red peppers (about 8 large)	1 small white onion
1 pound roma tomatoes (about 10 medium)	2 tablespoons minced basil
	1 tablespoon sugar
2 large cloves garlic	1 teaspoon coarse salt
	½ cup red wine vinegar

Roast peppers under a broiler or on a grill at 425°F until skin wrinkles and chars in spots. Turn peppers over and roast opposite side. Remove peppers from heat. Place in a paper bag; secure opening; cool 15 minutes. Roast tomatoes, garlic and onion under a broiler or on a grill 10 to 15 minutes. Remove from heat. Place tomatoes in a paper bag; secure opening; cool 15 minutes. Peel garlic and onion. Finely mince garlic; set aside. Finely mince onion; measure ¼ cup; set aside. Peel and seed red peppers and tomatoes. Purée in a food processor or blender. Combine all ingredients in a large saucepot. Bring to a boil over medium-high heat, stirring to prevent sticking. Reduce heat; simmer until spread thickens. Ladle hot spread into hot jars, leaving ¼-inch headspace. Adjust two-piece caps. Process 10 minutes in a boiling-water canner.

Roasted Roma Tomatoes

Yield: about 4 quarts

12 pounds Roma tomatoes	1 teaspoon salt
4 bulbs garlic	½ teaspoon coarsely ground black pepper
¼ cup extra-virgin olive oil	
1½ cups chopped onion	Ball Citric Acid or bottled lemon juice
1 tablespoon minced fresh oregano	

Roast tomatoes on grill or in broiler until skins begin to wrinkle and become lightly blackened in spots, turning to roast evenly on all sides. Remove from heat. Place roasted tomatoes in a paper bag and close tightly. Cool until tomatoes are easy to handle, about 15 minutes. Slip skins off tomatoes, cut in half and remove seeds. Cut into ½-inch chunks; set aside. Place garlic on aluminum foil and drizzle olive oil over garlic. Wrap foil around garlic, sealing edges tightly. Roast garlic at 350° F until tender, about 30 minutes. Cool garlic until it is easy to handle. Separate cloves of garlic and remove papery skins. Add garlic to tomatoes. Stir in remaining ingredients and cook over medium heat until hot throughout. Add ½ teaspoon citric acid or 2 tablespoons bottled lemon juice to each quart jar. Ladle hot tomatoes into hot jars, leaving ½-inch headspace. Remove air bubbles. Adjust two-piece caps. Process quarts 1 hour and 25 minutes in a boiling-water canner.

Tomatillo Salsa

Yield: about 2 pints

5½ cups chopped, cored, husked tomatillos (about 2 pounds)	2 tablespoons minced cilantro
	2 teaspoons cumin
	½ teaspoon salt
1 cup chopped onion	½ teaspoon red pepper
1 cup chopped green chili peppers	½ cup vinegar
	¼ cup lime juice
4 cloves garlic, minced	

Combine all ingredients in a large saucepot. Bring mixture to a boil. Reduce heat and simmer 10 minutes. Ladle hot salsa into hot jars, leaving ½-inch headspace. Adjust two-piece caps. Process 15 minutes in a boiling-water canner.

Note: When cutting or seeding hot peppers, wear rubber gloves to prevent hands from being burned.

Spicy Tomato Salsa

Yield: about 6 pints

6 pounds tomatoes (about 12 large)	15 cloves garlic, minced
	6 jalapeño peppers, seeded and diced
9 dried hot chili peppers	
3 cups diced red onion	1 tablespoon salt
1½ cups chopped cilantro, tightly packed	¾ teaspoon dried red chili flakes
	¾ cup red wine vinegar

Wash tomatoes; drain. Peel, seed and dice tomatoes into ¼-inch pieces. Remove seeds from dried chili peppers; place chili peppers in a small bowl. Pour boiling water over chili peppers just to cover. Secure plastic wrap over bowl and allow to steep for 15 minutes. Drain half the water. Purée chili peppers and remaining water in a food processor or blender for 1 minute or until smooth. Combine all ingredients in a large saucepot. Bring to a boil. Reduce heat and simmer 10 minutes or until mixture thickens. Ladle hot salsa into hot jars, leaving ½-inch headspace. Adjust two-piece caps. Process 15 minutes in a boiling-water canner.

Note: When cutting or seeding hot peppers, wear rubber gloves to prevent hands from being burned.

Zesty Salsa

Yield: about 6 pints

10 cups chopped, seeded, peeled, cored tomatoes (about 6 pounds)	2½ cups chopped and seeded hot peppers (about 1 pound)
	3 cloves garlic, minced
5 cups chopped and seeded long green peppers (about 2 pounds)	2 tablespoons cilantro, minced
	3 teaspoons salt
5 cups chopped onions (about 1½ pounds)	1¼ cups cider vinegar
	1 teaspoon hot pepper sauce (optional)

Combine all ingredients in a large saucepot, adding hot pepper sauce, if desired. Bring mixture to a boil. Reduce heat and simmer 10 minutes. Ladle hot salsa into hot jars, leaving ½-inch headspace. Adjust two-piece caps. Process 20 minutes in a boiling-water canner.

Note: When cutting or seeding hot peppers, wear rubber gloves to prevent hands from being burned.

infusions & condiments

Apple-Cinnamon Syrup

Yield: about 6 pints

6 cups apple juice	4 cups water
3 sticks cinnamon, broken	3 cups corn syrup
5 cups sugar	¼ cup lemon juice

Combine apple juice and cinnamon sticks in a medium saucepot. Simmer 5 minutes; set aside. Combine sugar and water in a medium saucepot; boil to 230°F (adjust for altitude). Add apple juice, cinnamon stick and corn syrup to sugar syrup. Boil 5 minutes. Remove cinnamon sticks. Stir in lemon juice. Ladle hot syrup into hot jars, leaving ¼-inch headspace. Adjust two-piece caps. Process 10 minutes in a boiling-water canner.

Note: To prepare juice, see page 30. Fruit syrup is typically thin. If a thicker syrup is desired for serving, combine 1 cup syrup and 1 tablespoon cornstarch in a small saucepan. Bring to a boil, cooking until syrup thickens. Do not add cornstarch before canning.

Blackberry Liqueur Sauce

Yield: about 3 half-pints

4 cups blackberries	1 tablespoon lemon zest
½ cup Chambord	1 tablespoon lemon juice
¾ cup sugar	1 pouch Ball Liquid Pectin

Wash blackberries; drain. Combine blackberries, Chambord and sugar in a saucepan; let stand 2 hours, stirring occasionally. Add lemon zest and lemon juice. Bring to a boil. Stir in liquid pectin. Return mixture to a rolling boil. Boil hard 1 minute, stirring constantly. Remove from heat. Skim foam if necessary. Ladle hot sauce into hot jars, leaving ½-inch headspace. Adjust two-piece caps. Process 10 minutes in a boiling-water canner.

Blueberry Syrup

Yield: about 3 pints

2 quarts blueberries	3 cups sugar
6 cups water, divided	2 tablespoons lemon juice
1 tablespoon grated lemon peel	

Wash blueberries; drain. Crush blueberries. Combine blueberries, 2 cups water and lemon peel in a medium saucepot. Simmer 5 minutes. Strain through a damp jelly bag or several layers of cheesecloth. Combine sugar and 4 cups water in a medium saucepot; boil to 230°F (adjust for altitude). Add blueberry juice to sugar syrup. Boil 5 minutes. Stir in lemon juice. Ladle hot syrup into hot jars, leaving ¼-inch headspace. Adjust two-piece caps. Process 10 minutes in a boiling-water canner.

Note: Fruit syrup is typically thin. If a thicker syrup is desired for serving, combine 1 cup syrup and 1 tablespoon cornstarch in a small saucepan. Bring to a boil, cooking until syrup thickens. Do not add cornstarch before canning.

Blueberry-Basil Vinegar

Yield: about 2 pints

4 cups blueberries	1 cup basil, loosely packed
4 cups white wine vinegar, divided	Zest of 1 lemon

Wash blueberries; drain. Combine blueberries and 1 cup white wine vinegar in a glass bowl. Lightly crush blueberries. Add remaining vinegar. Crush basil. Add basil and lemon zest to vinegar. Cover bowl with waxed paper or plastic wrap and secure. Let vinegar steep in a cool, dark place for 4 weeks, stirring every 2 to 3 days. Strain vinegar through several layers of cheesecloth. Heat vinegar to 180°F. Ladle hot vinegar into hot jars, leaving ¼-inch headspace. Adjust two-piece caps. Process 10 minutes in a boiling-water canner.

Note: One-fourth cup fresh blueberries may be added to vinegar before canning.

Cranberry-Orange Vinegar

Yield: about 2 pints

1 pound fresh cranberries, divided	1 cup sugar
4 whole cloves	3 cups white wine vinegar
2 sticks cinnamon	2 orange slices

Wash cranberries; drain. Measure ½ cup cranberries; set aside. Prepare cranberry juice with remaining cranberries (*see page 30*). Measure 1 cup juice. Tie spices in a spice bag. Combine cranberry juice, spice bag and sugar in a large saucepot. Cook over medium heat, stirring until sugar is dissolved. Add reserved cranberries and white wine vinegar. Bring to a boil. Reduce heat and simmer, covered, 10 minutes. Remove spice bag. Place 1 orange slice in each jar as jars are being filled. Ladle hot vinegar into hot jars, leaving ¼-inch headspace. Adjust two-piece caps. Process 10 minutes in a boiling-water canner.

Danish Cherry Sauce

Yield: about 3 pints

4½ pounds cherries (3 pounds pitted)	1½ tablespoons almond extract
1½ cups sugar	1 cup water
3 sticks cinnamon	¾ cup corn syrup

Wash and pit cherries. Combine sugar, cinnamon sticks, almond extract, water and corn syrup in a large saucepot. Bring to a boil. Reduce heat to a simmer. Add cherries and simmer until hot throughout. Remove cinnamon sticks. Ladle hot sauce into hot jars, leaving ½-inch headspace. Adjust two-piece caps. Process 10 minutes in a boiling-water canner.

Note: To thicken sauce for serving, combine 1 tablespoon cornstarch and 2 tablespoons water in a saucepan. Add 1 pint Danish Cherry Sauce. Bring to a boil, cooking until sauce thickens. Do not add cornstarch before canning.

Lemon-Mint Vinegar

Yield: about 2 pints

4 cups white wine vinegar	Peel of 2 lemons
¼ cup sugar	
2 cups mint leaves, loosely packed	

Combine vinegar and sugar in a medium saucepot. Simmer mixture until sugar dissolves. Pour into a glass bowl. Crush mint leaves. Remove all white pith from lemon peel. Add mint and lemon peel to vinegar. Cover bowl with waxed paper or plastic wrap and secure. Let vinegar steep in a cool, dark place for 1 to 4 weeks, stirring every 2 to 3 days. Taste each week for desired strength. Strain vinegar through several layers of cheesecloth. Heat vinegar to 180°F. Ladle hot vinegar into hot jars, leaving ¼-inch headspace. Adjust two-piece caps. Process 10 minutes in a boiling-water canner.

Note: A fresh sprig of mint and a piece of lemon peel may be added to each jar before canning.

Loganberry Vinegar

Yield: about 2 pints

4 cups loganberries	4 cups red wine vinegar

Wash loganberries; drain. Combine loganberries and red wine vinegar in a glass bowl. Cover bowl with waxed paper or plastic wrap and secure. Let vinegar steep in a cool, dark place for 1 to 4 weeks, stirring every 2 to 3 days. Strain vinegar through several layers of cheesecloth. Heat vinegar to 180°F. Ladle hot vinegar into hot jars, leaving ¼-inch headspace. Adjust two-piece caps. Process 10 minutes in a boiling-water canner.

Maple-Walnut Syrup

Yield: about 4 half-pints

1½ cups corn syrup	½ cup sugar
1 cup maple syrup	2 cups walnut pieces
½ cup water	

Combine corn syrup, maple syrup and water in a large saucepot. Add sugar, stirring until dissolved. Bring to a boil, stirring occasionally. Reduce heat and simmer syrup until it begins to thicken, about 15 minutes. Stir in nuts; cook 5 minutes. Ladle hot syrup into hot jars, leaving ¼-inch headspace. Adjust two-piece caps. Process 10 minutes in a boiling-water canner.

Mulled Blackberry Vinegar

Yield: about 3 pints

4 cups blackberries	1 tablespoon whole cloves
4 cups cider vinegar, divided	1 tablespoon whole allspice
2 sticks cinnamon	

Wash blackberries; drain. Combine blackberries and 1 cup cider vinegar in a glass bowl. Lightly crush blackberries. Add remaining cider vinegar and spices. Cover bowl with waxed paper or plastic wrap and secure. Let vinegar steep in a cool, dark place for 4 weeks, stirring every 2 to 3 days. Strain vinegar through several layers of cheesecloth. Heat vinegar to 180°F. Ladle hot vinegar into hot jars, leaving ¼-inch headspace. Adjust two-piece caps. Process 10 minutes in a boiling-water canner.

Note: ¼ cup washed, fresh berries may be added to each jar before canning.

Pineapple Topping

Yield: about 5 half-pints

5 cups crushed, fresh or canned pineapple	4 cups sugar

Combine pineapple and sugar in a large saucepot. Bring slowly to a boil, stirring until sugar dissolves. Cook rapidly almost to gelling point. As mixture thickens, stir frequently to prevent sticking. Remove from heat. Skim foam if necessary. Ladle hot topping into hot jars, leaving ½-inch headspace. Adjust two-piece caps. Process 15 minutes in a boiling-water canner.

Note: Cook to gelling point for jam.

Plum Sauce

Yield: about 4 pints

4 pounds plums	1 ¼- x 1-inch piece fresh ginger, minced
2 cups brown sugar	1 tablespoon salt
1 cup granulated sugar	1 clove garlic, minced
¾ cup chopped onion (about 1 medium)	1 cup cider vinegar
2 tablespoons mustard seed	
2 tablespoons chopped green chili peppers	

Wash plums; drain. Pit and chop plums. Combine remaining ingredients in a large saucepot. Bring to a boil; reduce heat. Add chopped plums. Cook until thick and syrupy. Ladle hot sauce into hot jars, leaving ½-inch headspace. Adjust two-piece caps. Process 20 minutes in a boiling-water canner.

Note: When cutting or seeding hot peppers, wear rubber gloves to prevent hands from being burned.

Pomegranate Sauce

Yield: about 4 half-pints

5 cups pomegranate juice (about 10 large)	½ cup lemon juice
	1 cup sugar

To Prepare Juice: Cut pomegranates in half. Extract juice from red seeds with a juice reamer. Strain juice through a damp jelly bag or several layers of cheesecloth. Measure 5 cups juice.

To Make Sauce: Combine pomegranate juice, lemon juice and sugar in a large saucepot. Bring to a boil, stirring to dissolve sugar. Reduce heat; simmer until reduced by half. Ladle hot sauce into hot jars, leaving ½-inch headspace. Adjust two-piece caps. Process 10 minutes in a boiling-water canner.

Praline Syrup

Yield: about 4 half-pints

2 cups dark corn syrup	1 cup pecan pieces
½ cup water	½ teaspoon vanilla
⅓ cup dark brown sugar	

Combine syrup and water in a saucepan. Add sugar, stirring until dissolved. Bring to a boil; boil 1 minute. Reduce heat; stir in pecans and vanilla; simmer 5 minutes. Ladle hot syrup into hot jars, leaving ¼-inch headspace. Adjust two-piece caps. Process 10 minutes in a boiling-water canner.

Note: For a lighter molasses flavor, use light corn syrup and light brown sugar.

Spiced Honey

Yield: about 3 half-pints

1 lemon	3 sticks cinnamon
12 whole cloves	2⅔ cups honey

Cut lemon into 6 thin slices. Place 2 cloves in each slice. Put lemon slices, cinnamon sticks and honey in a saucepan. Bring to a boil, stirring occasionally. Place 2 lemon slices and 1 cinnamon stick in each jar. Ladle hot honey into hot jars, leaving ¼-inch headspace. Adjust two-piece caps. Process 10 minutes in a boiling-water canner.

Strawberry Syrup

Yield: about 3 pints

2½ quarts strawberries	2½ cups sugar
3 cups water, divided	3½ cups corn syrup
1 2-inch strip of lemon peel	2 tablespoons lemon juice

Wash strawberries; drain. Stem and crush strawberries. Combine strawberries, 1½ cups water and lemon peel in a medium saucepot. Simmer 5 minutes. Strain through a damp jelly bag or several layers of cheesecloth. Combine sugar and 1½ cups water in a medium saucepot; boil to 230°F (adjust for altitude). Add strawberry juice and corn syrup to sugar syrup. Boil 5 minutes. Stir in lemon juice. Ladle hot syrup into hot jars, leaving ¼-inch headspace. Adjust two-piece caps. Process 10 minutes in a boiling-water canner.

Note: Fruit syrup is typically thin. If a thicker syrup is desired for serving, combine 1 cup syrup and 1 tablespoon cornstarch in a small saucepan. Bring to a boil, cooking until syrup thickens. Do not add cornstarch before canning.

Sweet Cherry Vinegar

Yield: about 2 pints

4 cups pitted sweet cherries
4 cups white wine vinegar, divided
Zest of 1 lemon

Combine cherries and 1 cup white wine vinegar in a glass bowl. Lightly crush cherries. Add remaining white wine vinegar and lemon zest. Cover bowl with waxed paper or plastic wrap and secure. Let vinegar steep in a cool, dark place for 4 weeks, stirring every 2 to 3 days. Strain vinegar through several layers of cheesecloth. Heat vinegar to 180°F. Ladle hot vinegar into hot jars, leaving ¼-inch headspace. Adjust two-piece caps. Process 10 minutes in a boiling-water canner.

flavorful sampler

Almond Pears

Yield: about 5 pints

7 pounds pears
Ball Fruit-Fresh Produce Protector
2 cups sugar
4 cups water
⅓ cup blanched almonds
½ cup almond liqueur

Wash pears; drain. Peel pears, cut into halves and core. Treat with Fruit-Fresh to prevent darkening. Rinse and drain. Cook pears in water one layer at a time until hot throughout; set aside, keeping hot. Combine sugar and 4 cups water in medium saucepot, stirring until sugar dissolves. Bring to a boil. Reduce heat and simmer 5 minutes. Pack hot pears into hot jars, leaving ½-inch headspace. Add 1 tablespoon almonds to each jar. Remove syrup from heat; stir in almond liqueur. Ladle hot syrup over pears, leaving ½-inch headspace. Remove air bubbles. Adjust two-piece caps. Process 20 minutes in a boiling-water canner.

Blackberries In Framboise

Yield: about 4 half-pints

3 pints blackberries
2 cups sugar
1 stick cinnamon, broken
1 tablespoon grated lemon peel
½ teaspoon freshly grated nutmeg
2 cups water
½ cup Framboise, or other raspberry brandy

Extract juice from 1 pint blackberries (*see page 30*). Measure ½ cup juice; set aside. Combine sugar, cinnamon stick, lemon peel, nutmeg and water in a large saucepot. Bring to a boil. Reduce heat and simmer 5 minutes. Strain syrup; return to saucepot. Add blackberry juice, remaining blackberries and raspberry brandy; bring to a boil. Pack hot blackberries into hot jars, leaving ½-inch headspace. Ladle hot syrup over blackberries, leaving ½-inch headspace. Remove air bubbles. Adjust two-piece caps. Process 10 minutes in a boiling-water canner.

Brandied Apple Rings

Yield: about 3 pints

4½ pounds firm red apples
Ball Fruit-Fresh Produce Protector
4 cups sugar
3 cups water
Red food coloring (optional)
1 cup brandy

Wash and core apples; do not peel. Cut into ¼-inch rings. Treat with Fruit-Fresh to prevent darkening. Bring sugar and water to a boil; boil 5 minutes, stirring to dissolve sugar. Add food coloring, if desired. Rinse and drain apple rings. Add apple rings to syrup; bring to a boil. Reduce heat, simmer 30 minutes or until rings are desired color. Remove from heat; cool to room temperature. Remove apple rings from syrup. Bring syrup to a boil. Remove from heat and stir in brandy. Pack apple rings loosely into hot jars, leaving ½-inch headspace. Ladle hot syrup over apple rings, leaving ½-inch headspace. Remove air bubbles. Adjust two-piece caps. Process 15 minutes in a boiling-water canner.

Mango-Raspberry Soup

Yield: about 4 pints

4 quarts raspberries, crushed
4 large mangoes, peeled, pitted and chopped
2½ cups sugar

Combine raspberries and mangoes in a large saucepot. Cover; bring to a boil, stirring to prevent sticking. Reduce heat and simmer 10 minutes. Strain through a damp jelly bag. Let stand 12 to 24 hours in a cool place. Measure 7 cups juice. Put juice in a large saucepot. Add sugar, stirring until dissolved. Bring to a boil. Reduce heat and simmer until soup thickens. Ladle hot soup into hot jars, leaving ½-inch headspace. Adjust two-piece caps. Process 15 minutes in a boiling-water canner.

Papaya Soup

Yield: about 6 pints

6 cups diced, peeled, seeded papaya (about 4 small)
1 cup diced, peeled, pitted mango (about 2 medium)
1 cup diced, peeled, pitted peaches (about 2 medium)
1 cup golden raisins
8 cups peach nectar
½ cup lemon juice
½ cup honey
2 sticks cinnamon
1 tablespoon whole cloves

Combine all ingredients except cinnamon and cloves in a large saucepot. Tie spices in a spice bag. Add to soup. Bring soup to a boil. Reduce heat. Cover; simmer 15 minutes. Remove spice bag. Purée soup in a food processor or blender. Return soup to a large saucepot; simmer 5 minutes. Ladle hot soup into hot jars, leaving ½-inch headspace. Adjust two-piece caps. Process 20 minutes in a boiling-water canner.

Note: To prepare peach nectar, see page 22.

pickled & spicy

Apricot And Date Chutney

Yield: about 12 half-pints

2 pounds dried apricots
2½ cups pitted dates
3 cups brown sugar
2½ cups raisins
1 tablespoon mustard seed
1 tablespoon salt
2 teaspoons ginger
1 teaspoon coriander
2 cups white wine vinegar
2 cups water

Soak apricots in enough water to cover for 30 minutes. Drain and place in a large saucepot. Chop dates and add to apricots. Add remaining ingredients and simmer over low heat until thickened, stirring frequently. Ladle hot chutney into hot jars, leaving ½-inch headspace. Adjust two-piece caps. Process 10 minutes in a boiling-water canner.

Brandied Mincemeat

Yield: about 4 quarts

2 quarts diced, peeled, cored tart apples (about 8 large)
4 cups cranberries (about 1 pound)
1 (14-ounce) package golden raisins
1 (14-ounce) package dark raisins
1 (11-ounce) package currants
1 (12-ounce) package figs, chopped
1⅓ cups ground and seeded oranges (about 2 medium)
1 cup ground and seeded lemons (about 2 large)
½ cup minced candied orange peel
½ cup minced candied lemon peel
2 cups brown sugar
1 tablespoon cinnamon
2 teaspoons allspice
2 teaspoons nutmeg
1 teaspoon cloves
1 teaspoon ginger
1 quart apple cider
¾ cup brandy
½ cup dry sherry

Combine all ingredients, except brandy and sherry, in a large saucepot. Simmer 1 hour, stirring occasionally. Remove from heat; stir in brandy and sherry. Return to heat; simmer 30 minutes. Ladle hot mincemeat into hot jars, leaving ½-inch headspace. Remove air bubbles. Adjust two-piece caps. Process 30 minutes in a boiling-water canner.

Curried Fruit Compote

Yield: about 4 quarts

3 pounds peaches, peeled, pitted, sliced
2 pounds apricots, peeled, pitted, halved
Ball Fruit-Fresh Produce Protector
1 fresh pineapple, peeled and cut into 1-inch chunks (about 5 pounds)
1 cantaloupe, cut into 1-inch chunks or balls (about 4 pounds)
3 cups sugar
3 tablespoons curry powder
4 cups water
¼ cup lemon juice
½ cup thinly sliced lime (about 1 small)

Treat peaches and apricots with Fruit-Fresh to prevent darkening. Combine sugar, curry powder, water and lemon juice in a large saucepot. Bring to a boil; reduce heat. Drain peaches and apricots. Add all fruit to syrup. Simmer just until fruit is hot throughout. Pack hot fruit into hot jars, leaving ½-inch headspace. Add 1 lime slice to each jar. Ladle hot syrup over fruit, leaving ½-inch headspace. Remove air bubbles. Adjust two-piece caps. Process 30 minutes in a boiling-water canner.

Crab Apple Pickles

Yield: about 6 pints

2 quarts crab apples with stems (about 2½ pounds)
6 cups sugar
3 cups vinegar
3 cups water
2 sticks cinnamon
1½ tablespoons whole allspice
1½ tablespoons whole cloves

Prick apples to help prevent peel from bursting; set aside. Combine sugar, vinegar and water in a large saucepot. Bring to a boil, stirring until sugar is dissolved. Tie spices in a spice bag; add spice bag to vinegar mixture. Reduce heat and simmer 5 minutes. Add crab apples, one layer at a time, and simmer until tender. Remove crab apples from pickling liquid and set in a large bowl. Bring pickling liquid to a boil. Ladle pickling liquid over apples, cover and let stand 12 to 18 hours in a cool place. Remove spice bag. Return pickling liquid to a large saucepot and bring to a boil. Pack crab apples into hot jars, leaving ½-inch headspace. Ladle hot syrup over crab apples, leaving ½-inch headspace. Remove air bubbles. Adjust two-piece caps. Process 15 minutes in a boiling-water canner.

Pickled Green Tomato-Hot Pepper Mix

Yield: about 5 quarts

7 pounds green tomatoes, cored, cut into eighths (about 21 medium)
2 pounds Hungarian peppers, cut into ½-inch rings
1 pound banana peppers, cut into ½-inch rings
1 pound Anaheim peppers, cut into ½-inch rings
½ pound pearl onions, peeled
5 cloves garlic, peeled
1 tablespoon Ball Salt
1 cup sugar
2 quarts white vinegar
1 quart water
¼ cup Ball Mixed Pickling Spice
2 tablespoons mustard seed
Ball Pickle Crisp (optional)

Combine tomatoes, peppers, onions, garlic and salt in a large bowl; set aside. Combine sugar, vinegar and water in a large saucepot. Bring to a boil, stirring until sugar dissolves. Tie spices in a spice bag; add spice bag to vinegar mixture. Reduce heat and simmer 10 minutes. Add vegetables and simmer 10 minutes. Remove spice bag. Pack hot vegetables into hot jars, leaving ½-inch headspace. Add Pickle Crisp to each jar, if desired. Ladle hot liquid over vegetables, leaving ½-inch headspace. Remove air bubbles. Adjust two-piece caps. Process 15 minutes in a boiling-water canner.

Jardiniere

Yield: about 6 pints

1 pound sweet green peppers, cut into strips (about 3 medium)
1¼ pounds onions, sliced (about 3 medium)
¾ pound zucchini, sliced (about 4 small)
½ pound carrots, cut into sticks (about 5 medium)
3⅔ cups sliced celery (about 6 stalks)
4 banana peppers, cut into strips
½ pound mushrooms, sliced
1 cup sugar
2 tablespoons Ball Mixed Pickling Spice
2 teaspoons basil
1 teaspoon oregano
1 teaspoon peppercorns
1 clove garlic, minced
1 teaspoon Ball Salt
1 quart cider vinegar
1½ cups water
Ball Pickle Crisp (optional)

Combine vegetables; set aside. Combine sugar, spices, vinegar and water in a large saucepot. Bring to a boil; reduce heat to a simmer. Add vegetables and simmer until just tender. Pack hot vegetables into hot jars, leaving ½-inch headspace. Ladle hot liquid over vegetables, leaving ½-inch headspace. Add Pickle Crisp to each jar, if desired. Remove air bubbles. Adjust two-piece caps. Process 20 minutes in a boiling-water canner.

Note: When cutting or seeding hot peppers, wear rubber gloves to prevent hands from being burned.

Mango-Pineapple Relish

Yield: about 6 pints

4 cups chopped, seeded, peeled mangoes (about 8 small)
3 cups chopped, cored, peeled pineapple (about 1 medium)
½ cup diced sweet green pepper
½ cup diced sweet red pepper
¼ cup diced red onion
¼ cup cider vinegar
¼ cup lemon juice
¼ cup pineapple juice
1 tablespoon sugar
2 teaspoons cinnamon
¼ teaspoon ginger

Combine all ingredients in a large saucepot. Bring to a boil. Reduce heat and simmer 20 minutes, stirring frequently. Ladle hot relish into hot jars,

leaving ½-inch headspace. Remove air bubbles. Adjust two-piece caps. Process 15 minutes in a boiling-water canner.

Pickled Pineapple

Yield: about 4 pints

2 cups brown sugar	½ teaspoon whole allspice
1 cup red wine vinegar	¼ teaspoon whole cloves
1 cup unsweetened pineapple juice	2 fresh pineapples, peeled, cored and cut into spears (about 5 pounds each)
3 sticks cinnamon, broken	

Combine brown sugar, vinegar and pineapple juice in a large saucepot. Tie spices in a spice bag; add to saucepot. Cover; simmer 20 minutes. Add pineapple to syrup; simmer until hot throughout. Remove pineapple from syrup; keep hot. Heat syrup just to a boil; remove spice bag. Pack hot pineapple into hot jars, leaving ½-inch headspace. Ladle hot syrup over pineapple, leaving ½-inch headspace. Remove air bubbles. Adjust two-piece caps. Process 10 minutes in a boiling-water canner.

Pickled Three Bean Salad

Yield: about 5 pints

1½ pounds green beans	2½ cups sugar
1½ pounds wax beans	1 tablespoon mustard seed
1 pound lima beans	1 teaspoon celery seed
2 cups sliced celery (about 3 stalks)	4 teaspoons Ball Salt
½ pound onion, sliced (about 1 large)	3 cups vinegar
	1¼ cups water
1 cup diced sweet red pepper (about 1 medium)	Ball Pickle Crisp (optional)

Cut green and wax beans into 1½-inch pieces. Combine beans, celery, onion and pepper in a large saucepot. Cover with boiling water; cook 8 to 10 minutes. Drain; keep hot. Combine sugar, mustard seed, celery seed, salt, vinegar and water in a large saucepot. Bring to a boil. Reduce heat and simmer 15 minutes. Pack hot vegetables into hot jars, leaving ½-inch headspace. Ladle hot liquid over vegetables, leaving ½-inch headspace. Add Pickle Crisp to each jar, if desired. Remove air bubbles. Adjust two-piece caps. Process 15 minutes in a boiling-water canner.

Spicy Pickled Beets

Yield: about 4 pints

4 pounds beets, 1- to 1½-inch diameter	1 tablespoon mustard seed
	1 teaspoon whole allspice
3 cups thinly sliced onions (about 3 medium)	1 teaspoon whole cloves
	1 teaspoon Ball Salt
2 cups sugar	2½ cups cider vinegar
3 sticks cinnamon, broken	1½ cups water
	Ball Pickle Crisp (optional)

Trim beet stem and tap root to 2 inches. Cover beets with boiling water in a large saucepot; cook until tender. Drain. Peel and trim beets. Combine remaining ingredients in a large saucepot. Bring to a boil. Reduce heat and simmer 5 minutes. Add beets and cook until hot throughout. Remove cinnamon sticks. Pack hot beets into hot jars, leaving ½-inch headspace. Ladle hot liquid over beets, leaving ½-inch headspace. Add Pickle Crisp to each jar, if desired. Remove air bubbles. Adjust two-piece caps. Process 30 minutes in a boiling-water canner.

Sweet And Sour Pepper Relish

Yield: about 7 half-pints

4 cups finely chopped sweet green peppers (about 4 medium)	1 cup finely chopped banana peppers (about 6 large)
3 cups chopped green cooking apples (about 3 large)	2 tablespoons Ball Salt
	3 cups sugar
	1 teaspoon mustard seed
2 cups chopped cabbage (½ small head)	3 cups cider vinegar
	Ball Pickle Crisp (optional)

Combine green peppers, apples, cabbage, banana peppers, and salt in a large bowl. Let stand 2 hours; drain. Combine sugar, mustard seed and vinegar in a large saucepot; bring to a boil. Reduce heat and add vegetables. Simmer relish 10 minutes. Pack hot relish into hot jars, leaving ½-inch headspace. Add Pickle Crisp to each jar, if desired. Remove air bubbles. Adjust two-piece caps. Process 10 minutes in a boiling-water canner.

Zucchini Bread And Butter Pickles

Yield: about 5 pints

14 to 16 small zucchini, sliced	2 tablespoons mustard seed
8 small onions, sliced	1 teaspoon turmeric
2 medium sweet green peppers, seeded and diced	1 teaspoon celery seed
	1 teaspoon peppercorns
⅓ cup Ball Salt	3 cups vinegar
2 cups sugar	Ball Pickle Crisp (optional)

Combine zucchini, onions and peppers in a large bowl. Sprinkle salt over vegetables; stir. Cover with ice. Let stand 1½ hours. Drain and rinse. Combine remaining ingredients in a large saucepot. Bring to a boil. Add vegetables and simmer 10 minutes. Pack hot vegetables into hot jars, leaving ½-inch headspace. Ladle hot liquid over vegetables, leaving ½-inch headspace. Add Pickle Crisp to each jar, if desired. Remove air bubbles. Adjust two-piece caps. Process 10 minutes in a boiling-water canner.

featured prepared recipe

Linguine with Roasted Roma Sauce and Spinach

Makes about 4 servings

3 tablespoons extra virgin olive oil, divided	⅛ teaspoon coarsely ground pepper
2 cloves garlic, minced	½ cup (4 ounces) heavy cream
1 quart jar Roasted Roma Tomatoes *(recipe on page 82)*	8 ounces linguine
	1 cup (4 ounces) freshly shaved parmesan cheese
5 ounces baby spinach	
¼ teaspoon salt	

Heat 2 tablespoons olive oil over medium heat in a 10-inch sauté pan. Stir in garlic and cook until tender but not browned. Add tomatoes and cook over medium-high heat until heated through. Layer spinach over tomatoes, cover pan and continue cooking about 5 minutes. Add salt and pepper. Stir in cream, reduce heat and gently simmer until thickened, about 3 minutes. Cook pasta according to package directions while tomatoes and spinach cook. Drain pasta then toss with remaining olive oil. Ladle tomato and spinach mixture over pasta. Sprinkle with parmesan cheese.

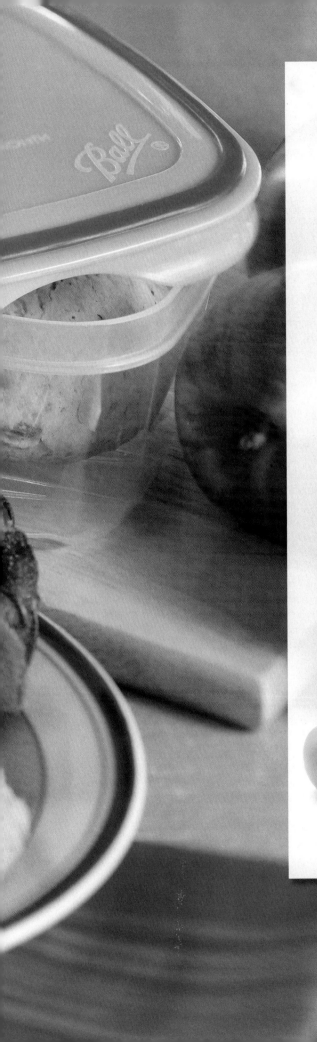

freezing

Spreads, Meats, Vegetables & Prepared Foods

The little league game is over. In the bottom of the ninth, your team eked out a surprising win over a long-time rival. Sweet victory. It's time to celebrate.

Bring the whole team home and pop Savory Pocket Pies from your freezer into the microwave or oven. Even before they're warm, your mouth waters in anticipation as the cheddar cheese melts over the smoked ham, punctuated with tart Granny Smith apples and spicy mustard. Then, score big, serving up a sweet ending of peanut butter bar cookies drizzled with homemade Banana-Strawberry Freezer Jam. No-cook freezer jam recipes are simple to make using Ball RealFruit Instant Pectin and convenient to store in Ball Plastic Freezer Jars – a winning combination every time.

With our exclusive line of Ball Plastic Freezer Containers, you're always prepared with delicious foods at the ready. Fill your home with the irresistible aroma of a home-baked cherry pie, with fruit filling frozen when tree branches hung low with summer's bountiful harvest. Or invite a friend over for lasagna for two. Whether freezing canapés, desserts, meats, jams, or sauces, Ball stain-resistant plastic freezer containers seal in flavor and freshness. And the date dials on the lid let you record the exact month and date your foods were frozen. It's easy and quick—wholesome foods stored in individual or meal-sized portions, awaiting your call.

The day is done. The team has gone home. What remains are happy memories that last a lifetime—memories of high fives, toothless grins, and bursts of laughter. It was a gathering made all the more special by the ready-to-go frozen foods you preserved, just for a night like tonight.

Pictured, Savory Pocket Pie made with Savory Pastry Crust. Recipe for Savory Pastry Crust is found on page 100. Recipe for the Savory Pocket Pie is found on page 104.

getting started

Freezing has many advantages over other methods of food preservation. Frozen foods are more like fresh foods than those either canned or dried. Freezing keeps the natural color, fresh flavor and nutritive qualities of most foods better than any other known method of preservation. Freezing is also one of the simplest and least time-consuming ways to preserve foods.

To be successful in freezing foods, start with a quality product that has been handled under the most sanitary conditions. The quality of the original product is the single most important factor in determining its quality when it is served.

The Spoilers

Preservation by freezing is based on the principle that extreme cold retards growth of microorganisms and slows down enzyme activity and oxidation. Freezing does not sterilize food.

Freezing is an effective and safe method for preserving fruits, vegetables, meats and precooked foods. Directions for each product have been established to minimize changes in frozen food caused by:

a) bacteria, yeasts and molds   **d)** formation of large ice crystals
b) enzymes   **e)** oxidation
c) freezer burn

Bacteria, Yeasts And Molds

All fresh foods contain bacteria, yeasts and molds. These spoilers will multiply rapidly and cause spoilage if not stopped. This can be accomplished by:

a) using only quality products
b) preparing the food under the most sanitary conditions
c) storing food at or below 0°F
d) preparing foods according to directions in this book
e) using containers and wrap specifically designed for freezing foods

Enzymes

Foods contain enzymes which cause chemical changes. Some of these changes are desirable. Beef, for example, is aged in a chill room about one week to give the enzymes a chance to tenderize the meat. However, enzymes can cause an off-color product and destroy the fresh flavor in vegetables if they are not inactivated before vegetables are frozen. Retarding the growth of enzymes in vegetables is easily achieved by a short heat treatment referred to as blanching. Since blanching may have a softening effect on the texture of fruits, controlling enzyme activity in fruits is best accomplished by the addition of sugar and an antioxidant such as Ball Fruit-Fresh Produce Protector.

Freezer Burn

Is a condition that can occur if food is improperly wrapped. Dry air in the freezer circulates over exposed surfaces, removing moisture from the food and causing a dry, pithy, tough surface to develop. Chemical changes from exposure to air also include loss of color, development of off-flavors, absorption of odors and loss of vitamins. Moisture/vapor-resistant packaging materials prevent drying and protect the frozen product from contact with air. Be sure package is free of air and has an airtight seal.

Formation Of Large Ice Crystals

Is caused by freezing foods too slowly. When foods are quickly frozen, at 0°F or lower, the cells in the food fiber retain their normal structure. Slower freezing causes moisture from the fibers to form ice crystals between groups of fibers. As a result, physical changes may occur, including loss of liquid, diminished weight and dark appearance.

Oxidative Changes

These are commonly encountered chemical changes in frozen foods. If the product is exposed to oxygen as the result of incorrect storage or packaging is permeable by air, it will suffer losses in quality.

Equipment And Utensils

The equipment needed for freezing foods at home includes those used everyday for meal preparation. As with all food-storage methods, it is important to keep bacterial contamination to a minimum by using clean equipment and work surfaces.

Packaging designed specifically for freezing foods minimizes the affect "spoilers" have during freezer storage. While it is not necessary for frozen foods to be hermetically sealed, the package must be moisture/vapor-proof, odorless, tasteless, grease-proof and capable of being tightly closed. There are two types of packaging materials for home freezing use: rigid containers and flexible bags or wraps.

Package food leaving no air pockets. For dry pack, leave no headspace. For packs that are liquid at room temperature, leave ¼- to ½-inch headspace to allow for expansion during freezing. Seal container airtight. Keep record of storage date.

To reuse jars and plastic freezer boxes wash in hot, soapy water. Rinse and drain. Do not reuse traditional flexible bags or wraps.

Rigid Containers—Excellent results can be achieved in home freezing when using Ball plastic freezer jars (*see page 105*). Plastic freezer jars come in 8, 16, and 32 ounce sizes. Ball tapered glass jars may also be used for freezing all types of foods (*see page 8*). Rigid containers should be used for most frozen foods and are recommended for all foods that are soft or liquid at room temperature. Products suitable for storage in rigid containers include fruits packed in syrup or sugar, butter, eggs, stews, creamed foods and meats with gravy.

Flexible Bags And Wraps—Flexible bags are best for packaging products with irregular shapes such as roasting turkeys or hens, fish and all cuts of meat. Bags can be used for vegetables and fruits without syrup or added sugar. Bags are also suitable for precooked foods that are not liquid at room temperature.

Plastic freezer bags come in the following sizes: pint, quart, two-quart, and one-gallon. These are closed by pressing out the air, twisting the top, doubling it over and wrapping it several times with handy ties included in the package or closing the plastic-channeled seal.

Wrapping materials are similar to flexible bags except they are available in rolls and are cut to the desired size as they are used. Plastic wrap, paper and foil must be secured with freezer tape.

The Freezer

Regardless of the style of freezer being used—chest, upright or refrigerator-freezer combination—it should be placed in a convenient, cool, dry and well ventilated location. The freezer temperature must be held at 0°F or lower at all times. Keeping the temperature at -10°F will help keep the temperature below 0°F when unfrozen food is placed in the freezer. Use a freezer thermometer to register the freezer temperature. Make necessary adjustments to maintain 0°F.

For economical use of your freezer, all foods should be used within one year. Most of them should be held for much less time. By continuously using foods from the freezer and replacing them with other foods as they come in season, the space in the freezer may be effectively utilized during the entire year. The higher the rate of turnover, the lower the cost per pound for storing frozen foods.

Store like foods together, placing the most recently frozen foods at the bottom or back of the freezer. At the same time, move foods that have been in freezer storage longer toward the top or front.

The quantity of food that can be successfully frozen at one time depends on the type of food, its size, type of package and design of freezer. Put no more unfrozen food into a freezer than will freeze within 24 hours (usually about 2 or 3 pounds of food per cubic foot of capacity). Overloading slows down the rate of freezing causing foods that freeze too slowly to lose quality or spoil. Also, overloading can raise the temperature above 0°F and affect the quality of frozen food already in the freezer. When packing the freezer, place each package in direct contact with a refrigerated surface leaving space between containers. The original fresh flavor, color, texture and nutritive value of the frozen product will be retained if it is properly prepared and protected at 0°F during storage.

Follow your freezer instruction manual for defrosting, deodorizing and cleaning the freezer.

General Information

1. Vegetables must be properly blanched to preserve quality. Exceptions are rhubarb and vegetables used exclusively for flavoring, such as peppers, onions, horseradish, and herbs. If you live 5,000 feet or more above sea level, blanch 1 minute longer than times specified in recipes.

2. All meats and poultry must be chilled quickly after slaughter. Beef must be aged about one week at 33° to 38°F to become tender and flavorful.

3. Fruits in syrup, stews and other foods liquid at room temperature should be tightly closed in rigid freezer containers, such as plastic freezer jars, plastic freezer containers and tapered glass jars for all food types. Crumble a piece of freezer wrap and place it on top of food in container to hold food under liquid. Vegetables should be packed in moisture/vapor-resistant packaging, such as plastic freezer bags, plastic freezer jars, plastic freezer containers or tapered glass jars. Meats should be wrapped as "skintight" as possible in moisture/vapor-proof materials; secure wrap with freezer tape.

4. Freezing must be rapid to preserve the natural color, flavor and texture of fruits and vegetables and to prevent spoilage of meats and prepared foods. Cool hot foods quickly before freezing. After blanching vegetables, immerse vegetables in ice-cold water to stop the cooking process. Cool vegetables for the same length of time used for blanching. Foods which are cooked and have a soft texture can be placed in a bowl and set in ice-cold water to cool; stir the product to cool quickly. If it is not practical to cool the cooked product in ice-cold water, allow the product to cool at room temperature, not to exceed 2 hours.

Freezer Storage Expectancy

Gradual loss of quality occurs in all frozen foods. Controlling the factors that diminish the quality of frozen foods will help to maintain the best quality for the longest possible storage period. The relationship between temperature of storage and the length of time foods are frozen is important. Deterioration of frozen foods accelerates rapidly with a rise in storage temperature. Freezer temperature must be maintained at 0°F or lower.

How foods are prepared and wrapped for freezer storage also determines the length of time foods can be held in the freezer before the quality begins to diminish. Approximate storage time guidelines provided in figure 9 are for foods packaged in can-or-freeze jars, plastic freezer boxes, freezer foil, film or paper.

figure 9 | Recommended Length Of Storage At 0°F

Bakery	Months	Meat, Poultry, Seafood & Game	Months
Breads, Quick (*Baked*)	2	Ground Meat	3-4
Breads, Yeast (*Baked*)	4-8	Liver	3
Breads, Yeast (*Unbaked*)	½	Rabbit, Squirrel	6-8
Cakes	6	Crab, Fish Roe, Lobster, Oysters	3-4
Cakes, Fruit	12	Pork (*Cured*)	1-2
Cookies (*Baked*)	6	Pork (*Fresh*)	6-8
Cookies (*Unbaked*)	4	Sausage	4-6
Pastry (*Unbaked*)	2	Shrimp	6
Pies (*Baked*)	1	Turkey, Chicken	12
Pies (*Unbaked*)	3	**Prepared Foods**	**Months**
Dairy	**Months**	Candies	12
Butter	5-6	Gravy	2
Cheese, Cottage	1	Pizza	1
Cheese, Hard or Semi-Hard	6-12	Prepared Main Dishes	3-6
Cheese, Soft	4	Salads	2
Eggs	12	Sandwiches	1
Ice Cream, Sherbet	1-3	Soups, Stews	6
Milk	1	**Soft Spreads**	**Months**
Fruits	**Months**	Freezer Jams & Jellies	12
Fruits, Citrus	3-4	**Vegetables**	**Months**
Fruits (*Except Citrus*)	12	Onions	3-6
Meat, Poultry, Seafood & Game	**Months**	Vegetables (*Cooked*)	1
Beef, Lamb, Mutton, Veal, Venison	8-12	Vegetables (*Except Onions*)	12
Fish	2-3		

Labeling

Label packaging with the name of the product, a description of how it was prepared, the number of servings and the storage date.

It's a good idea to keep a record of the frozen foods stored in the freezer. Post the list near the freezer so it can be easily kept up-to-date by regular recordings as you put foods in or take them out. Such a list will let you know exactly what foods you have on hand and how long they have been stored in the freezer, thus helping you use all frozen foods within the recommended storage period (see page 91).

Thawing And Preparing

Methods Of Thawing

Do not thaw more food at one time than is actually needed; when frozen food is thawed, it spoils more rapidly than fresh foods. Thaw each product to the desired point by placing the sealed package:

a) in the refrigerator (this is the best method)

b) at room temperature for two hours; complete thawing in refrigerator

c) in the microwave oven on the defrost cycle, following manufacturer's instructions

d) in cold water (never in hot water)

Cooking And Serving

Frozen foods must be cooked immediately after thawing and should be served as soon as the correct internal temperature is reached. Prepared or cooked foods may be thawed and made ready for serving by one of the following ways:

1. Serve while still frozen: cookies, candies, ice cream, salads and similar foods.
2. Serve immediately after thawing: cakes, sandwiches and similar foods.
3. Heat to serving temperature: soups, meat dishes, stews and similar dishes.
4. Cook frozen: uncooked pies, rolls and combination dishes.

Refreezing

Complete or partial thawing of foods can occur unexpectedly such as during a power outage. Foods considered partially thawed are those that still have a large percentage of ice crystals remaining in the product. Partially thawed foods may be safely refrozen. However, even partial thawing has an adverse affect on quality. Foods refrozen for a second time will likely undergo additional deterioration and yield a very poor quality product. Refrozen foods should be used as soon as possible.

Foods that have completely thawed should not be refrozen. Foods that thawed within two hours of a power outage but remain chilled under 40°F may be refrigerated for immediate use.

Gradual thawing and warming of foods to a temperature of 40°F over a period of several days is not suitable for refreezing. Under these conditions, the food may be unsafe to eat.

It is best not to take chances when in doubt about any thawed foods. Eating foods that have begun to spoil may result in serious illness. Dispose of food so that no other human or animal will come in contact with it. Carefully clean containers and surfaces that were exposed to the questionable food.

Care Of Foods In Emergencies

When you know or suspect that power will be off in your home, immediately set the freezer control at its coldest setting. The lower temperature of the freezer and food will delay thawing if the power does go off.

If the freezer stops operating because of a power outage or any other reason, try to find out how long it will be inoperative. If normal operation of the freezer will not resume before the food will thaw, use dry ice to keep the food cold or transfer the food in insulated boxes to a freezer plant or another low temperature storage space until the problem is resolved.

A fully-loaded freezer at 0°F usually will stay cold enough to keep foods frozen for a couple days; in a freezer filled to half capacity, food may not stay frozen for more than one day.

Fifty pounds of dry ice placed in the freezer soon after the power goes off should keep the temperature of food in a 20-cubic-foot freezer filled to capacity below freezing for 3 to 4 days; in a freezer filled to half capacity or less, the food should remain frozen for 2 to 3 days. Tip: Keep the phone number and address of a dry ice source handy.

Work quickly when putting dry ice in the freezer. Place it on thick cardboard or boards on top of the frozen food or on shelves. Never put dry ice directly on frozen food packages. Handle dry ice with care. Be sure the room is well ventilated to allow air circulation. Never touch dry ice with bare hands; short exposure can cause severe frostbite!

Do not open the freezer door while the freezer is inoperative except as part of food-saving procedures.

Foods That Do Not Freeze Well

- Cake icings made with egg whites become frothy or "weep" when thawed.
- Cream fillings and soft frostings are unsatisfactory when frozen.
- Custards and cream-pie fillings become watery and lumpy.
- Egg whites become cracked, tough and rubbery when frozen.
- If too much fat is used in proportion to the starch and flour when making gravy, the fat may separate. Use less fat when making gravy to be frozen. Stir well when reheating.
- Fried foods lose their crispness and become soggy. (Exceptions are French-fried potatoes and onion rings.)
- Fruit jelly in sandwiches may soak into the bread.
- Macaroni, spaghetti and some rice (frozen separately) have a warmed-over flavor and often are mushy.
- Mayonnaise separates during freezing and thawing, except when used in some salads.
- Meringue toughens and sticks to paper after a few days of freezing.
- Peppers, onions, cloves and synthetic vanilla become strong and bitter when frozen as a part of a prepared food.
- Potatoes (Irish) cooked in stews and soups become mushy and may darken.
- Salt loses flavor when frozen.
- Sauces tend to separate unless beaten or stirred when reheated.
- Vegetables (raw) lose their crispness.

dairy products

Butter

Freeze only high-quality butter made from pasteurized cream. Mold into desired shapes or freeze in sticks. Wrap butter tightly in freezer film and pack into plastic freezer bags or plastic freezer containers. Seal, label and freeze.

Cheese

Hard Or Semi-Hard Cheese: Cut in ½- to 1-pound pieces. Wrap tightly in freezer film and pack cheese into plastic freezer bags or plastic freezer containers. Seal, label and freeze.

Soft Cheese: Wrap tightly in freezer film and pack cheese into plastic freezer bags or plastic freezer containers. Seal, label and freeze.

Cottage Cheese: Pack cottage cheese into plastic freezer jars or plastic freezer containers. Seal, label and freeze.

Cream

Freeze only heavy cream containing 40 percent or more butterfat. Heat from 170° to 180°F for 15 minutes. Add 3 tablespoons sugar per pint of cream. Cool quickly and ladle cream into plastic freezer jars or plastic freezer containers, leaving ½-inch headspace. Seal, label and freeze.

Eggs

Select eggs as fresh as possible. Wash eggs in clear water; break each egg separately into a small bowl; examine eggs by smell and appearance for spoilage before mixing with other eggs.

Whole: Gently mix the whites and yolks without forming air bubbles by putting them through a sieve or colander. Pack eggs into plastic freezer jars or plastic freezer containers, leaving ½-inch headspace. Seal, label and freeze.

Yolks: Gently mix the yolks without forming air bubbles. To each 6 yolks add 1 teaspoon sugar or ½ teaspoon salt to reduce coagulation. Pack same as Eggs, Whole.

Whites: Gently mix whites without forming air bubbles. Pack same as Eggs, Whole.

Measuring: Use these measurements for frozen eggs:
- 3 tablespoons whole egg = 1 egg
- 2 tablespoons egg white = 1 egg white
- 1 tablespoon egg yolk = 1 egg yolk

Ice Cream And Sherbet

Homemade: Prepare your favorite recipe and freeze in a hand-turned or electrically turned ice cream freezer. Pack ice cream or sherbet into plastic freezer jars or plastic freezer containers. Label and freeze.

Commercially Made: Place original carton in plastic freezer bag or repack ice cream into plastic freezer jars or plastic freezer containers. Seal, label and freeze.

Milk

Freeze only pasteurized milk. Ladle milk into plastic freezer jars or plastic freezer containers, leaving ½-inch headspace. Seal, label and freeze.

Thawing And Preparing Dairy Products

Place the frozen product in the refrigerator to thaw. After thawing, use as fresh.

fruits & fruit fillings

One method of packing fruits for freezing requires the use of a sugar syrup. The chart below gives guidelines for preparing extra-light to heavy syrup. Follow individual recipes for using sugar syrup.

figure 10	Syrups For Freezing			
Type of Syrup	Approx. % of Sugar	Sugar	Water	Yield of Syrup
Extra-Light	20	1¼ cups	5½ cups	6 cups
Light	30	2¼ cups	5¼ cups	6½ cups
Medium	40	3¼ cups	5 cups	7 cups
Heavy	50	4¼ cups	4¼ cups	7 cups

Apples

Select apples that are crisp and firm. Wash, peel and core. Cut into ¼-inch slices. Treat with Fruit-Fresh to prevent darkening.

Syrup Pack: Use heavy syrup; add 1 teaspoon Fruit-Fresh (*see page 9*) to each cup of syrup. Ladle ½ cup cold syrup into plastic freezer jars or plastic freezer containers. Press apple slices down in container and add enough syrup to cover, leaving ½-inch headspace. Seal, label and freeze.

Pie Apples: Place apple slices in boiling water 2 minutes and cool in ice water. Drain. Pack apples into plastic freezer bags, plastic freezer jars or plastic freezer containers. Seal, label and freeze.

Applesauce: Wash apples; peel, if desired; core and slice. To each quart of apples, add ⅓ cup water and 1 tablespoon Fruit-Fresh (*see page 9*). Cook apples until tender; purée. To each quart of hot purée, add ¼ cup sugar, stirring until dissolved. Cool. Ladle applesauce into plastic freezer jars or plastic freezer containers, leaving ½-inch headspace. Seal, label and freeze.

Apple Pie Filling

Yield: about 6 pints

6 pounds apples	¼ cup flour
Ball Fruit-Fresh	1½ teaspoons cinnamon
Produce Protector	¼ teaspoon nutmeg
2 cups sugar	2 tablespoons lemon juice

Wash, peel, core and slice apples. Treat with Fruit-Fresh to prevent darkening. Combine sugar, flour and spices. Rinse and drain apples; stir into sugar mixture. Let stand until juices begin to flow, about 30 minutes. Stir in lemon juice. Cook over medium heat until mixture begins to thicken. Ladle pie filling into plastic freezer jars or plastic freezer containers, leaving ½-inch headspace. Cool at room temperature, not to exceed 2 hours. Seal, label and freeze.

Berries

Blackberries, Mulberries, Raspberries

Select fully-ripe, firm berries. Wash berries in cold water. Drain and dry berries. Discard soft, under-ripe or defective berries. Remove stems. Pack using one of the following methods:

Sugar Pack: Mix 1 part sugar with 4 parts berries until fruit is coated with the sugar. Pack into plastic freezer jars or plastic freezer containers. Seal, label and freeze.

Syrup Pack: Prepare a heavy syrup (*see page 93*). Pack drained berries into plastic freezer jars or plastic freezer containers. Shake the container gently to pack berries. Cover berries with syrup, leaving ½-inch headspace. Seal, label and freeze.

Purée: Select fully-ripe berries. Purée using a food processor or food mill. Ladle berry purée into plastic freezer jars or plastic freezer containers, leaving ½-inch headspace. Seal, label and freeze.

Note: Berry juice may be used in place of water when making syrup.

Blueberries, Huckleberries, Elderberries And Gooseberries

Wash berries; drain. Dry berries. Remove stems and under-ripe or defective berries. Pack using one of the following methods:

Dry Pack: Pack berries into plastic freezer bags, plastic freezer jars or plastic freezer containers. Seal, label and freeze.

Sugar Pack: Mix one quart berries and ⅔ cup sugar. Pack into plastic freezer jars or plastic freezer containers. Seal, label and freeze.

Syrup Pack: Pack same as Berries, Syrup Pack.

Blueberry Pie Filling

Yield: about 5 pints

12 cups blueberries	1 tablespoon grated
3 cups sugar	lemon peel
¾ cup cornstarch	¼ cup lemon juice

Wash and drain blueberries. Combine sugar and cornstarch. Stir in blueberries; let stand until juice begins to flow, about 30 minutes. Add lemon peel and lemon juice. Cook over medium heat until mixture begins to thicken. Ladle pie filling into plastic freezer jars or plastic freezer containers, leaving ½-inch headspace. Cool at room temperature, not to exceed 2 hours. Seal, label and freeze.

Cherries—Sour

Select tender-skinned, bright red cherries with a characteristic tart flavor. Wash cherries; drain. Stem and pit. Pack using one of the following methods:

Sugar Pack: Mix 1 part sugar to 4 parts cherries. Pack cherries into plastic freezer jars or plastic freezer containers. Seal, label and freeze.

Syrup Pack: Prepare heavy syrup (*see page 93*). Pack drained cherries into plastic freezer jars or plastic freezer containers. Shake the container gently to pack cherries. Cover cherries with syrup, leaving ½-inch headspace. Seal, label and freeze.

Cherries—Sweet

Select bright, fully-ripe sweet cherries of a dark color variety. Wash cherries; drain. Stem and pit.

Syrup Pack: Prepare heavy syrup (*see page 93*). Add 4 teaspoons Fruit-Fresh (*see page 9*) to each quart of heavy syrup. Pack cherries into plastic freezer jars or plastic freezer containers. Shake container gently to pack cherries. Cover cherries with syrup, leaving ½-inch headspace. Seal, label and freeze.

Cherry Pie Filling

Yield: about 4 pints

8 cups tart cherries	5 tablespoons cornstarch
2½ cups sugar	

Wash cherries; drain. Pit cherries. Combine sugar and cornstarch. Stir in cherries; let stand until juices begin to flow, about 30 minutes. Cook over medium heat until mixture begins to thicken. Ladle pie filling into plastic freezer jars or plastic freezer containers, leaving ½-inch headspace. Cool at room temperature, not to exceed 2 hours. Seal, label and freeze.

Coconut

Grate coconut by hand or in a food processor. Pack using one of the following methods:

Dry Pack: Pack grated coconut into plastic freezer bags, plastic freezer jars or plastic freezer containers. Seal, label and freeze.

Sugar Pack: Mix 1 part sugar to 8 parts shredded coconut. Pack coconut into plastic freezer jars or plastic freezer containers. Seal, label and freeze.

Milk Pack: Mix grated coconut with its own milk. Pack coconut into plastic freezer jars or plastic freezer containers, leaving ½-inch headspace. Seal, label and freeze.

Cranberries

Select firm cranberries of uniform color with glossy skins. Wash cranberries in cold water; drain. Dry and stem. Pack cranberries into plastic freezer bags, plastic freezer jars or plastic freezer containers. Seal, label and freeze.

Sauce: Prepare selected recipe as for serving. Pack into plastic freezer jars or plastic freezer containers, leaving ½-inch headspace. Cool at room temperature, not to exceed 2 hours. Seal, label and freeze.

Currants

Select ripe currants. Wash currants in cold water; drain. Stem. Pack using one of the following methods:

Dry Pack: Pack currants into plastic freezer bags, plastic freezer jars or plastic freezer containers. Seal, label and freeze.

Sugar Pack: Crush currants lightly. Mix 3 parts currants with 1 part sugar. Allow to stand until sugar dissolves, about 10 minutes. Pack currants and syrup into plastic freezer jars or plastic freezer containers, leaving ½-inch headspace. Seal, label and freeze.

Figs

Select fully-ripe figs. Wash figs; drain. Peel figs. Prepare using one of the following methods:

Dry Pack: Pack figs into plastic freezer bags, plastic freezer jars or plastic freezer containers. Seal, label and freeze.

Sugar Pack: Leave figs whole or cut in half. Combine 1 part sugar to 4 parts figs. Pack into plastic freezer jars or plastic freezer containers. Seal, label and freeze.

Syrup Pack: Prepare a heavy syrup (see page 93). Pack whole or halved figs into plastic freezer jars or plastic freezer containers. Ladle heavy syrup over figs, leaving ½-inch headspace. Seal, label and freeze.

Fruit Juices

Most fruit juices make excellent frozen products and retain their fresh flavor. Prepare juice using your favorite recipe. Cool. Ladle into plastic freezer jars or plastic freezer containers, leaving ½-inch headspace. Seal, label and freeze.

Fruit Sorbet

Yield: about 7 half-pints

4 cups sliced fruit (any soft variety)	1 cup orange juice
2 cups sugar	2 tablespoons lemon juice

Purée fruit in a food processor or blender. Combine sugar, orange juice and lemon juice in a saucepot. Cook over medium heat, stirring until sugar dissolves. Remove from heat. Stir in purée. Pour sorbet into a 13 x 9-inch pan. Freeze. Working in small batches, process frozen purée in a food processor or blender until light and fluffy. Ladle sorbet into plastic freezer jars or plastic freezer containers, leaving ½-inch headspace. Seal, label and freeze.

Note: Any soft fruit such as peaches, strawberries, raspberries or melon can be used for sorbet. Prepare fruit as for eating fresh.

Grapefruit And Oranges

Select firm, tree-ripened fruit. Heaviness of fruit indicates maturity. Wash fruit; drain. Chill. Peel and section fruit, removing membrane and seeds.

Syrup Pack: Prepare a medium syrup (see page 93). Pack fruit into plastic freezer jars or plastic freezer containers. Ladle syrup over fruit, leaving ½-inch headspace. Seal, label and freeze.

Note: Grapefruit juice may be used in place of part or all of water in syrup.

Grapes

Select ripe, firm, sweet grapes. Wash grapes; drain. Stem. Prepare using one of the following methods:

Syrup Pack: Prepare medium syrup (see page 93). Pack grapes into plastic freezer jars or plastic freezer containers. Ladle medium syrup over grapes, leaving ½-inch headspace. Seal, label and freeze.

Purée: Slightly crush grapes. Heat grapes to a boil, adding just enough water to prevent sticking. Press through a sieve or food mill to remove seeds and peels. Add 1 part sugar to 5 parts purée. Cool. Pack purée into plastic freezer jars or plastic freezer containers, leaving ½-inch headspace. Seal, label and freeze.

Juice: Prepare and heat grapes same as for Purée. Strain juice through a damp jelly bag or several layers of cheesecloth. Sweeten to taste with sugar. Cool. Ladle juice into plastic freezer jars or plastic freezer containers, leaving ½-inch headspace. Seal, label and freeze.

Kiwi

Select firm, ripe kiwi. Peel. Cut kiwi into ¼-inch slices. Pack kiwi into plastic freezer jars or plastic freezer containers. Seal, label and freeze.

Melons

Cantaloupe, Cranshaw, Honeydew, Persian and Watermelon

Select fully-ripe, firm melons. Remove seeds and peel. Cut melon into ¾-inch cubes, slices or balls. Pack melon into plastic freezer jars or plastic freezer containers. Seal, label and freeze.

Note: Serve before completely thawed.

Peaches, Nectarines And Apricots

Select fully-ripe fruit and handle carefully to avoid bruising. Wash fruit; drain. Peel, pit and slice fruit. Treat with Fruit-Fresh to prevent darkening. Prepare using one of the following methods:

Sugar Pack: Combine ⅔ cup sugar and 2 teaspoons Fruit-Fresh (see page 9); set aside. Measure 1 quart sliced fruit; sprinkle with sugar mixture. Gently toss to coat fruit with sugar. Allow fruit to stand until sugar dissolves, about 10 minutes. Pack sliced fruit and syrup into plastic freezer jars or plastic freezer containers, leaving ½-inch headspace. Seal, label and freeze.

Syrup Pack: Prepare a heavy syrup (see page 93). Add 4 teaspoons Fruit-Fresh (see page 9) to each quart of syrup. Ladle ½ cup syrup into plastic freezer jars or plastic freezer containers. Fill container with sliced fruit, gently shaking to pack fruit, leaving ½-inch headspace. Add more syrup if needed, leaving ½-inch headspace. Seal, label and freeze.

Purée: Combine 2 cups sliced fruit, 2 tablespoons sugar and 1½ teaspoons Fruit-Fresh (see page 9). Place mixture in a food processor and purée. Pack purée into plastic freezer jars or plastic freezer containers, leaving ½-inch headspace. Place a piece of freezer wrap over the top of purée to prevent discoloration. Seal, label and freeze.

Peach Pie Filling

Yield: about 4 pints

6 pounds peaches	1 teaspoon cinnamon
Ball Fruit-Fresh Produce Protector	½ teaspoon nutmeg
2¼ cups sugar	2 teaspoons lemon peel
½ cup flour	¼ cup lemon juice

Wash peaches; drain. Peel, pit and slice peaches. Treat with Fruit-Fresh to prevent darkening. Combine sugar, flour and spices. Rinse and drain peaches. Stir into sugar mixture. Let stand until juices begin to flow, about 30 minutes. Stir in lemon peel and lemon juice. Cook over medium heat until mixture begins to thicken. Ladle pie filling into plastic freezer jars or plastic freezer containers, leaving ½-inch headspace. Cool at room temperature, not to exceed 2 hours. Seal, label and freeze.

Pears

Select full-flavored pears that are crisp and firm. Wash pears; drain. Peel and core pears. Leave in halves or cut into quarters or slices. Treat with Fruit-Fresh to prevent darkening. Prepare a medium syrup (see page 93). Bring syrup to a boil. Drain pears. Blanch pears in syrup for 2 minutes. Cool pears and syrup. Pack pears into plastic freezer jars or plastic freezer containers. Ladle syrup over pears, leaving ½-inch headspace. Seal, label and freeze.

Pineapple

Select fruit of bright appearance, dark yellow-orange color and fragrant aroma. If top pulls out easily, pineapple is ripe. Wash pineapple; drain. Peel, core, dice, slice or cut into wedges. Prepare using one of the following methods:

Dry Pack: Pack slices into plastic freezer jars or plastic freezer containers layering two pieces of freezer paper between slices. Seal, label and freeze.

Sugar Pack: Mix 1 part sugar to 8 parts pineapple. Allow pineapple to set until sugar is dissolved. Pack pineapple into plastic freezer jars or plastic freezer containers. Seal, label and freeze.

Syrup Pack: Prepare a light syrup (see page 93). Pack pineapple into plastic freezer jars or plastic freezer containers. Ladle syrup over pineapple, leaving ½-inch headspace. Seal, label and freeze.

Plums

Select firm, ripe plums soft enough to yield to slight pressure. Wash plums; drain. Leave plums whole or cut into halves, slices or dice. Prepare using one of the following methods:

Dry Pack: Wash and drain plums. Pack whole plums into plastic freezer bags, plastic freezer jars or plastic freezer containers. Seal, label and freeze.

Sugar Pack: Mix 1 part sugar to 5 parts plums. Allow to set until sugar is dissolved. Pack plums into plastic freezer jars or plastic freezer containers. Seal, label and freeze.

Syrup Pack: Prepare heavy syrup (see page 93). Pack halved, sliced or diced plums into plastic freezer jars or plastic freezer containers. Ladle syrup over plums, leaving ½-inch headspace. Seal, label and freeze.

Prepared Fruits

Cooked fruits such as baked apples, baked pears and applesauce may be prepared as for serving. Cool. Pack into plastic freezer jars or plastic freezer containers. Seal, label and freeze.

Rhubarb

Select rhubarb with crisp, tender, red stalks. Early spring cuttings are best for freezing. Remove leaves and woody ends; discard blemished and tough stalks. Wash rhubarb well under running water; cut into 1-inch lengths. Prepare using one of the following methods:

Dry Pack: Pack rhubarb into plastic freezer bags, plastic freezer jars or plastic freezer containers. Seal, label and freeze.

Sugar Pack: Mix 1 part sugar to 4 parts rhubarb. Allow to stand until sugar is dissolved. Pack rhubarb into plastic freezer jars or plastic freezer containers. Seal, label and freeze.

Syrup Pack: Prepare a heavy syrup (see page 93). Pack rhubarb into plastic freezer jars or plastic freezer containers. Ladle syrup over rhubarb, leaving ½-inch headspace. Seal, label and freeze.

Stewed: Stew or steam rhubarb according to your favorite recipe; sweeten to taste. Cool. Pack same as Rhubarb, Syrup Pack.

Strawberries

Select fully-ripe, firm strawberries with a deep-red color. Discard immature and defective fruit. Wash strawberries; drain. Remove caps. Prepare using one of the following methods:

Dry Pack: Pack berries into plastic freezer bags, plastic freezer jars or plastic freezer containers. Seal, label and freeze.

Sugar Pack: Slice berries lengthwise in halves or thirds. Mix 1 part sugar to 6 parts strawberries. Allow to stand until sugar is dissolved, about 10 minutes. Gently stir. Pack strawberries and syrup into plastic freezer jars or plastic freezer containers, leaving ½-inch headspace. Seal, label and freeze.

Syrup Pack: Prepare a heavy syrup (see page 93). Leave strawberries whole or slice. Pack strawberries into plastic freezer jars or plastic freezer containers. Ladle syrup over berries, leaving ½-inch headspace. Seal, label and freeze.

Purée: Combine 1 pint strawberries, 4 tablespoons sugar and 1 teaspoon lemon juice in food processor and purée. Pack purée into plastic freezer jars or plastic freezer containers, leaving ½-inch headspace. Seal, label and freeze.

Thawing And Preparing Fruits

When serving frozen fruits for dessert, serve while there are still a few ice crystals remaining. Frozen fruits may be used the same as fresh fruits in most recipes. When using frozen fruits in cooking, an allowance should be made for any sugar added at the time of freezing.

Some fruits, especially youngberries and boysenberries, make better jellies when frozen than when fresh because freezing and thawing causes juices and the natural fruit color to be released from the cells. However, soft spreads made with fresh fruit are usually superior in flavor, color and texture to those made from frozen fruits. Soft spreads made with frozen fruits may have a softer set, depending on the type and quality of the fruit after freezing.

freezer spreads

Recipes in this section are made using Ball RealFruit Instant Pectin. For more information about this product see page 9.

Banana-Strawberry Freezer Jam

Yield: about 5 half-pints

3 large bananas	1½ cups sugar
3 cups crushed strawberries (about 1½ quarts)	5 tablespoons Ball Instant Pectin

Preheat oven to 400°F. Cover a baking sheet with aluminum foil. Place bananas on baking sheet; do not peel. Bake for 15 minutes at 400°F. Cool. Peel and crush bananas. Measure 1 cup crushed bananas. Combine bananas and strawberries in a medium bowl; set aside. Stir sugar and instant pectin together in a large bowl until well blended. Add fruit mixture to sugar mixture and stir 3 minutes. Ladle jam into plastic freezer jars, leaving ½-inch headspace. Adjust caps. Let jam stand 30 minutes to thicken. Label and freeze.

Lemony Blueberry-Nectarine Freezer Jam

Yield: about 5 half-pints

3 cups chopped, pitted, peeled nectarines (about 4 medium)	1 tablespoon grated lemon peel
	1 teaspoon lemon juice
1 cup crushed blueberries (about 1 pint)	1½ cups sugar
	5 tablespoons Ball Instant Pectin

Combine nectarines, blueberries, lemon peel and lemon juice in a medium bowl; set aside. Stir sugar and instant pectin together in a large bowl until well blended. Add fruit mixture to sugar mixture and stir 3 minutes. Ladle jam into plastic freezer jars, leaving ½-inch headspace. Adjust caps. Let jam stand 30 minutes to thicken. Label and freeze.

Plum-Orange Freezer Jam

Yield: about 5 half-pints

3 pounds plums (about 10 medium)	¼ cup orange pulp (about 1 medium)
½ cup water	1½ cups sugar
1 teaspoon grated orange peel	½ teaspoon mace
	5 tablespoons Ball Instant Pectin

Wash plums; drain. Pit and finely chop plums. Combine plums and water in a saucepot. Cover and simmer 5 minutes. Measure 3¾ cups cooked plums. Combine cooked plums, orange peel, orange pulp and mace in a medium bowl; set aside. Stir sugar and instant pectin together in a large bowl until well blended. Add fruit mixture to sugar mixture and stir 3 minutes. Ladle jam into plastic freezer jars, leaving ½-inch headspace. Adjust caps. Let jam stand 30 minutes to thicken. Label and freeze.

Spiced Apple-Pear Freezer Jam

Yield: about 5 half-pints

4 cups chopped, peeled, cored apples (about 5 medium)	1 cup granulated sugar
	½ cup brown sugar
	¾ teaspoon cinnamon
4 cups chopped, peeled, cored pears (about 5 medium)	¼ teaspoon nutmeg
	¼ teaspoon allspice
¼ cup water	5 tablespoons Ball Instant Pectin

Combine apples, pears and water in a saucepot. Cover and simmer 5 minutes. Lightly crush fruit. Measure 4 cups cooked fruit. Combine cooked fruit and spices in a medium bowl; set aside. Stir sugar and instant pectin together in a large bowl until well blended. Add fruit mixture to sugar mixture and stir 3 minutes. Ladle jam into plastic freezer jars, leaving ½-inch headspace. Adjust caps. Let jam stand 30 minutes to thicken. Label and freeze.

Triple Berry Freezer Jam

Yield: about 5 half-pints

2 cups crushed strawberries (about 1 quart)	1 cup crushed blackberries (about 1 pint)
1 cup crushed red raspberries (about 1 pint)	1½ cups sugar
	5 tablespoons Ball Instant Pectin

Combine strawberries, raspberries and blackberries in a medium bowl; set aside. Stir sugar and instant pectin together in a large bowl until well blended. Add fruit mixture to sugar mixture and stir 3 minutes. Ladle jam into plastic freezer jars, leaving ½-inch headspace. Adjust caps. Let jam stand 30 minutes to thicken. Label and freeze.

meats

Freezing preserves the natural, fresh qualities of meat better than any other method of preservation. Freezing may tenderize meat slightly, but it will not make tough meat tender.

While beef, lamb, pork, chicken and turkey may be produced on the farm and frozen in the home, it is advisable slaughtering, chilling and preparation of beef, lamb and pork be done in commercial establishments. The advantages of commercial meat packing are that animals may be slaughtered at any time of the year and the meat can be handled under sanitary conditions, controlled temperatures and inspected by local authorities.

Equipment for handling meat products should be as free of seams and cracks as possible; equipment should be scrubbed in hot water with a good detergent and sanitizer after each use.

Many families prefer to select cuts of their choice from the market and freeze these at home. All store-packaged, fresh meats must be repackaged in freezer wrap at home since "store wrap" usually is not moisture/vapor-proof and contains air pockets.

Beef, Lamb, Mutton, Veal And Venison

Use only high-quality meat from carcasses that have been aged at 35°F about one week in a relatively dry room. Cut meats as for cooking, removing as much bone and fat as possible and package in family-size servings. Keep meat cold while being cut and wrapped. Pack using one of the following methods:

Large Cuts: Wrap individually in plastic freezer bags, freezer foil, film, paper or vacuum package. Seal, label and freeze.

Steaks Or Chops: Wrap individually in plastic freezer bags, freezer foil, film, paper or vacuum package with a double layer of moisture/vapor-proof material placed between each piece of meat to make separation for cooking easier. Seal, label and freeze.

Ground Meat: Pack in family-size servings and wrap same as Large Cuts.

Pork, Rabbit And Squirrel

Select cuts suitable for roasting, broiling, frying, stewing and ground meat. Pork meat products should be frozen or prepared for curing as soon as chilled. Hold no longer than 1 day after slaughter before freezing. Pack using one of the following methods:

Fresh Meat: All cuts of this type should be frozen fresh except ham, bacon, jowls and sausage. These may be cured instead. Cut into cooking-size pieces, removing as much bone and fat as possible. Wrap in plastic freezer bags, freezer foil, film, paper or vacuum package. Seal, label and freeze.

Cured Pork: Freshly cured pork loses desirable color and flavor during freezer storage; therefore, it has a very short storage period in the freezer. Wrap in plastic freezer bags, freezer foil, film, paper or vacuum package. Seal, label and freeze.

Sausage: Make sausage from trimmings of lean portions of pork. Sausage to be frozen should contain approximately three times as much lean as fat. Prepare the sausage using your favorite recipe. Pack sausage tightly into plastic freezer bags, plastic freezer jars, plastic freezer containers or vacuum package. Seal, label and freeze.

Recipe Variation: For country-style flavor, cure stuffed sausage 5 days at 35°F before freezing. Wrap in plastic freezer bags, freezer foil, film, paper or vacuum package. Seal, label and freeze.

Prepared Meats

Stews, creamed meats, meat sauces, casserole dishes, meat with vegetables, pies, roasted and baked meats, meatballs and meatloaf may be frozen. Pack into plastic freezer jars, plastic freezer containers or vacuum package. Seal, label and freeze.

Thawing And Preparing
Beef, Pork, Lamb, Mutton, Veal And Venison
Leave package wrapped until ready to cook. The refrigerator is the best place to thaw meats. Slow thawing allows the meat to absorb the thawed ice crystals. Also, the meat is less likely to spoil and develop an off-flavor. If you must thaw meat fast, thaw in a microwave oven on the defrost setting or seal in plastic wrap and submerge in cold water. Thaw frozen meat just long enough for the ice to disappear in the center. Never thaw meat and allow it to return to room temperature. It is best to cook meat while it still contains a few ice crystals. Usually roasts and steaks over 1½-inch thick should be thawed before cooking. Thin steaks, chops or patties may be cooked from the frozen stage, but the cooking time must be longer to allow for thawing the meat. Use a recommended meat cooking chart for accurate times and temperatures for completely thawed meats. Add from 12 to 21 minutes per pound for roasting meats still frozen.

poultry
Chicken And Turkey

Select choice birds that have grown rapidly and are well fattened. If practical, starve birds overnight before slaughtering. Allow carcass of whole turkey to chill two days. Pack using one of the following methods:

Whole: Wrap whole chicken or turkey in freezer foil, film, paper, or vacuum package. Seal, label and freeze.

Cut Up: Cut chicken or turkey in pieces. Pack pieces in plastic freezer jars, plastic freezer containers, freezer foil, film, paper or vacuum package. Seal, label and freeze.

Halves: Cut chicken or turkey in half. Wrap in freezer foil, film, paper or vacuum package. Seal, label and freeze.

Prepared Poultry

Frozen creamed chicken, chicken a la king, pies, baked chicken, broth, chicken chopped for salad, barbecued...all keep well. Do not freeze stuffed poultry. Cover chicken with a cream sauce or gravy if possible. Cool. Pack into plastic freezer jars or plastic freezer containers. Seal, label and freeze.

Thawing And Preparing Chicken and Turkey
Whole Or Halves: Thaw wrapped whole or halved chicken or turkey in refrigerator or submerge in cold water. Never thaw poultry at room temperature. Prepare and cook as fresh.

Cut-Up: Thaw chicken or turkey pieces in the refrigerator until pieces can be easily separated. Prepare and cook as fresh.

prepared foods
Breads—Quick

Biscuits, Fruit And Nut Breads, Muffins And Waffles: Prepare, bake and cool. Pack into plastic freezer bags or plastic freezer containers. Seal, label and freeze.

Breads—Yeast

Unbaked: Shape as desired. Freeze on baking sheet. Pack into plastic freezer bags or plastic freezer containers. Seal, label and return to freezer.

Baked: Prepare, bake and cool. Pack same as Yeast Breads, Unbaked.

Brown-And-Serve: Bake 20 minutes at 275°F. Cool. Package same as Yeast Breads, Unbaked.

Pizza: Prepare pizza. Do not bake. Flash freeze; remove from freezer. Wrap in freezer film, foil, paper or vacuum package. Seal, label and return to freezer.

Cakes

Layer, Loaf, Cupcakes, Angel, Chiffon, Sponge And Fruit: Prepare, bake and cool. May be frozen whole or in meal-size portions or slices. Pack into plastic freezer bags or plastic freezer containers. Seal, label and freeze.

Frosted: Prepare, bake, cool and frost. Place in freezer to harden the frosting. Remove from freezer and pack into plastic freezer bags or plastic freezer containers. Seal, label and return to freezer.

Candies—Homemade

Fudge, Divinity, Brittle, Taffy, Creams And Caramels: Wrap each piece individually in freezer film and pack into plastic freezer containers to avoid crushing. Seal, label and freeze. Allow to thaw in the package.

Combination Dishes

Baked Beans, Stew, Ravioli And Meat Sauce Casseroles: Prepare as usual, keeping fat to a minimum. Cool. Pack into plastic freezer jars or plastic freezer containers. Seal, label and freeze.

Cookies

Unbaked: For bar cookies, form into a long roll; for drop cookies, place cookies close together on a baking sheet. Flash freeze cookie roll and drop cookies; remove from freezer. Wrap in plastic freezer bags, freezer film, foil, paper or vacuum package. Seal, label and return to freezer.

Baked: Prepare, bake and cool. Pack into plastic freezer bags or plastic freezer containers, placing freezer paper between cookie layers. Or, vacuum package in a rigid container, placing freezer paper between cookie layers. Seal, label and freeze.

Desserts

Mousse: Mix and pour into plastic freezer jars or plastic freezer containers. Seal, label and freeze.

Cheesecake, Baked: Prepare, bake and cool. Wrap in freezer film and pack in plastic freezer containers. Seal, label and freeze.

Pudding, Steamed: Prepare, cook and cool. Pack in covered baking mold, securing lid with freezer tape. Pack mold in plastic freezer bag. Seal, label and freeze.

Doughnuts

Deep-Fried: Fry in high-quality fat. Cool. Package same as Cookies, Baked.

Freezer Slaw

Yield: about 5 pints

2 pounds cabbage	2 cups sugar
1 large green pepper	1 teaspoon dry mustard
3 large carrots	1 teaspoon celery seed
¾ cup chopped onion	1 cup vinegar
1 teaspoon salt	½ cup water

Shred cabbage, green pepper and carrots. Add onion. Sprinkle with salt; let stand 1 hour. Drain. Combine remaining ingredients in a saucepot. Bring to a boil; boil 3 minutes. Cool. Ladle liquid over cabbage mixture; let stand 5 minutes. Stir well. Pack slaw into plastic freezer jars or plastic freezer containers, leaving ½-inch headspace. Seal, label and freeze.

Gazpacho

Yield: about 7 pints

2 pounds tomatoes (about 6 medium)	5 cups tomato juice
	½ cup red wine vinegar
1 pound cucumbers (about 2 medium)	2 tablespoons olive oil
	½ teaspoon hot pepper sauce
1 cup chopped onion	1 clove garlic, minced
1 cup chopped green pepper	1 teaspoon salt
½ cup chopped celery	¼ teaspoon pepper

Peel, core, seed and chop tomatoes. Peel, seed and chop cucumbers. Combine all ingredients. Ladle Gazpacho into plastic freezer jars or plastic freezer containers, leaving ½-inch headspace. Seal, label and freeze.

Gravy

It is better to freeze broth and thicken while reheating than to freeze gravy. Prepare broth according to favorite recipe; cool. Ladle broth into plastic freezer jars or plastic freezer containers, leaving ½-inch headspace. Seal, label and freeze.

Herb Pizza Crust

Yield: about three 10- to 14-inch pizza crusts

2 tablespoons sugar	1 tablespoon coarse salt
2¼ teaspoons active dry yeast	1 tablespoon basil
1½ cups warm water (105° to 115°F or according to yeast packet)	1 tablespoon oregano
	1 tablespoon thyme
	3 tablespoons extra-virgin olive oil
3½ cups all-purpose flour	
½ cup bread flour	

Dissolve sugar and yeast in warm water. Let stand until mixture starts to foam, about 5 minutes. Combine flours, salt and herbs in a large bowl. Mound flour mixture, then make a well in the center. Pour yeast mixture into the flour well. Add olive oil. With a fork, stir in circular motion to gradually incorporate dry ingredients into liquid ingredients. Continue stirring until dough forms. Shape dough into a ball. Grease a large bowl with olive oil. Place dough in bowl, turning to cover entire surface of dough with a thin coating of olive oil. Cover bowl with plastic wrap and let dough rise at room temperature until double in size, 45 minutes to

1 hour. Punch down dough. Turn dough onto a floured surface and shape into three balls. Lightly brush individual dough balls with olive oil and cover with plastic wrap. Let rise at room temperature 30 to 45 minutes. Shape dough by hand working from center to outer edge. For a crispy crust, form a ¼-inch thickness. For a soft crust, form a ½-inch thickness. Transfer dough to a cardboard round. Freeze pizza crust plain or with toppings. Wrap crusts individually in plastic freezer bags, freezer foil, film, paper or vacuum package. Seal, label and freeze.

Lemon Curd

Makes one 9-inch tart

6 large egg yolks	1 cup fresh lemon juice
¾ cup sugar	½ cup (¼ pound) cold unsalted butter, cut into 8 pieces
Grated peel of one lemon	

Press egg yolks though a sieve set over a heavy saucepan to remove all egg whites. Add sugar, lemon peel and lemon juice. Whisk just to combine. Cook over medium heat, stirring constantly with a wooden spoon. Make sure to stir down the sides of the saucepan. Cook until mixture coats the back of the wooden spoon, about 20 minutes. Remove saucepan from heat. Add butter, one piece at a time, stirring after each addition to ensure the mixture is smooth. Ladle lemon curd into plastic freezer jars or plastic freezer containers, leaving ½-inch headspace. Chill until set, about 1 hour. Seal, label and freeze.

Onion Soup

Yield: about 5 pints

2 pounds onions, sliced	3 tablespoons flour
6 tablespoons butter	2 quarts beef broth
1 teaspoon sugar	1 cup white cooking wine
1 teaspoon dry mustard	Salt and pepper to taste

Cook onions in butter until transparent but not browned. Add sugar and dry mustard. Blend in flour; cook 1 minute, stirring to prevent burning. Gradually stir in beef broth and wine; simmer 30 minutes. Add salt and pepper to taste. Cool. Ladle soup into plastic freezer jars or plastic freezer containers, leaving ½-inch headspace. Seal, label and freeze.

Pastry Circles, Squares Or Rectangles

Roll out dough; cut circles, squares or rectangles large enough for pie or tart pan, adding 2 inches. Place pastry onto a piece of cardboard cut to the shape of the pastry then wrap in freezer foil, film or paper. Separate layers with a double thickness of freezer foil, film or paper. Flash freeze. Place in plastic freezer bags or vacuum package. Seal, label and return to freezer.

Note: Pastry can be placed in foil baking pans, then wrapped for freezing.

Pesto

Yield: about 2 half-pints

1 cup pine nuts	1 cup grated Parmesan cheese
4 cups fresh basil leaves, firmly packed	
	1 cup plus 1 tablespoon extra-virgin olive oil
2 cloves garlic, crushed	

Spread pine nuts on a baking sheet and toast in oven at 450°F until lightly browned. Purée toasted pine nuts, basil and garlic in a food processor or blender until smooth. Add Parmesan cheese, processing just to blend. Add 1 cup olive oil through feed tube of food processor or lid of blender in a slow steady stream while machine is running. Pour pesto into plastic freezer jars or plastic freezer containers, leaving ½-inch headspace. Drizzle 1½ teaspoons olive oil over pesto. Seal, label and freeze.

Recipe Variation: One-half cup of fresh flat leaf parsley can be used to substitute for ½ cup fresh basil. Garlic may be increased to 4 cloves, if desired.

Pickled Horseradish

Yield: about 2 half-pints

¾ pound horseradish root	1½ teaspoons Ball Fruit-Fresh
1 cup vinegar	Produce Protector
½ teaspoon salt	

Wash horseradish root; drain. Peel and finely grate horseradish root. Combine 2 cups grated horseradish, vinegar, salt and Fruit-Fresh in a bowl. Ladle pickled horseradish into plastic freezer jars or plastic freezer containers, leaving ½-inch headspace. Seal, label and freeze.

Note: The pungency of horseradish root fades quickly. Prepare only the amount of pickled horseradish that will be used within three months.

Pie Crust

Yield: about 4 pie crusts

4½ cups flour	1 egg, beaten
2 teaspoons salt	1 tablespoon vinegar
4 teaspoons sugar	½ cup water
1¾ cups shortening	

Combine dry ingredients; cut in shortening until mixture is uniformly coarse. Combine egg, vinegar, and water. Gradually add to flour mixture, stirring until mixture forms a ball. Divide dough into 4 equal parts. Roll dough out on a floured surface; cut into circles the size of the pie pan plus 2 inches. Place pastry onto cardboard round covered with freezer foil, film or paper. Separate layers with a double thickness of freezer foil, film or paper. Place in plastic freezer bags. Seal, label and freeze. Or, flash freeze; remove from freezer. Vacuum package. Label and return to freezer.

Note: Pie crust can be placed on foil baking pans, then wrapped for freezing.

Pies

Double-crust pies, raw or cooked, as well as single-crust pies (coconut, nut, potato and similar pies) may be frozen. The pie filling to be frozen should be slightly thicker than usual. Flash freeze; remove from freezer. Pack into plastic freezer bags. Seal, label and return to freezer.

Salads

Fruit and gelatin salads that freeze well are those made with a base of cream, cottage cheese, whipped cream or mayonnaise. Prepare as a single dish or individual servings. Most containers suitable for freezer storage can be used to freeze the salad or gelatin. Salad molds, serving bowls, custard cups or muffin tins are just a few of the containers that can be used. So that the container can be used for another purpose after the salad or gelatin is frozen, line it with freezer foil or film before filling. Flash freeze the salad or gelatin. After salad or gelatin is frozen, remove it from the dish and over-wrap the salad or gelatin using plastic freezer bags, plastic freezer containers, freezer foil or film. Seal, label and return to freezer.

Sandwiches

Filled: Sandwiches suitable for freezing include those made with cheese, chicken, meat, peanut butter, nut paste, egg-yolk mixtures and fish. Use day-old bread; spread bread with butter; add filling. Wrap sandwiches individually in freezer film or foil. Flash freeze. Overwrap with plastic freezer bags. Label and return to freezer.

Open-Face Canapés: Make canapés according to recipe. Be sure to spread filling to very edge of bread. Place canapés on a baking sheet and flash freeze. Pack frozen canapés into plastic freezer containers, separating layers with freezer foil, film or paper. Seal, label and return to freezer.

Savory Pastry Crust

Yield: about 4 five-inch crusts

2 cups all-purpose flour	3 tablespoons sugar
½ cup shredded cheddar cheese	½ teaspoon salt
2 tablespoons minced flat leaf parsley	½ cup butter, chilled and cut into ½-inch cubes
	⅓ cup cold water

Combine flour, cheese, parsley, sugar and salt in a medium bowl. Cut in butter until mixture is uniformly coarse. Gradually add water, one tablespoon at a time, stirring gently with a fork after each addition. Use just enough water for dough to form a ball. Divide dough into 4 equal parts. Roll one part of dough out on a floured surface into a 5-inch circle; repeat for each part. Place pastry onto a cardboard round covered with freezer foil, film or paper. Separate layers with a double thickness of freezer foil, film or paper. Place in plastic freezer bag or plastic freezer container. Seal, label and freeze.

Soups

Most soups freeze well. These include dried beans, split pea, oyster and those made from poultry, meats and vegetables.

Stock-Based: Prepare as usual. Cool. Pack into plastic freezer jars or plastic freezer containers, leaving ½-inch headspace. Seal, label and freeze.

Spaghetti Sauce

Yield: about 6 pints

2 cups chopped onions	3 (8-ounce) cans tomato sauce
2 cups chopped green peppers	1 (29-ounce) can whole tomatoes, chopped
1 cup chopped celery	2 bay leaves
4 cloves garlic, minced	2 teaspoons oregano
2 tablespoons oil	1 teaspoon basil
2 pounds ground beef	1 teaspoon salt
3 (6-ounce) cans tomato paste	¼ teaspoon pepper

Sauté onions, green peppers, celery and garlic in oil until onions are tender. Add ground beef; cook until browned. Drain off fat. Add remaining ingredients; simmer 1 hour. Remove bay leaves. Cool. Ladle sauce into plastic freezer jars or plastic freezer containers, leaving ½-inch headspace. Seal, label and freeze.

seafoods

It is important that only fresh seafood be used for freezing. Seafood must be cleaned and prepared for freezing shortly after being caught. Since seafood is a perishable commodity, it must be kept under refrigeration at all times.

Crab, Lobster And Oysters

Prepare seafood as for using fresh. Pack meat into plastic freezer jars or plastic freezer containers, or vacuum package. Seal, label and freeze.

Fish

Select any fresh eating variety of fish.

Whole: Prepare fish for freezing the same as for cooking. Wrap each fish tightly in freezer film, foil or paper, then pack into plastic freezer bags, plastic freezer jars or plastic freezer containers. Or, vacuum package. Seal, label and freeze.

Fish may also be frozen in plastic freezer jars or plastic freezer containers and covered with cold water. Seal, label and freeze.

Steaks Or Fillets: Dip fish 30 seconds in a 5 percent salt solution (⅔ cup salt to 1 gallon water). Pack same as Fish, Whole.

Fish Roe

Thoroughly wash roe. Pack roe into plastic freezer jars or plastic freezer containers. Seal, label and freeze.

Shrimp

Fresh Frozen: Remove head from shrimp; wash shrimp in cold water. Pack shrimp in plastic freezer bags, plastic freezer jars or plastic freezer containers or vacuum package. Seal, label and freeze.

Cleaned: Remove head from shrimp. Peel, de-vein and wash shrimp in cold water. Pack same as for Shrimp, Fresh Frozen.

Cooked: Prepare shrimp as for Cleaned. Boil 5 minutes in 1 gallon water and 3 tablespoons salt. Pack same as for Fresh Frozen.

Breaded: Remove head, peel and de-vein. Wash shrimp in cold water. Coat with breading. Pack same as for Fresh Frozen.

Thawing And Preparing Seafood Products

Place unopened package in the refrigerator until thawing begins and the product softens slightly. Cook as for fresh.

special diet & baby foods

Freezing foods is an excellent way to meet specialized meal requirements and save time. However, ready-to-serve meals do not retain quality, flavor or texture as long as foods frozen as separate ingredients. Careful management of ready-to-serve meals will help meet individual dietary needs and still provide nutritious meals.

Foods for diabetics can be prepared and frozen without sugar or sweetened with a non-sugar sweetener. Consult your physician and follow manufacturer's instructions for use of non-sugar sweeteners.

It is often convenient to freeze single portions without salt or without fat for individuals on special diets. Plastic freezer jars and plastic freezer containers make convenient freezer storage containers for foods that are soft or liquid at room temperature. They are available in sizes that are perfect for one serving.

Purées of vegetables, fruits and meats for babies and convalescents may be made and frozen when the foods are in season. These foods require a rigid container due to the soft texture. Four-ounce tapered glass jars or 8-ounce plastic freezer jars are most suitable for freezing baby food, while 8-ounce tapered glass or plastic jars make a perfect single serving size for adults.

vegetables

Excellent frozen products may be prepared from most vegetables when: the proper varieties are used; they are harvested at the correct time; they are adequately blanched and cooled, and they are packaged correctly. Practically all frozen vegetables may be stored for one year.

If you harvest vegetables from your own garden, pick tender vegetables at their peak of flavor and texture. Process the same day harvested or bought; never use vegetables which become over-mature either before or after harvesting. The fresher the vegetables when frozen, the more satisfactory the frozen product.

If it is necessary to store vegetables for a short time, store in a cool, well-ventilated area or in the refrigerator. Prompt cooling in ice water after blanching followed by storage in the refrigerator will help retain flavor and other qualities.

Most fully-cooked vegetables lose flavor rapidly and should be stored for only a few days. Loss of flavor may be retarded by covering the vegetables with a cream sauce.

Blanching

Blanching is a critical step in preparing vegetables for freezing and must be done carefully. This is a "must" for all vegetables to be stored frozen for more than four weeks. However, those vegetables used exclusively for their flavor, such as green onions, hot peppers and herbs, do not have to be blanched. Blanching cleanses off surface dirt and microorganisms, brightens the color, helps retain vitamins and reduces the action of enzymes which can destroy the fresh flavor after four weeks. It also shrinks the product, making packing easier.

Immediately before blanching, wash, drain, sort, trim and cut the vegetables as for cooking fresh. Use 1 gallon water per 1 pound vegetables—2 gallons for leafy greens. Put vegetables into blancher (wire basket, coarse mesh bag or perforated metal strainer) and lower into vigorously boiling water. Begin counting the time as soon as vegetables are placed in the boiling water. Keep the heat on high and stir water or keep container covered during blanching. Follow the blanching time given in the recipe for each vegetable. Underblanching stimulates the activity of enzymes and is worse than no blanching at all. Prolonged blanching causes loss of vitamins, minerals, flavor and color.

As soon as blanching is complete, the vegetables should be cooled quickly to stop the cooking process. This may be achieved by immersing the vegetables in ice water. The vegetables should be stirred several times during cooling, which should not be longer than the blanching time.

With a large quantity, determine how many vegetables can be blanched in 15 minutes. Prepare this amount, leaving the others in the refrigerator; blanch and cool vegetables before packaging.

Vegetables usually are packed loosely without seasoning. Immediately after blanching and cooling, pack vegetables into meal-size, airtight, moisture/vapor-proof containers.

Place sealed packages into freezer in single layers, leaving 1-inch space between packages. Use coldest part of freezer for freezing foods. Foods should freeze in 12 to 24 hours.

When completely frozen, packages may be compactly stacked. Keep the freezer at 0°F or lower at all times.

Artichoke—Globe

Select globe artichokes with uniform green color, compact globes and tightly adhering leaves. Size has little to do with quality or flavor. Remove outer bracts until light yellow or white bracts are reached. Cut off tops of bud, and trim to a cone. Wash the hearts in cold water as soon as trimming is complete. Drain. Blanch 7 minutes. Cool. Drain. Pack globe artichokes in plastic freezer jars, plastic freezer bags, plastic freezer containers or vacuum package. Seal, label and freeze.

Artichoke—Jerusalem

Select mature, unblemished Jerusalem artichokes. Wash thoroughly; peel or scrape; wash again. Blanch 3 to 5 minutes, depending on size. Cool. Drain. Pack artichokes into plastic freezer jars, plastic freezer containers or vacuum package. Seal, label and freeze.

Asparagus

Select young, tender asparagus with tightly closed tips. Wash thoroughly and sort into sizes. Trim stalks by removing scales with a sharp knife. Cut into even lengths to fit freezer containers. Blanch small spears 1½ minutes, medium spears 2 minutes and large spears 3 minutes. Cool. Drain. Pack asparagus into plastic freezer bags, plastic freezer jars, plastic freezer containers or vacuum package. Seal, label and freeze.

Beans—Lima

Select lima beans while the seed is in the green stage. Wash in cold water. Shell and wash again. Sort according to size. Blanch small beans 1 minute, medium beans 2 minutes and large beans 3 minutes. Cool. Drain. Pack beans into plastic freezer bags, plastic freezer jars, plastic freezer containers or vacuum package. Seal, label and freeze.

Beans—Snap

Select young, tender bean pods when the seed is first formed. Wash in cold water. Trim ends; cut into 2- to 4-inch lengths or lengths to fit freezer container. The longer cuts are the best quality. Blanch 3 minutes. Cool. Drain. Pack beans into plastic freezer bags, plastic freezer jars, plastic freezer containers or vacuum package. Seal, label and freeze.

Beets

Select uniformly-deep red, tender beets. Leave 2-inch stem and tap root; wash; cook until tender. Cool and remove skins, stem and tap root. Leave whole, quarter, slice or dice. Pack beets into plastic freezer jars, plastic freezer containers or vacuum package. Seal, label and freeze.

Broccoli

Select tender-firm broccoli stalks with compact heads. Wash and remove leaves and woody portions. Separate heads into convenient-size sections and immerse in brine (1 cup salt to 1 gallon water) 30 minutes to remove insects. Rinse and drain. Blanch medium-size sections 3 minutes and large-size sections 4 minutes. Cool. Drain. Pack broccoli into plastic freezer jars, plastic freezer containers or vacuum package. Seal, label and freeze.

Brussels Sprouts

Select Brussels sprouts with dark green, compact heads. Remove coarse outer leaves; wash and sort into small, medium and large sizes. Blanch small-size 3 minutes, medium-size 4 minutes and large-size 5 minutes. Cool. Drain. Pack Brussels sprouts into plastic freezer jars, plastic freezer containers or vacuum package. Seal, label and freeze.

Cabbage

Select solid cabbage heads with crisp green leaves. Wash, discard the coarse outer leaves and cut the head into wedges or coarsely shred. Blanch wedges 3 minutes, shredded cabbage 1½ minutes. Cool. Drain. Pack cabbage into plastic freezer jars or plastic freezer containers. Seal, label and freeze.

Carrots

Select young, tender, coreless, medium-length carrots. Wash, peel, wash again and dice or quarter. Small carrots may be frozen whole. Blanch cut carrots 3 minutes, whole carrots 5 minutes. Cool. Drain. Pack carrots into plastic freezer jars, plastic freezer containers or vacuum package. Seal, label and freeze.

Cauliflower

Select cauliflower with compact heads. Trim; break into flowerets of uniform size, about 1-inch across. Wash and drain. Immerse in brine (1 cup salt to 1 gallon water) 30 minutes to remove insects. Rinse and drain. Blanch medium-size sections 3 minutes, large-size sections 4 minutes. Cool. Drain. Pack cauliflower into plastic freezer jars, plastic freezer containers or vacuum package. Seal, label and freeze.

Corn

Select only tender, freshly-gathered corn in the milk stage. Husk and trim the ears; remove silks and wash.

Corn-On-The-Cob: Blanch ears 1½ inches in diameter 6 minutes, 2 inches in diameter 8 minutes and larger ears 10 minutes. Cool. Drain. Wrap ears individually in moisture/vapor-proof film. Pack wrapped ears of corn into plastic freezer bags or vacuum package. Seal, label and freeze.

Whole Kernel: Blanch 5 to 6 minutes, depending on size of ears. Cool; drain; cut corn from cob. Pack into plastic freezer bags, plastic freezer jars, plastic freezer containers or vacuum package. Seal, label and freeze.

Cream-Style Corn: Blanch ears the same as Corn, Whole Kernel. Cool. Drain. Cut kernels, leaving tip ends; scrape cob to extract milk and pulp. Pack corn into plastic freezer jars or plastic freezer containers, leaving ½-inch headspace. Seal, label and freeze.

Precooked Corn: Cut and scrape corn from the cob without blanching. Put small amount of water in saucepot, add cut corn and cook over low heat, stirring constantly, about 10 minutes or until it thickens. Pour corn into a pan; set pan in ice water to cool. Do not cook more than 3 quarts at a time. Pack same as Corn, Cream-Style.

Eggplant

Harvest uniformly dark color eggplant before seeds become mature.

Plain: Wash, peel and slice ⅓-inch thick. Prepare just enough eggplant for 1 blanching at a time. Blanch 4 minutes in 1 gallon boiling water

containing 3 tablespoons Fruit-Fresh (see page 9) or ½ cup lemon juice. Cool. Drain. Pack eggplant into plastic freezer jars or plastic freezer containers. Seal, label and freeze.

For Frying: Pack same as Eggplant, Plain. Separate drained slices with freezer wrap.

Greens

Pick young, tender, green leaves. Wash thoroughly and cut off woody stems. Blanch 2 minutes and avoid matting leaves. Cool. Drain. Pack into plastic freezer jars or plastic freezer containers, leaving ½-inch headspace. Seal, label and freeze.

Herbs—Fresh

Many fresh herbs may be frozen. Wash, drain and dry herbs. Do not blanch. Wrap a few sprigs or leaves in freezer film and place in plastic freezer bags, plastic freezer jars or plastic freezer containers. Seal, label and freeze.

Note: These usually are not suitable for garnish since the frozen product becomes limp when it thaws. Chop and use in cooked dishes.

Mushrooms

Select cultivated mushrooms that are firm and of even color. Work quickly with mushrooms as they deteriorate rapidly. Do not allow mushrooms to soak in water.

Plain: Wash and remove base of the stem. Sort mushrooms by size. Smaller mushrooms may be frozen whole; larger mushrooms should be sliced. Add Fruit-Fresh (see page 9) to blanching water to help prevent discoloration. Blanch small, whole mushrooms 4 minutes and sliced mushrooms 3 minutes. Cool. Drain. Pack mushrooms into plastic freezer jars or plastic freezer containers. Seal, label and freeze.

Sautéed: Cut into slices and sauté in butter about 3 minutes. Cool. Pack same as Mushrooms, Plain. Seal, label and freeze.

Note: If mushrooms are sautéed, no blanching is required.

Okra

Select tender okra pods. Wash and separate into two sizes: under 4 inches and larger than 4 inches. Remove stems at the end of the seed cells. Blanch small pods 3 minutes, large pods 5 minutes. Cool. Drain. Leave small pods whole, cut large pods into 1-inch lengths. Pack okra into plastic freezer jars or plastic freezer containers. Seal, label and freeze.

Onions

Mature Bulbs: Choose mature bulbs and clean as for eating. Blanch onions 3 to 7 minutes or until the center is heated. Cool. Drain. Pack onions into plastic freezer jars or plastic freezer containers. Seal, label and freeze. These are suitable for cooking only.

Green: Wash and chop. Freeze without blanching. Pack same as Onions, Mature Bulbs.

Note: Green onion will not be crisp and may become slightly tough. Use in cooked dishes.

Parsnips And Turnips

Choose parsnips or turnips that are firm with a smooth skin. Remove tops, wash thoroughly and peel. Slice, dice or cut lengthwise. Blanch 3 minutes. Cool. Drain. Pack parsnips or turnips into plastic freezer jars, plastic freezer containers or vacuum package. Seal, label and freeze.

Peanuts

Select fully-mature peanuts.

Green In The Shell: Wash. Leave in shell. Blanch 10 minutes. Cool. Drain. Pack peanuts into plastic freezer jars or plastic freezer containers. Seal, label and freeze.

Shelled: Shell. Pack peanuts into plastic freezer jars, plastic freezer containers or vacuum package. Seal, label and freeze.

Note: These peanuts may be removed from the freezer, thawed and used as fresh-shelled peanuts in any recipe.

Peas

Field (Blackeye): Select pods when seeds are tender and barely grown. Wash peas. Shell. Wash again. Blanch smaller sizes 1 minute and larger sizes 2 minutes. Cool. Drain. Pack peas into plastic freezer jars or plastic freezer containers. Seal, label and freeze.

Green Or Garden: Harvest when pods are filled with young, tender peas that have not become starchy. Wash peas. Shell. Wash again. Blanch 2 minutes. Cool. Drain. Pack peas into plastic freezer jars or plastic freezer containers. Seal, label and freeze.

Snow Or Sugar Snap: Select firm, unblemished pods. Wash and blanch 2 minutes. Cool. Drain. Pack pea pods into plastic freezer jars, plastic freezer containers or vacuum package. Seal, label and freeze.

Peppers

Hot: Select crisp, tender, green or bright-red pods. Wash and drain. Pack peppers into plastic freezer jars, plastic freezer containers or vacuum package. Seal, label and freeze.

Pimientos: Select fully-ripe pods of deep-red color. Wash; cut out stems; remove seeds. Peel by roasting in oven at 400°F until skins blister or cover with water and boil until peppers are tender. Cool. Drain. Peel. Pack pimientos into plastic freezer jars or plastic freezer containers. Seal, label and freeze.

Sweet: Select crisp, tender, green or bright-red pods. Wash; cut out stems; remove seeds. Freeze whole, as halves, strips or diced. Do not blanch. Pack peppers into plastic freezer jars, plastic freezer containers or vacuum package. Seal, label and freeze.

Note: When cutting or seeding hot peppers, wear rubber gloves to prevent hands from being burned.

Potatoes—Irish

Select smooth new potatoes.

Plain: Wash thoroughly. Peel. Wash again. Blanch 3 to 5 minutes, depending on size. Drain. Cool. Pack potatoes into plastic freezer jars, plastic freezer containers or vacuum package. Seal, label and freeze.

Baked Or Stuffed: Prepare as usual; top with melted cheese. Cool quickly. Wrap individually in freezer foil or film. Freeze. Pack individually wrapped frozen potatoes in plastic freezer bags, plastic freezer containers or vacuum package. Seal, label and return to freezer.

French Fried: Cut potatoes into thin strips. Blanch potatoes 2 minutes; cool on a paper towel. Fry in fresh, high-quality oil (370°F) until very light brown. Drain. Cool. Pack into plastic freezer bags, plastic freezer containers or vacuum package. Seal, label and freeze.

Scalloped: Bake potatoes in dish suitable for baking and freezing until pale in color but not quite done. Cool at room temperature, not to exceed 2 hours. Wrap cooled dish with freezer foil or film. Place wrapped dish in plastic freezer bags or vacuum package. Seal, label and freeze.

Potatoes—Sweet

Allow sweet potatoes to cure for a minimum of one week after harvesting. Wash and dry potatoes.

Baked: Grease peel with cooking oil; bake at 350°F until slightly soft. Cool. Wrap individually in freezer foil or film. Place in plastic freezer bags, plastic freezer containers or vacuum package. Seal, label and freeze.

Sliced: Cook unpeeled potatoes in water at 130°F for 30 minutes. Peel and cut lengthwise into ½-inch slices. Blanch 3 minutes in boiling syrup to cover (1½ cups water to 1 cup sugar and 1 tablespoon lemon juice). Cool. Pack potatoes into plastic freezer jars or plastic freezer containers. Ladle syrup over potatoes, leaving ½-inch headspace. Seal, label and freeze.

Purée: Bake potatoes at 350°F until soft. Cool. Peel sweet potatoes. Purée in a food processor or food mill. For each 5 pounds of potatoes puréed, add ½ cup sugar, ½ cup cold water and 1 tablespoon lemon juice. Cool. Pack purée into plastic freezer jars or plastic freezer containers, leaving ½-inch headspace. Seal, label and freeze.

Pumpkin

Select mature cooking pumpkin that has uniform color and the stem breaks easily from the vine. Wash; peel and remove seeds. Cut pumpkin into sections; steam until soft. Purée using a food processor or food mill. Add 1 part sugar to 6 parts purée, if desired. Cool. Pack purée into plastic freezer jars or plastic freezer containers, leaving ½-inch headspace. Seal, label and freeze.

Squash—Spaghetti

Cut squash in half; remove seeds. Place squash in baking dish, cut side down. Add ½-inch water and bake at 350°F until fork tender. Using a fork, rake pulp away from peel. Squash should separate into strands. Cool. Pack squash into plastic freezer jars or plastic freezer containers. Seal, label and freeze.

Squash—Summer

Raw: Choose young squash with tender skin. Wash; slice; blanch 3 minutes. Cool. Pack squash into plastic freezer jars, plastic freezer containers or vacuum package. Seal, label and freeze.

Squash—Winter

Select fully-mature squash with a hard rind. Wash; cut into halves; scoop out seeds and membrane. Place squash cut side down in a shallow baking dish; add ¼-inch water and bake at 375°F until tender. Scoop out pulp. Purée in a food processor or food mill. Cool. Pack purée into plastic freezer jars or plastic freezer containers. Seal, label and freeze.

Tomatoes

Sauce: Select firm, ripe tomatoes. Wash, core, quarter and seed tomatoes. Cook tomatoes until soft, stirring to prevent sticking. Purée in food processor or food mill. Return to saucepot and simmer until reduced by half. Cool. Pack sauce into plastic freezer jars or plastic freezer containers. Seal, label and freeze.

Juice: Select firm, ripe tomatoes. Wash, core, quarter and seed tomatoes. Simmer tomatoes until soft, stirring to prevent sticking. Purée in a food processor or food mill. Cool. Pack juice into plastic freezer jars or plastic freezer containers. Seal, label and freeze.

Tomatoes—Green

Select firm, green tomatoes. Wash; core; slice ¼-inch thick. Pack tomatoes into plastic freezer jars or plastic freezer containers with freezer wrap between slices. Seal, label and freeze.

Thawing And Preparing Vegetables

Most vegetables can be cooked without thawing. The exception is corn-on-the-cob, the only vegetable which should be completely thawed before being cooked. All greens should be partially thawed so as to separate them before cooking. Precooked vegetables should also be partially thawed.

To maintain quality, cook frozen vegetables as you would fresh. However, cook them for a shorter period of time since they were blanched before freezing. Use the smallest amount of water possible. Cook vegetables immediately before serving. Nutrients in frozen vegetables are quickly lost if they are allowed to stand after cooking. Cook only the amount that can be consumed at one meal.

featured prepared recipe

Savory Pocket Pie

Makes about 4 pocket pies

4 (5-inch) frozen Savory Pastry Crusts, thawed (*recipe on page 100*)	⅓ cup shredded Cheddar cheese
¼ cup spicy mustard, divided	¼ cup sliced green onions
⅓ pound smoked ham, diced	½ teaspoon salt
⅓ cup shredded Granny Smith apple	¼ teaspoon white pepper
	1 egg, beaten

Spread 1 tablespoon spicy mustard on each pastry round. Combine ham, apple, cheese, onion, salt and pepper in a small bowl. Place an equal portion of filling onto half of each pastry round, spreading evenly to within ¼ inch from edge. Lightly brush entire edge of pastry with beaten egg. Fold unfilled half of pastry over the opposite side aligning edges so they are even; crimp edges together to seal. Individually wrap pocket pies with freezer foil, film or wrap. Place in a plastic freezer bag or plastic freezer container. Seal, label and freeze.

To Serve: Bake frozen pies at 350°F about 25 minutes or until pies are golden brown and filling is heated through.

Note: Savory Pocket Pies may be pre-baked then frozen. Reheat frozen pocket pies in conventional or microwave oven until hot throughout.

freezing corn step-by-step

1. Read recipe instructions; assemble equipment and ingredients before starting. Follow guidelines for recipe preparation, type and size of packaging and freezing method. Do not make changes in recommended guidelines.

2. Select appropriate moisture/vapor-resistant packaging for the type of food being frozen: rigid containers for foods which are liquid at room temperature; flexible wrap for foods which are solid at room temperature.

3. Select fresh ears of corn at the peak of quality and flavor. Husk and trim ears. Remove silks and wash.

4. Bring 6 to 8 quarts of water to a boil. Submerge several ears of corn in boiling water to blanch. Do not crowd corn. When freezing corn-on-the-cob, blanch ears of corn having a 2-inch diameter for 8 minutes. For whole-kernel corn (corn cut from the cob), blanch ears 5 to 6 minutes. Start counting the blanching time when ears of corn are submerged in boiling water.

5. Remove corn from boiling water and immediately submerge in cold water to cool. Allow corn to remain in cold water for the same amount of time used for blanching. Drain; dry corn.

6. To cut corn from cob, hold cob upright, resting one end on a cutting board. Cut kernels from the cob with a knife. For whole-kernel corn: cut kernels from cob, leaving tip ends. For cream-style corn: cut kernels from cob, leaving tip ends. Scrape the cob with the edge of a knife to extract the milk.

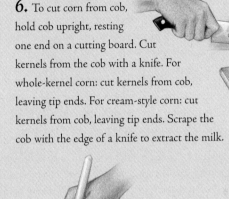

7. Pack whole-kernel corn into plastic freezer jars, plastic freezer containers or tapered glass jars, leaving as little head-space as possible. If cream-style corn is being frozen, allow ½-inch headspace for expansion of the liquid. Or, wrap individual ears of corn that have been blanched and cooled in freezer wrap, removing as much air as possible; secure tightly. Pack ears of corn into plastic freezer bags or vacuum package.

8. Label containers with the date and name of product. Place containers in freezer, near the coldest spot, in a single layer. Stack containers after corn is frozen solid. Frozen foods must be stored at 0°F. Refer to figure 9 for proper storage time.

dehydrating

Fruit Leathers, Jerky & Rubs

On a cold wintry evening, when a bowl of hot soup sounds like heaven, it's no further away than your pantry. There you have stored, at the peak of freshness, dried vegetables ready at a moment's notice.

In no time at all, White Bean-Chicken Soup is simmering on the stove. As the leeks, mushrooms and zucchini rehydrate, the soup comes to life with rich aromas of butternut squash, plum tomatoes, and fresh herbs and spices.

The oldest method of food preservation, food dehydration is a long-practiced art. The list of summer's harvest that can be dried includes fruits, vegetables, fruit leathers, beef jerky and your favorite herb rubs. Dehydrating foods is simple to do and easy to store, in both traditional Ball Canning Jars or Ball Plastic Freezer Jars.

Dried vegetables and fruits make the perfect on-the-go snack for busy families. And who can resist the fun-to-eat treat of chewy beef jerky and fruit leathers? Snacks that are both delicious and nutritious—now that's an unbeatable combination.

When the soup is ready, you slice a loaf of whole grain bread and toss a salad, as the appetizing smells beckon the family to gather. The harvest season is short, but with home-dried foods, you reap the benefits all year long.

Pictured, White Bean-Chicken Soup
made with dried leeks, mushrooms & zucchini.
Recipe for White Bean-Chicken Soup is found on page 114.
Instructions for drying vegetables begin on page 112.

getting started

Drying food at home is simple to do. Dried foods are easy to use and convenient to store. However, unlike the exact methods needed for canning and freezing, finding the best technique for drying may require the trial-and-error approach. Various factors, such as the drying method used, the quality of the produce, pretreatment techniques and even the climate, may affect the finished product. Follow the general guidelines given for each specific food and then make the necessary adjustments.

Successful home food dehydration is dependent on three basic principles:

- **Heat:** controlled temperature high enough to force out moisture, but not hot enough to cook the food.
- **Dry Air:** to absorb the released moisture.
- **Air Circulation:** to carry the moisture away.

When food is dehydrated, 80 to 95% of the moisture is removed, inactivating the growth of bacteria and other spoilage microorganisms. This makes it a useful method of preservation.

Ingredients And Preparation

Fresh, high-quality, ripe produce is best for dehydrating. Dry foods during the peak harvest season for the specific food type, especially if produce must be purchased from farm stands or supermarkets. During peak season the quality will be higher and the price lower.

Properly dried produce will weigh much less and take up less volume than fresh produce, depending on the natural moisture content of the fruit or vegetable and the discarded inedible portions (such as peelings, cores, seeds, pits, pods and stems). As an example, apples are usually peeled and cored prior to drying; so, a purchased weight of 10 pounds will be reduced to 1 to 1½ pounds when dried.

Pretreatment Techniques

Most vegetables and some fruits benefit from pretreatment techniques, such as blanching and dipping. Although the drying process slows down the action of enzymes, chemical substances that cause fruits and vegetables to mature and ripen, it does not stop the action entirely. Simple pretreating can retard this action. Blanching (heating in steam or water for a specific time, then cooling quickly) is the most common method of pretreating vegetables. Steam blanching is preferred because more water-soluble vitamins and minerals are preserved. In steam blanching, vegetables or fruits are placed in a colander that is suspended above boiling water and heated by the steam. In water blanching, the vegetables or fruits are placed directly in the boiling water. Blanching shortens the drying and rehydration time, sets color, retards enzyme action and kills many spoilage microorganisms.

Dipping is a pretreatment used to prevent fruits such as apples, bananas, peaches and pears from oxidizing. Oxidation is the process that causes fruits to turn brown and lose some Vitamin A and C when exposed to the oxygen in air. Common antioxidants are Ball Fruit-Fresh Produce Protector, lemon or lime juice and ascorbic acid.

Ball Fruit-Fresh Produce Protector: is a blend of ascorbic and citric acids. Dissolve 2 tablespoons in 2 quarts of water. Hold produce in solution for no longer than 30 minutes, drain before drying.

Lemon Or Lime Juice: the most natural pretreatment. Use 1 cup juice to 1 quart water. Soak fruit no longer than 10 minutes; drain before drying.

Ascorbic Acid: also known as Vitamin C. Dissolve 1 tablespoon ascorbic acid to each quart water. Hold produce in solution no longer than 30 minutes; drain before drying.

Equipment And Utensils

Other than an electric dehydrator, most equipment needed for drying food is found in the kitchen. The list includes: sharp paring knife, colander or steamer for washing and blanching produce, cutting board, vegetable peeler, food processor or vegetable slicer for evenly cut slices, grater, blender and measuring utensils.

Food dehydration can be done by several methods. Natural methods, such as sun and room drying, require warm days of 90°F or more, low humidity, little air pollution and control of insects for a quality finished product. Oven drying is a good choice only for small quantities of food because the energy costs of operating a gas or an electric oven are high compared to the cost of operating an electric food dehydrator. And, a conventional oven only heats food and does not carry away moisture.

Commercial or homemade electric dehydrators provide the most reliable and consistent results, often without pretreatment, because of the controlled temperature and air flow. Food dehydrated by this method dries quickly and evenly. The quality of the finished product can be excellent. Food can be dried 24 hours a day, summer or winter, rain or shine.

Quality, cost, efficiency and personal needs should be assessed when considering the purchase of a food dehydrator. Inexpensive dehydrators may not operate efficiently, resulting in greater energy costs than the actual savings of preserving foods by dehydration. Selecting a dehydrator that offers greater capacity than will be practical for your needs will also waste energy dollars. If a food dehydrator is used frequently and to its maximum capacity each time it is operated, dehydration can be a very cost-effective way to preserve foods.

When looking for a dehydrator to purchase, or if you plan to build a dehydrator, be certain the following features are built into the dehydrator to ensure quality results:

Heat Source: heating element should be efficient and durable, enclosed for safety and have sufficient wattage for the entire drying area, about 70 watts per tray.

Fan: to blow heated air evenly over all the food. Its size should be proportional to the dryer's capacity, and it should be quiet.

Thermostat: an adjustable temperature control with a range from 85° to 160°F.

Drying Trays: should be made of safe, food-grade material, such as stainless steel, nylon, Teflon-coated fiberglass or plastic. Copper, aluminum or plated metal (such as cadmium or zinc plated) should not come in contact with drying food. Copper reduces Vitamin C in many foods. Aluminum discolors some fruits. Cadmium and zinc (galvanized) plated metal can be dissolved by fruit acids to cause the fruit to become toxic. Trays should have adequate spaces for air circulation and be easy to load, unload and clean.

Construction Quality: of plastic or metal approved for food contact that is durable and easy to clean. Electrical components must be UL approved. The dehydrator should come with a warranty and information for factory repair service. Dehydrators may be made at home. Contact your state or county Cooperative Extension Service for building plans.

The Drying Process

Temperature plays a key role in the drying process. If the temperature is too high, food may case harden; that is, cook and harden on the outside while trapping moisture on the inside. Generally, vegetables are dried at 125°F, fruits at 135°F and meats at 145°F.

There are other variables to consider when timing foods in a dehydrator: the amount of natural water in the food, the size and thickness of the food, the relative humidity of the air and the efficiency of the dehydrator. Vegetables may take as little as 3 to 4 hours or up to 14 hours to dry, depending on the above variables. For example, sliced cultivated mushrooms may dry in an average of 4 to 6 hours, while beets may take as long as 12 to 14 hours to dry.

Determining Weight Of Dehydrated Foods

Testing fruits and vegetables for dryness can be done simply by tasting and touching. The following equation will also be helpful in determining if the correct amount of moisture has been removed from foods.

figure 11	Fresh Weight Vs. Dried Weight		
Fruits		**Vegetables**	
20 Pounds Prepared Produce	Yield Dehydrated Pounds	20 Pounds Prepared Produce	Yield Dehydrated Pounds
Apples	6½	Beans (*Green, Wax*)	3
Cherries (*Sweet*)	7	Carrots	3 to 3½
Peaches	6½ to 7	Corn	6
Pears	6½ to 7	Onions	3
Prune Plums	7½	Peas	5 to 5½
		Squash (*Summer*)	2

1. After peeling, coring, etc., weigh prepared produce. (For example, peeled, cored, sliced apples weigh 10 pounds.)

2. See the recipe for the water content of fruits or vegetables (apples = 84%).

3. The total weight of water equals the weight of prepared fruit multiplied by the percent of water content (10 x 0.84 = 8.4 pounds of water).

4. Most fruits need 80% of water removed; most vegetables need 95% of water removed. To find the weight of water to be removed, multiply the total weight of water by the percent of water to be removed. (For apples, 8.4 x 0.80 = 6.72 pounds of water to remove.)

5. To find how much the produce should weigh after dehydration, subtract the weight of water to be removed from the weight of the fresh product. (For apples, 10 pounds prepared apples - 6.72 pounds of water = 3.28 pounds of dried apples.) In this technique, if one starts out with 10 pounds of prepared apples, the apples will be sufficiently dehydrated when they weigh about 3¼ pounds.

Storage

Any food-safe container that protects from air, moisture, light and insects will extend the shelf life of dried foods. Home canning jars have the advantage of keeping out these spoilers while providing a convenient "see-through" container. Jars should be washed in hot, soapy water (a dish-washer may be used), rinsed, dried and allowed to cool completely before filling. Screw on two-piece caps, label and date the finished product.

Plastic jars with twist-on lids, plastic storage containers with locking lids and vacuum packaging also keep dehydrated foods protected from air, moisture and insects.

Store dried foods in a cool, dry, dark place. The best storage temperature for dehydrated foods is between 50° and 70°F. Most fruits and vegetables can be safely stored from 6 months to 1 year, depending on storage temperature, humidity and storage container. Check dried fruits and vegetables occasionally for moisture. If moisture is apparent, dispose of food.

Rehydrating Dried Foods

Fruits and vegetables can be rehydrated and used like fresh foods for side dishes, salads, etc. Directions for rehydrating fruits and vegetables are given at the beginning of the sections for drying fruits and vegetables (*see page 109 and page 112*). Foods may be rehydrated before use or as a part of the cooking and baking process. Follow individual recipe guidelines for using dehydrated foods in cooking and baking.

Understanding the following points which apply to dehydrated fruits and vegetables will help you achieve successful results when rehydrating foods.

- Vegetables dried to 5% residual moisture take longer to rehydrate than fruit dried to 20% residual moisture content.
- Small or thin pieces of fruits and vegetables rehydrate in less time than large pieces.
- Blanched vegetables rehydrate more quickly than unblanched vegetables.
- Boiling water shortens rehydration time.
- Rehydration is quicker in soft water than in hard water.
- Sugar and salt increase time for food rehydration; add at final 5 minutes for best results.

fruits

Sweet, ripe fruits in their natural state will be sweet and delicious when dried. As a rule, most fruits can be successfully dried. However, a few fruits, such as avocados, citrus fruits and melons, are best if eaten fresh.

Some fruits, such as grapes, plums and blueberries, have a waxy coating or "bloom" that must be "checked" or removed by dipping in boiling water before beginning the drying process. Other fruits, such as peaches, plums and apricots, benefit by using a technique called "popping the backs." That is pushing the peel side inward to expose more of the pulp surface to dry. It may take up to 24 hours to properly dry stone fruit.

Uniformly cutting slices or pieces of fruit will help fruit to dry more evenly. Dried fruit should retain some moisture, about 15 to 20%. To test for dryness, cut a piece in half; no visible moisture should be present. The piece of fruit should be pliable and chewy. Bananas and strawberries should be almost crisp for best protection against mold.

Pack dehydrated fruits in home canning jars, plastic jars, plastic storage containers or vacuum package. Label and date.

Dried fruit is a natural, sweet-tasting snack. However, there may be times when you will want to rehydrate the fruit for eating and serving. Just barely cover the fruit with boiling water; wait 10 minutes; serve immediately or use in a favorite recipe.

Apples

Choose any tart, firm-textured apple. Wash, peel and core apples. Cut into ¼- to ½-inch slices or rings. Pretreat with Fruit-Fresh by dipping. Dry at 130° to 135°F until pliable. Use as a snack, for applesauce or in baked goods, such as pies, cobblers or crisps. Water content 84%.

Apricots

Choose any firm, ripe apricot with a deep-yellow to orange color. Wash, cut in half and remove pits. Pretreat with Fruit-Fresh by dipping, if desired. Dry at 130° to 135°F until pliable with no moisture pockets. Use as a snack, in meat dishes, salads or baked goods. Water content 85%.

Bananas

Choose any large, slightly brown-speckled, yellow variety. Peel and cut into ¼- to ½-inch slices. Pretreat with Fruit-Fresh by dipping, if desired. Dry at 130° to 135°F until pliable to almost crisp. Use in trail mixes, cookies, cakes, breads, on cereal or as a snack. Water content 76%.

Blueberries

Choose large, firm blueberries with deep-blue color. Wash and remove stems. Dip in boiling water 30 seconds to "check" skins. Blueberries dried without boiling first have a puffy appearance. Dry at 130° to 135°F until leathery. Use like raisins in baked goods. Water content 83%.

Cherries

Choose sweet or sour varieties. Wash, cut in half and remove pits. Dry at 165°F 2 to 3 hours; then dry at 135°F until leathery and slightly sticky. Use sweet cherries as a snack or like raisins in baked goods. Use sour varieties in baked goods. Water content: sweet 80%, sour 84%.

Citrus Peel

Choose peels from grapefruit, lemon, lime, orange or tangerine. Do not use fruit labeled "Color Added". Wash well to remove surface dirt and pesticides. Cut a thin layer of peel from fruit, avoiding the bitter, white pith. Dry at 135°F until crisp. Use as a flavoring in baked goods.

Coconuts

Choose fresh coconuts heavy and full of coconut milk. Pierce eyes to remove milk; crack the hard, outer shell with a hammer. Remove coconut meat, discarding dark, outer skin. Grate or thinly slice. Dry at 135°F until crisp. Use in pies, cakes, candy and trail mix. Water content 51%.

Grapes

Home-Dried Raisins

Choose Thompson seedless or red seedless varieties. Wash, remove stems and leave whole. Dip in boiling water 30 to 60 seconds to "check" skins. Dry at 130° to 135°F until pliable with no moisture pockets. Use raisins as a snack or in baked goods. Water content 81%.

Nectarines

Choose bright-looking, plump fruit with an orange-yellow color between red areas. Wash, cut in half and remove pits. Cut into ¼- to ½-inch slices.

Pretreat with Fruit-Fresh by dipping, if desired. Place on drying trays peel-side down. Dry at 130° to 135°F until pliable with no moisture pockets. Use as a snack or in baked goods. Water content 82%.

Peaches

Choose either Clingstone or Freestone varieties. Peaches must be firm and ripe with no green color. Wash peaches; dip in boiling water 1 minute, then dip in cold water to loosen peels. Slip off peels. Remove pits; cut into ½-inch slices or circles. Pretreat with Fruit-Fresh by dipping. Dry at 130° to 135°F until pliable with no moisture pockets. Use as a snack or in baked goods, salads or desserts. Water content 89%.

Pears

Choose any summer or winter variety. Allow pears to ripen at home before drying. Wash, peel and core. Cut into ½-inch slices, quarters or halves. Pretreat with Fruit-Fresh by dipping, if desired. Dry at 130° to 135°F until leathery with no moisture pockets. Use as a snack or in baked goods. Water content 83%.

Pineapples

Choose only fully-ripe pineapples with a yellowish-brown peel. Wash, peel and core pineapple. Cut into ½-inch slices. Dry at 130° to 135°F until leathery but not sticky. Use as a snack or in baked goods and granolas. Water content 86%.

Plums

Choose any variety ripe, sweet plums. Wash, cut in half and remove pits. Cut into ¼- to ½-inch slices. Dry at 130° to 135°F until pliable. Use as a snack, in puddings, muffins or breads. Water content 87%.

Prune Plums

Homemade Prunes

Remember, all prunes are plums, but not all plums can be prunes. Ripe prune plums are slightly soft with a sweet flesh. Wash, cut in half and remove pits. "Pop the back" of fruit to increase surface area (*see page 109*). Dry peel side down at 130° to 135°F until pliable with no moisture pockets. Use in breads, stuffings, salads or as a snack. Water content 79%.

Strawberries

Choose ripe, juicy, red berries. Gently wash. Remove caps. Cut into ½-inch slices. Dry at 130° to 135°F until pliable to almost crisp. Use in puddings, yogurt, desserts or as a snack. Water content 90%.

Note: Strawberries do not rehydrate well.

fruit leathers

Fruit leather is puréed fruit which is dried and rolled into a chewy fruit taffy. It is a delicious, nutritious snack for lunch boxes, after school snacks or to tote along anywhere.

Apples, apricots, berries (all kinds), cherries, nectarines, peaches, pears, pineapple and plums make excellent fruit leathers. Be sure to remove excess seeds from berries. Bananas are wonderful blended with other fruits for a smooth, naturally sweet, finished product. Fresh fruit in

season has the best flavor; however, do not overlook canned or frozen fruits which may be used any time of the year.

Pack dehydrated fruit leather rolls or pieces in home canning jars or vacuum package. Label and date.

Assorted Fruit Leathers

Wash fruit; cut away blemished areas; peel, if necessary; remove pits or seeds. Purée fruit in a blender until smooth. If too thick, thin with a little water or fruit juice. Add 1 tablespoon honey or corn syrup if fruit is too tart, if desired. Spices or flavorings may be added at this time. Fruits that oxidize (apples, nectarines, peaches and pears) should be heated to 190°F and allowed to cool before proceeding. Cover drying trays with a heavy, food-grade plastic wrap or use specifically designed sheets that come with most dehydrators. Spread purée evenly, about ⅛-inch thick in the center to ¼-inch thick at the edges, on dehydrator trays. Dry at 135°F until fruit purée feels pliable and leather-like. Check center to be sure there are no sticky spots. Roll, jelly-roll style, while still warm; cut in pieces and seal securely in plastic wrap. Store fruit leather in home canning jars for long-term storage.

Mango Leather

2 pounds mangoes	1 tablespoon lemon juice
2 tablespoons corn syrup	

Wash mangoes; drain. Peel, pit and dice mangoes. Purée mangoes using a food processor or food mill. Add corn syrup and lemon juice; blend. Spread purée evenly on dehydrator trays to ¼-inch thick. Dry at 135°F until pliable, about 12 to 14 hours. Cut mango leather into 6-inch circles. Place parchment paper or plastic wrap between circles. Pack into a plastic storage container or vacuum package. Label and date.

beef jerky

Jerky is raw meat or fish which is salted or marinated and dried. Although most any type of lean meat (beef, lamb, pork or game) or fish may be used, beef jerky is the easiest to make with the most reliable results. Choose any lean cut of beef. Flank, round or sirloin tip are excellent choices. Rump, if it is lean, is also a good choice. Use only a commercial or homemade electric food dehydrator. Do not attempt to dry meat in the sun due to risk of spoilage and contamination.

Freeze meat slightly to aid in slicing. Cut beef in strips, ½-inch thick, across the grain for a tender, slightly brittle finished product. Cut with the grain for a chewy end product.

The meat must be "cured"; that is, treated in such a way to prevent spoilage. Dry cures are salt and seasonings rubbed on the meat surface. Brine cures are marinades or liquid seasoning mixtures in which the meat is soaked for a period of time. Vacuum packaging sliced meat and marinade will reduce the length of time it takes for the marinade to penetrate the meat. Not only is this method quicker, but it allows the marinade to penetrate deeper, locking in the great taste.

Dry meat in an electric dehydrator at 145°F. If fat droplets appear during the drying process, blot meat with a paper towel. To test a slice of meat, allow to cool. It should bend but not break.

Jerky must be brought to an internal temperature of 160°F just prior to drying or immediately after drying. Two methods are recommended: heat meat strips in marinade before drying by boiling 5 minutes. Or, heat

dehydrated meat strips in an oven at 275°F for 10 minutes after the drying process is completed. Check the internal temperature of the jerky with a prong type meat thermometer to assure it has reached 160°F. Heating strips of meat in a marinade before dehydrating reduces the drying time.

Jerky that has been properly dehydrated and brought to an internal temperature of 160°F can be stored on the shelf. Pack in home canning jars or plastic storage containers. If the jerky is slightly moist after dehydrating, store in the freezer. Check jerky that is stored on the shelf occasionally for indications of moisture and fat weeping from meat tissue. If moisture or fat is apparent, dispose of jerky.

Barbecued Beef Jerky

Yield: about 12 ounces of jerky

3 pounds lean beef (flank, round or sirloin tip)	2 teaspoons dry mustard
1 cup ketchup	1 teaspoon onion powder
½ cup red wine vinegar	1 teaspoon salt
¼ cup brown sugar	¼ teaspoon cracked pepper
2 tablespoons Worcestershire sauce	Dash of hot pepper sauce

Cut beef into strips ½-inch thick. Combine all marinade ingredients in a large, glass baking dish. Add strips of beef; cover and refrigerate overnight. Drain beef slices. Dry in an electric dehydrator at 145°F until pliable. Package in home canning jars, plastic storage containers or vacuum package. Label and date.

Soy Jerky

Yield: about 12 ounces of jerky

3 pounds lean beef (flank, round or sirloin tip)	1 teaspoon onion powder
¾ cup soy sauce	1 clove garlic, crushed
¼ cup Worcestershire sauce	½ teaspoon cracked pepper
¼ cup brown sugar	¼ teaspoon liquid smoke (optional)

Cut beef into strips ½-inch thick. Combine marinade ingredients in a large, glass baking dish. Add strips of beef; cover and refrigerate overnight. Drain beef slices. Dry in an electric dehydrator at 145°F until pliable. Package in home canning jars, plastic storage container or vacuum package. Label and date.

rubs

Dry rubs are used for the intense complement of flavors they impart, and the crusty coating they wrap around a wide variety of meat, poultry, seafood and game. Rubs made fresh surpass the spice blends or seasoning packets available in stores. They are easy to make even if you do not grow all the ingredients in your back yard. However, you can take full advantage of fresh herbs and other edibles you do grow. When purchasing ingredients to fill-in where you do not have your own supply, select whole spices and herbs, grinding them as needed.

Preparing dry rubs takes no more than a few minutes. Ingredients can be crushed with a mortar and pestle, ground in a hand-held grinder or pulsed in a food processor. Be careful when using a food processor that the mixture does not break down too far, causing natural oils to release. If this happens the rub will need to be used quickly because the oils will turn rancid.

Dry rubs store on the shelf for 1 to 3 months, depending on the blend of ingredients. Not all ingredients will age at the same rate, so the flavor of the rub may change the longer it is stored. This is one reason why it is best to prepare small amounts and use them quickly. Rubs are sensitive to light and heat. Keep dry rubs in a home canning jar or plastic storage container and place in a cabinet to protect the rub from light and heat.

The seasoning or flavoring characteristics of a dry rub is great. Only a small amount, 1 tablespoon or less, is needed to season a single fish fillet, chicken breast or steak. Larger cuts of meat or whole portions of poultry and fish use about ¼ cup. Depending on how the dry rub is to be used, there may be some remaining for a second use. To prevent the contamination of remaining rub during initial use, measure only the amount of rub needed for one application in a separate dish.

Rubs are often prepared using fresh ingredients. But many of the same ingredients can be used in their dry state. The time required to air-dry fresh ingredients can be minimized using a dehydrator.

Island Jerk Rub

6 dried habañero peppers	1½ teaspoons ground cinnamon
6 dried scallions	1 teaspoon ground coriander
2 tablespoons whole allspice	1 teaspoon ground nutmeg
1 tablespoon coarse salt	1 teaspoon coarse
2 teaspoons cayenne pepper	ground black pepper

Crush or grind habañero peppers, scallions and whole allspice to a coarse powder. Add remaining ingredients and grind to a uniformly coarse powder. Store in home canning jar or plastic storage container. Label and date.

Recommended Use: Shrimp, chicken breast, pork chops, spareribs and beef or lamb kabobs. Drench meat in a sauce prepared with ⅓ cup red wine vinegar, 2 tablespoons canola oil and 1 tablespoon soy sauce. Apply rub. Let shrimp stand 2 to 4 hours; chicken, beef and lamb cubes 4 to 6 hours; pork 3 to 4 hours and ribs overnight in a cool place. Grill.

Note: When cutting or seeding hot peppers, wear rubber gloves to prevent hands from being burned.

Kitchen Herb Garden Rub

1 cup dried parsley	2 tablespoons dried thyme
½ cup dried oregano	1 tablespoon coarse salt
¼ cup dried rosemary	1 teaspoon coarse ground
2 tablespoons dried tarragon	black pepper

Crush or grind herbs to a coarse powder. Stir in salt and pepper. Store in home canning jar or plastic storage container. Label and date.

Recommended Use: Chicken and fish. Coat meat lightly with olive oil. Apply rub. Let chicken and fish stand 2 to 4 hours in a cool place. Grill.

Lemon-Cumin Spice Rub

¼ cup ground cumin	1 tablespoon ground cinnamon
2 tablespoons grated lemon peel	1 tablespoon coarse ground black pepper
2 tablespoons paprika	
2 tablespoons ground cardamom	1 tablespoon cayenne pepper
	2 tablespoons dried oregano

Crush or grind all ingredients to a coarse powder. Store in home canning jar or plastic storage container. Label and date.

Recommended Use: Shrimp, chicken breast and lamb kabobs. Drench meat in a syrup prepared with 1 tablespoon brown sugar and 2 tablespoons water. Apply rub, using 1 tablespoon for chicken breast and 4 tablespoons for 1 pound of shrimp or lamb cubes. Let shrimp stand 2 to 4 hours; chicken and lamb cubes 4 to 6 hours in a cool place. Grill.

vegetables

Most vegetables, from asparagus to zucchini, can be dehydrated at home. Select garden-fresh, top-quality produce for the best results. Remember, although dried vegetables retain most of their vitamin and mineral content and good flavor, the original quality cannot be improved.

All vegetables require some preparation, such as removing stems, peel or seeds, before drying. Like fruits, uniformly cut slices or pieces result in even drying. Unlike fruits, vegetables are better cut slightly smaller to hasten drying time. Vegetables lose flavor and tenderness if the drying time is prolonged. Drying time varies from about 4 to 14 hours. A temperature of 125°F is recommended for most vegetables. Finished vegetables should contain about 5% moisture. When tested, vegetables should look and feel crisp or brittle.

Vegetables can be eaten dried, but they are usually reconstituted before using. An equal volume of water and vegetables is needed. Boiling water will shorten the rehydration time.

Generally, it takes 15 minutes to 3 hours for reconstituting vegetables, depending on the texture and thickness of the vegetables.

If a vegetable is not listed in the following pages, freezing or canning may be a more suitable method of food preservation.

Pack dehydrated vegetables in home canning jars, plastic storage containers or vacuum package. Label and date.

Asparagus

Choose young, tender stalks. Wash; cut off tough end. Slice into 1-inch pieces. Steam blanch 3 to 4 minutes. Dry at 125°F until brittle. Rehydrate and serve in soups or with seasoned cream sauce. Water content 92%.

Beans—Green Or Wax

Choose any variety with crisp, thick walls and small seeds. Wash; snap off ends; cut diagonally into 1-inch pieces or French cut to expose more surface area. Steam blanch 4 to 6 minutes. Freeze beans 30 minutes to tenderize; dry at 125°F until brittle. Rehydrate and use in casseroles, soups and stews. Water content 90%.

Beets

Choose any variety with deep-red color and smooth skins. Wash; remove all but one inch of stem and tap root. Steam about 30 minutes or until tender. Cool; peel; trim stem and tap root. Cut into ¼-inch slices or dice. Dry at 125°F until leathery. Use in soups or reconstitute as a vegetable. Water content 87%.

Carrots

Choose any deep-orange, mature variety. Wash, trim tops and peel. Slice crosswise or dice. Steam blanch 3 to 4 minutes. Dry at 125°F until almost brittle. Use in soups, stews and carrot cake. Water content 88%.

Corn

Choose any yellow variety with tender, sweet kernels. Husk corn; remove silks and wash. Steam until milk is set. Cool. Carefully cut corn from cob. Dry at 125°F until brittle. Use in soups, chowders, fritters or to make cornmeal. Water content 73%.

Mushrooms

Choose only edible, cultivated mushrooms with small, closed caps. Wash quickly to remove dirt; cut into ¼-inch slices. Dry at 125°F until brittle. Use in soups, sauces and casseroles. Water content 90%.

Okra

Choose any firm pod 2 to 4 inches long. Wash; cut off ends; slice cross-wise ¼-inch thick. Dry at 125°F until leathery. Use in soups and gumbos. Or, rehydrate and bread okra for deep-fat frying . Water content 89%.

Onions And Leeks

Choose red, white or yellow onions; white varieties dry best. Choose leeks about 1- to 1½-inch diameter at bulb end. Trim ends off onions; peel off paper shell; cut into slices ¼-inch thick. Trim root end off leeks; cut white and light green portion into ¼-inch thick slices; discard dark leafy top. Dry at 145°F until crisp. Use in soups, stews, casseroles or use powdered (or flaked) for seasoning. Water content 89%.

Peas

Choose a medium-size pea. Shell and wash peas. Steam blanch 3 minutes. Dry at 125°F until brittle. Use in soups, stews or rehydrate for other uses. Water content 78%.

Peppers—Hot

Choose any hot variety. Wash; cut into pieces about ¼- to 1-inch thick. Dry at 125°F until crisp. Crush or grind and use as a seasoning in soups, stews, casseroles and Mexican foods. Water content 93%.

Note: When cutting or seeding hot peppers, wear rubber gloves to prevent hands from being burned.

Peppers—Sweet

Choose any well-shaped sweet pepper. Wash; remove stems and seeds; dice. Dry at 125°F until leathery. Use to season a variety of foods. Water content 93%.

Popcorn

Choose varieties specifically grown for popping. Leave kernels on cob until dried. Dry at 130°F until shriveled. Test a few kernels to see if they pop. Popcorn should have a dehydrated moisture content of 10%. Water content 73%.

Potatoes—Sweet And Yams

Choose thick, orange potatoes free from decay and blemishes. Wash, peel and cut into ¼-inch slices. Steam blanch 3 minutes. Dry at 125°F until brittle. Use to make candied yams or bake in pies and breads. Water content 71%.

Potatoes—White Or Irish

Choose any white variety. Wash well to remove dirt. Peel. Cut into slices ¼-inch thick. Steam blanch 5 to 6 minutes. Rinse well in cold water to remove starch. Dry at 125°F until crisp. Use in soups, casseroles and potato dishes. Water content 80%.

Pumpkin

Choose a cooking variety. Wash, peel and remove fibers and seeds. Cut into small, thin strips. Steam blanch 2 to 3 minutes or until tender. Dry at 125°F until brittle. Use in pies and baked goods. Water content 90%.

Tomatoes

Choose paste-type varieties. Wash; dip in boiling water 30 seconds; then dip in cold water to remove skins. Core. Cut into slices ¼-inch thick. Dry at 145°F until crisp. Use in soups, sauces or combined with other vegetables for flavor. Can be powdered and used to make tomato sauces, paste or ketchup. Water content 94%.

Turnips And Rutabagas

Choose firm, round turnips and rutabagas. Wash, remove tops and peel. Cut into slices ¼- to ½-inch thick. Steam blanch 3 to 5 minutes. Dry at 125°F until brittle. Use in soups or with potatoes. Thinly sliced turnip chips are an excellent snack. Water content: turnips 92%, rutabagas 87%.

Zucchini

Choose young, slender zucchini. Wash zucchini. Cut into ¼-inch slices or ⅛-inch slices for chips. Dry at 125°F until brittle. Use in soups and casseroles. Sprinkle zucchini chips with seasoned salt and serve with dips. Water content 94%.

cooking with
dehydrated foods

Many dehydrated foods are excellent to eat in their dried form, while others require reconstitution or rehydration. In some cases this is done in the cooking process of the recipes you choose. In others, the dried fruits, vegetables or meats are reconstituted before they are added to recipes for cooking and baking. Using these delicious recipes, you will discover that dehydration is a tasty, simple and practical method of food preservation.

Apricot Lite Jam

Yield: about 6 half-pints

2 cups dried apricots
1½ cups crushed pineapple, unsweetened (if using canned, drain)
½ cup chopped orange pulp (about 1 large)
2 tablespoons lemon juice
3½ cups sugar

Cover apricots with cold water and let soak overnight. Simmer apricots in soaking water, uncovered, until tender. Mash apricots with a potato masher or in a food processor. Add pineapple, orange pulp, lemon juice and sugar to apricot mixture. Simmer until sugar has dissolved, stirring frequently; then, cook over high heat until thick, about 20 to 30 minutes. Skim foam if necessary. Ladle hot jam into hot jars, leaving ¼-inch headspace. Adjust two-piece caps. Process 10 minutes in a boiling-water canner.

Banana Nut Bread

Makes one 9-inch loaf

1 cup dried banana chips or pieces	2/3 cup sugar
1 cup water	1/3 cup shortening
1¾ cups flour	2 eggs, slightly beaten
2¼ teaspoons baking powder	½ cup chopped pecans or walnuts
½ teaspoon salt	

Rehydrate bananas in 1 cup water. Let stand 1 hour. Grease a 9 x 5 x 3-inch loaf pan. Sift together flour, baking powder and salt. Cream sugar and shortening. Add dry ingredients to sugar mixture. Stir in bananas, eggs and nuts until blended. Pour batter into greased pan. Bake at 350°F for 1 hour or until done. Cool.

Dried Apple Snacks

Makes about 4 cups

3½ pounds apples, peeled, cored and sliced	2 cups granulated sugar
	1 cup brown sugar
Ball Fruit-Fresh Produce Protector	2 teaspoons cinnamon

Pretreat apples with Fruit-Fresh by dipping *(see page 108)*. In a large bowl, combine sugars and cinnamon. Drain apples. Toss apples in sugar mixture. Dry at 130°F for 21 hours or until pliable.

Note: Apples must be turned halfway through the drying process.

Granola

Makes about 8 cups

4 cups regular or quick oats	1 teaspoon cinnamon
½ cup wheat germ	½ teaspoon salt
1 cup coconut	¾ cup vegetable oil
1 cup slivered almonds	½ cup honey
1 cup sunflower seeds	1 teaspoon vanilla
½ cup brown sugar	1 cup raisins

Combine all ingredients, except raisins; mix until well blended. Spread on a shallow baking sheet and bake at 300°F for 25 to 30 minutes, stirring every 10 minutes. Mixture may also be dried in an electric dehydrator at 145°F about 3 hours or until mixture is crunchy. Stir in raisins. Cool.

Peach And Pineapple Jam

Yield: about 6 half-pints

1 pound dried peaches	½ cup chopped orange pulp (about 1 large)
Peel of ½ orange	
2½ cups water	½ teaspoon ginger
3½ cups sugar	¼ teaspoon salt
1½ cups crushed pineapple with juice	

Rinse, drain and cut peaches into small pieces. Cut orange peel into 3 pieces. Combine peaches and orange peel in a medium bowl. Cover fruit and peel with water; let stand overnight. Put fruit mixture in a large saucepot. Add the remaining ingredients and bring the mixture to a rolling boil, stirring occasionally until mixture thickens. Discard orange peel. Skim foam if necessary. Ladle hot jam into hot jars, leaving ¼-inch headspace. Adjust two-piece caps. Process 10 minutes in a boiling-water canner.

Trail Mix

Makes 4½ cups

½ cup each: almonds, dried apples, dried apricots, dried banana chips, coconut flakes, dried pears, dried pineapple, raisins and sunflower seeds.

Cut fruit into ½-inch pieces. Combine all ingredients; mix well.

Vegetable Beef Soup

Makes 8 servings

1 large soup bone with meat or 2 (10¾-ounce) cans beef broth	2 cups boiling water
	1 cup tomato purée, sauce or whole tomatoes, crushed
Water	1 beef bouillon cube
2 cups dried mixed vegetables (carrots, peas, corn, potatoes, green beans, onions, etc.)	1 tablespoon parsley
	1 teaspoon salt
	¼ teaspoon pepper
	¼ cup rice, barley or soup pasta

Cover soup bone with water; bring to a boil. Reduce heat and simmer, covered, 1 to 2 hours. Meanwhile, rehydrate vegetables in 2 cups boiling water. Let stand about 2 hours. Remove soup bone; cut off meat; set aside. Measure 3 to 4 cups stock or use canned broth. Combine beef stock, meat pieces, tomato purée, bouillon cube and seasonings; bring to a boil. Reduce heat and simmer 30 minutes. Add reconstituted vegetables and rice, barley or soup pasta. More water may be added if soup is too thick. Simmer about 1 hour or until vegetables are tender.

featured prepared recipe

White Bean-Chicken Soup

Makes about 8 servings

2 cups (about 1 pound) dried navy beans	2 tablespoons minced flat leaf parsley
Water	2 sprigs fresh thyme
8 cups Chicken Stock *(recipe on page 63)*	1 sprig fresh rosemary
	1 bay leaf
1 cup diced butternut squash	1½ cups diced white meat chicken
½ cup dried sliced leeks *(recipe on page 113)*	1 cup diced plum tomatoes
	1 tablespoon salt
½ cup dried sliced mushrooms *(recipe on page 113)*	½ teaspoon coarsely ground black pepper
½ cup dried sliced zucchini *(recipe on page 113)*	

Put beans in a large stockpot; add water to cover by two inches. Bring beans to a boil; boil 2 minutes. Remove from heat and let beans soak for 1 hour. Drain. Add chicken stock to beans and cook 1 hour or until beans are tender. Stir in squash, leeks, mushrooms, and zucchini. Add parsley, thyme, rosemary and bay leaf. Cook mixture over medium heat until dried vegetables are reconstituted, about 1 hour. Add chicken, tomatoes, salt and pepper. Continue cooking for 30 minutes. Remove whole herbs.

dehydrating apples step-by-step

1. Read recipe instructions; assemble equipment and ingredients before starting. Follow guidelines for recipe preparation, drying and storage. Do not make changes in recommended guidelines.

2. A commercial or homemade electric dehydrator is the best method for drying food. An electric dehydrator yields the most reliable and consistent results.

3. Select fresh, high-quality, fully-ripe apples for drying. Wash, peel and core apples. Cut into uniform ¼- to ½-inch rings or slices.

4. To prevent darkening, pretreat apple rings or slices by dipping into an antioxidant solution. Use 2 tablespoons Fruit-Fresh Produce Protector (*see page 9*) and 2 quarts water. Do not allow apples to remain in dipping solution more than 10 minutes. Drain before drying.

5. Arrange apple rings or slices evenly on dehydrator trays, allowing space between pieces for air circulation. Dry at 130° to 135°F until pliable. Drying time will vary depending on the moisture content of the apples, quality of the apples, volume being dried at one time, method of drying and the climate.

6. Store dehydrated apples in an airtight, moisture-proof container. Glass home canning jars and plastic jars make excellent storage containers. Store in a cool, dry, dark place. Cooler temperatures, 50° to 70°F, will help prolong shelf life. Most fruits and vegetables will keep 6 months to 1 year.

7. Follow recipe guidelines when rehydrating fruits and vegetables. To rehydrate apples, cover apple rings or slices with boiling water; let stand 10 minutes or until fully rehydrated. Use as fresh apples.

home canning planning guide

Seasonal availability is dependent on growing conditions and location within a region. Weight of purchase unit may vary based on individual state standards. The actual weight or number needed to yield one quart jar is an approximate amount and may vary based on size of produce, recipe preparation and cooking method.

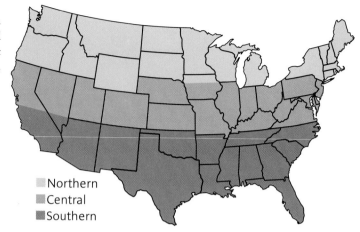

■ Northern
■ Central
■ Southern

Fresh Produce	Peak Season Northern	Peak Season Central	Peak Season Southern	Purchase Unit	Purchase Weight	Number Per Pound	Pounds Per Quart
Vegetables							
Beets	July-November	May-November	April-November	Topped, Sack	25 lbs	5-6 Medium	2-3½
Cabbage	July-November	June-November	January-April	Sack	50 lbs	⅓ Head	2½-3
Carrots	July-November	May-November	Year Round	Sack	50 lbs	5-6 Medium	2-3
Cucumbers, Pickling	July-September	July-October	March-November	Crate	55 lbs	6-7 Medium	1½-2
Green Beans	July-September	June-October	Year Round	Bushel	28-32 lbs		1½-2½
Green Peas	June-September	May-August	Year Round	In Shell, Bushel	28-32 lbs		3-6
Lima Beans	August-September	June-October	Year Round	In Shell, Bushel	28-32 lbs		3-5
Okra	June-September	June-October	May-October	Carton	18 lbs	50 Small	1½-2
Summer Squash	June-September	June-October	February-October	Box	24 lbs	3 Medium	2
Sweet Corn	July-September	June-October	April-November	Carton	50 lbs	3 Medium	3-6
Sweet Potatoes	August-November	September-October	July-November	Carton	40 lbs	3 Medium	2-3
White Potatoes	June-December	June-December	Year Round	Sack	100 lbs	3 Medium	2
Fruits							
Apples	June-December	June-November	May-November	Bushel	48-50 lbs	4 Medium	2½-3
Apricots	July-September	June-August	May-August	Lug	24 lbs	12-13 Medium	2-2½
Berries	June-October	June-October	May-October	12, ½ Pint	6 lbs	2 Cups	1½-3
Cherries	June-August	May-August	May-August	Lug	18 lbs	3 Cups	2-2½
Figs	Market Availability	Market Availability	June-October	Single Layer Flat	6 lbs	12-13 Small	2½
Grapes	September-October	July-October	June-November	Lug	22-23 lbs	3 Cups	2
Nectarines	Market Availability	Market Availability	April-October	Lug	22 lbs	3 Medium	2-2½
Peaches	July-September	June-October	April-September	Two-Layer Carton	22 lbs	4 Medium	2-3
Pears	August-October	August-October	April-November	Carton	36 lbs	3 Medium	2-3
Plums	August-October	July-September	May-August	½ Carton	28 lbs	9 Medium	1½-2½
Strawberries	June-August	May-September	January-October	12, Pint	12 lbs	25 Medium	2½-3
Tomatoes	July-October	May-October	January-December	Two-Layer Flat	20 lbs	3-4 Medium	2½-3½

equivalents guide

Weight & Measure Equivalents

Dry Measure

3 teaspoons = 1 tablespoon

4 tablespoons = ¼ cup

5 tablespoons + 1 teaspoon = ⅓ cup

8 tablespoons = ½ cup

10 tablespoons + 2 teaspoons = ⅔ cup

12 tablespoons = ¾ cup

16 tablespoons = 1 cup

1 cup = ½ pint

2 cups = 1 pint

4 cups or 2 pints = 1 quart

4 pints or 2 quarts = ½ gallon

4 quarts or 2 half-gallons = 1 gallon

8 quarts = 1 peck

4 pecks = 1 bushel

Liquid Measure

1 fluid ounce = 2 tablespoons or ⅛ cup

2 fluid ounces = 4 tablespoons or ¼ cup

4 fluid ounces = 8 tablespoons or ½ cup

6 fluid ounces = 12 tablespoons or ¾ cup

8 fluid ounces = 16 tablespoons or 1 cup

16 fluid ounces = 2 cups or 1 pint

32 fluid ounces = 2 pints or 1 quart

64 fluid ounces = 2 quarts or ½ gallon

Dry Weight

4 ounces = ¼ pound

8 ounces = ½ pound

16 ounces = 1 pound

Helpful To Know Equivalents

Ascorbic Acid (Vitamin C)

1 teaspooon powdered = 3,000 mg tablet

Dill

1 head fresh dill = 2 teaspoons dill seed

Garlic

1 small clove = ½ teaspoon minced

1 medium clove = 1 teaspoon minced

Lemon

1 medium = 2-3 tablespoons juice

5-6 medium = 1 cup juice

1 medium = 2 tablespoons grated rind

Orange

1 medium = 5-6 tablespoons juice

3-4 medium = 1 cup juice

1 medium = 2 tablespoons grated rind

Sugar

5 pounds granulated = about 11¾ cups

1 pound brown, packed = about 2¼ cups

Tomatoes

add 1 teaspoon sugar to off-set acidity
— For —
each tablespoon lemon juice or vinegar added per jar

How To Measure Ball RealFruit Pectin

Measurements

6 tablespoons Ball RealFruit Classic Pectin = 1 (1.75 oz) package Ball original pectin

2 (3 oz) pouches Ball RealFruit Liquid Pectin = 2 (3 oz) pouches Ball liquid pectin

3 tablespoons Ball RealFruit Low or No-Sugar Needed Pectin = 1 (1.75 oz) package Ball no-sugar needed pectin

5 tablespoons Ball RealFruit Instant Pectin = 1 (1.59 oz) package Ball freezer jam pectin

the problem solver

The general information in Learning About Canning (*see pages 2-13*) and the tested recipes in this book will guide you to successful home canning results. However, should you experience a problem, refer to the list below. It identifies some conditions which might occur in home canned foods, the causes for them and how they can be remedied. Please review the cause and prevention for your particular problem and make the necessary adjustments in your canning procedures. If the condition of any home canned food indicates spoilage, dispose of it in a manner that no human or animal will come in contact with the product (*see page 122*).

Condition*	Cause	Prevention
Food darkens in top of jar.	1. Liquid did not cover food product.	1. Completely cover food product with brine, syrup, juice or water before adjusting two-piece cap.
	2. Food not processed long enough to inactivate enzymes.	2. Process each food for recommended length of time.
	3. Manner of packing and processing did not expel enough air.	3. Use hot pack when indicated in the recipe.
	4. Air was sealed in the jar either because headspace was too large or air bubbles were not removed.	4. Use headspace recommended in recipe. Slide a nonmetallic spatula between food and jar; press back gently on the food to release trapped air.
Fruit darkens after removed from jar.	Fruit has not been processed long enough to inactivate enzymes.	Process each fruit by recommended method and for recommended length of time. Time is counted when water reaches a rolling boil in the boiling-water canner.
Corn turns brown after processing.	1. Variety of corn was not suitable for canning or corn was not harvested at the correct time.	1. Select only varieties of corn recommended for preserving and choose ears-of-corn with plump, shiny kernels filled with milk.
	2. Liquid did not cover corn.	2. Cover corn with liquid before adjusting two-piece cap.
	3. Jars were processed at too high a temperature.	3. Keep pressure in canner at recommended pounds; dial gauge may be faulty and must be checked.
Pink, red, blue or purple color in canned apples, pears, peaches and quinces.	A natural chemical change which occurs in cooking the fruit.	None.
Some foods become black, brown or gray.	Natural chemical substances (tannins, sulfur compounds and acids) in food react with minerals in water or with metal utensils used in preparing the food.	Use soft water. Avoid using brass, copper, iron, aluminum, zinc or chipped enamelware and utensils from which tin plate is worn.
Crystals in grape products.	Formed by tartaric acid which is naturally found in grapes.	Grape juice should stand overnight after straining; ladle juice from container so as not to disturb sediment that has settled to the bottom; strain again.
White crystals in canned spinach.	Calcium and oxalic acid in spinach combine to form harmless calcium oxalate.	None.

Condition*	Cause	Prevention
White sediment in bottom of jar of vegetables. *(If sediment denotes spoilage, do not use.)*	1. Starch from the food. 2. Minerals in water used. 3. Bacterial spoilage; liquid is usually murky and food is soft. *(Do not use.)*	1. None. 2. Use soft water. 3. Process each food by recommended method and for recommended length of time.
Fruit floats in jar.	Fruit is lighter than the syrup.	Use firm, ripe fruit. Heat fruit before packing. Use a light to medium syrup. Pack fruit as closely as possible without crushing.
Cloudy liquid. *(If cloudiness denotes spoilage, do not use.)*	1. Food spoilage from underprocessing. 2. Minerals in water. 3. Starch in vegetables. 4. Fillers in table salt.	1. Process each food by recommended method and for recommended length of time. 2. Use soft water. 3. None. 4. Use canning and pickling salt or a salt without additives.
Jar seals, then comes unsealed. *(Do not use.)*	1. Spoilage from underprocessing or not processing the food. 2. Particles of food left on the sealing surface. 3. Crack or chip in jar rim. 4. Incorrect headspace used. 5. Air bubbles not removed before adjusting two-piece cap.	1. Process each food by recommended method and for recommended length of time. 2. Wipe jar rim and threads of the jar before adjusting two-piece cap. 3. Check jars: discard ones unsuitable for canning. 4. Use recommended headspace in recipe *(see page 11).* 5. Slide a nonmetallic spatula between food and jar; press back gently on food to release trapped air.
Loss of liquid during processing. *(Do not open jar to replace liquid.)*	1. Food not heated before packing into jars. 2. Food packed too tightly. 3. Air bubbles not removed before adjusting two-piece cap. 4. Pressure canner not operated correctly. 5. Jars not covered with water in boiling-water canner. 6. Starchy foods absorbed liquid.	1. Use hot pack method. 2. Pack food loosely. 3. Slide a nonmetallic spatula between food and jar; press back gently on food to release trapped air. 4. Pressure should not be allowed to fluctuate during processing time. Allow pressure to drop to zero naturally. Remove gauge or open petcock. Allow canner to continue cooling for 10 minutes before opening lid. 5. Jars must be covered with water by 1 to 2 inches throughout the processing period. 6. None.
Jar of food fails to seal. *(Reprocess unspoiled food within 24 hours using a new lid and processing for the full time. Or, refrigerate food and use within a few days.)*	Many factors can contribute to seal failure: not preparing lids correctly, improper adjustment of caps, food particles on jar rim, not processing food or underprocessing food.	Carefully follow instructions for using home canning jars and two-piece caps and follow correct processing methods and times for the recipe. Refer to Learning About Canning *(see pages 2-13).*
Hollow pickles.	Faulty growth of cucumbers.	None. Hollow cucumbers are best if used for relish. They can be identified during cleaning, as hollow cucumbers will float in water.
Black spots on underside of metal lid.	Natural compounds in some foods cause a brown or black deposit on the underside of the lid. This deposit is harmless and does not mean the food is unsafe to eat.	None.
White sediment in bottom of jar of pickles. *(If spoilage is evident, do not use.)*	1. Harmless yeasts have grown on the surface and then settled. 2. Additives in salt.	1. None. The presence of a small amount of white sediment is normal. 2. Use canning and pickling salt or a salt without additives.

*Product usable unless spoilage is indicated.

Condition*	Cause	Prevention
Shriveled pickles.	1. Too much salt, sugar or vinegar was added to the cucumbers at one time. 2. Whole pickles were not pricked before canning. 3. Cucumbers had a wax coating that prevented the brine from penetrating the peel.	1. Gradually add salt, sugar or vinegar until the full amount has been incorporated. 2. Prick whole pickles before canning to allow the brine to saturate and plump the flesh of the cucumber. 3. Use unwaxed pickling cucumbers.
Soft or slippery pickles. *(If spoilage is evident, do not use.)*	1. Blossom end was not removed from cucumber. 2. Brine or vinegar was too weak. 3. Scum was not removed daily from top of brine. 4. Pickles not completely covered with brine. 5. Pickles were underprocessed.	1. Cut ¹⁄₁₆-inch off blossom end of cucumber before pickling. 2. Use pure granulated salt or canning and pickling salt, 5 percent acidity vinegar and a tested recipe. 3. Completely remove scum daily during the brining process. 4. Pickles must be completely covered with liquid during fermentation and in the home canning jar. 5. Process all pickled foods in a boiling-water canner.
Darkened and discolored pickles.	1. Minerals present in hard water used in making the pickles. 2. Brass, iron, copper, aluminum or zinc utensils were used in making the pickles. 3. Ground spices used. 4. Whole spices left in jars of pickles.	1. Use soft water. 2. Use enamelware, glass, stainless-steel or stoneware utensils. 3. Use whole spices. 4. Whole cloves, cinnamon sticks and other whole spices used for flavoring the pickling liquid should be removed before canning.
Soft spread is tough or stiff.	1. Too much natural pectin in fruit. 2. Soft spread was cooked too long. 3. Too much sugar used.	1. Use fruit that is fully ripe. 2. When commercial pectin is not added, use Gelling Test (*see page 29*). 3. If commercial pectin is not used, ¾ to 1 cup sugar for each cup of juice or fruit should be adequate. Use standard dry measuring cups and level sugar even with the top edge of the cup.
Soft spread ferments. *(Do not use.)*	Soft spread was not brought to the correct temperature before filling jars and/or was underprocessed, preventing all spoilage microorganisms such as yeasts from being destroyed.	Bring soft spread to a rolling boil when using commercial pectin or 220°F when preparing a recipe without added pectin. Fill jars and adjust two-piece caps one at a time. Process in a boiling-water canner. Refer to recipe for correct processing time.
Soft spread contains glass-like particles.	1. Too much sugar was used. 2. The mixture may have been undercooked. 3. The mixture may have been cooked too slowly or too long. 4. Undissolved sugar that was sticking to the pan washed into the soft spread as it was poured. 5. If jelly is grape, the crystals may be tartaric acid, the natural substance in grapes from which cream of tartar is made.	1. Follow instructions for Soft Spreads (*see pages 26-43*). 2. Too short a cooking time results in sugar not dissolving completely and not mixing thoroughly with the juice or fruit. 3. Long, slow cooking results in too much evaporation of the water content of the fruit. 4. Carefully wipe side of pan free of sugar crystals with a damp cloth before filling jars. Ladle soft spread into jars instead of pouring. 5. Allow juice to stand in the refrigerator 12 to 24 hours. Ladle juice from bowl, being careful not to disturb sediment that may have settled in the bottom, and strain through a damp jelly bag or several layers of cheesecloth.

Condition*	Cause	Prevention
Soft spread "weeps".	1. Syneresis or "weeping" occurs in quick-setting soft spreads and is due to the quantity of acid and quality of pectin in the fruit. 2. Storage conditions were not ideal.	1. None. 2. Store soft spread in a dry, dark place between 50° and 70°F.
Soft spread made with added pectin is too soft. (See page 122 for Remake Instructions.)	1. Proportions of sugar, juice or fruit, acid and pectin were not in balance. 2. Too large a batch was made at one time. 3. Fruit used was too ripe. 4. Soft spread was not boiled at a "rolling boil" for the time indicated in the recipe. 5. The wrong type of pectin was used. 6. The wrong amount of pectin was used.	1. Follow instructions for Soft Spreads (see pages 26-43). 2. Use no more than 4 to 6 cups of juice or fruit in each batch. Never "double batch" the recipe. 3. Fruit selected should include some fruit that is slightly under-ripe (but not green) along with some fruit that is fully-ripe. 4. Soft spread must be brought to a hard boil, one that cannot be stirred down, and boiled hard for the length of time indicated in the recipe. 5. Classic, liquid, low or no-sugar needed and instant pectin are not interchangeable. Use only the type of pectin indicated in the recipe. 6. Package weight for different brands of commercial pectin is not uniform. Use only the amount of pectin called for in the recipe.
Soft spread made without added pectin is too soft. (See page 122 for Remake Instructions.)	1. Proportions of sugar, juice or fruit, acid and pectin were not in balance. 2. Too large a batch was made at one time. 3. Fruit used was too ripe. 4. Soft spread was not boiled to the correct temperature.	1. Follow instructions for Soft Spreads (see pages 26-43). 2. Use no more than 4 to 6 cups of juice or fruit in each batch. Never "double batch" the recipe. 3. Fruit selected should include some fruit that is slightly under-ripe (but not green) along with some fruit that is fully-ripe. 4. Use Gelling Test (see page 29).
Soft spread is cloudy.	1. Fruit used was too green. 2. Fruit may have been cooked too long before straining. 3. Some fruit pulp may have been extracted when juice was squeezed from fruit. 4. Soft spread was ladled into jars too slowly. 5. Soft spread mixture was allowed to stand before it was ladled into the jars.	1. Fruit should be firm and ripe. 2. Fruit should be cooked only until it is tender. 3. To obtain the clearest jelly possible, let juice drain through a damp jelly bag or several layers of cheesecloth. Do not squeeze jelly bag. 4. Work quickly to fill jars before soft spread starts to gel. 5. When cooking period is complete, ladle soft spread into jars and process immediately.
Bubbles in soft spread. (If bubbles denote spoilage, do not use.)	1. If bubbles are moving when the jar is stationary, the soft spread is spoiling. 2. If bubbles are not moving when the jar is stationary, air was trapped in the soft spread as it gelled.	1. Process all soft spreads in a boiling-water canner for the time indicated in the recipe. 2. Ladle soft spread quickly into the jar, holding ladle near the rim of the jar or funnel.
Soft spread molds. (Do not use.)	1. Headspace was too great. 2. Soft spread was not processed long enough to destroy molds, allowing them to grow on the surface of the soft spread.	1. Leave ¼-inch headspace. 2. Process soft spread in a boiling-water canner for the time indicated in the recipe.

*Product usable unless spoilage is indicated.

Remake Instructions
For Cooked Soft Spreads

Not all soft spread recipes set within 24 hours. If the soft spread in question was properly processed in a boiling-water canner, and the jar is vacuum sealed, it is safe to wait to determine if the product will gel. If after two weeks the product does not have a good set, it can be re-cooked in order to achieve a firmer set.

Classic Pectin

Measure the unset soft spread to be re-cooked. Re-cook no more than 2 quarts (8 cups) at one time. For each cup of unset soft spread, measure 1½ teaspoons classic pectin, 1 tablespoon water and 2 tablespoons sugar; set sugar aside. Combine pectin and water in a large saucepot and bring to a boil over medium-high heat, stirring constantly to prevent scorching. Add the unset soft spread and sugar, stirring to blend evenly. Bring to a boil, stirring constantly. Boil hard for 30 seconds. Remove from heat. Skim foam if necessary. Ladle hot soft spread into hot jars, leaving ¼-inch headspace. Adjust new lids and bands onto jars. Process in a boiling-water canner for the full length of time indicated in the original recipe.

Liquid Pectin

Measure the unset soft spread to be re-cooked. Re-cook no more than 2 quarts (8 cups) at one time. For each cup of unset soft spread, measure 3 tablespoons sugar, 1½ teaspoons lemon juice and 1½ teaspoons liquid pectin. Bring soft spread to a boil over medium-high heat in a large saucepot, stirring constantly. Quickly stir in sugar, lemon juice and liquid pectin. Return to a rolling boil. Boil hard for 1 minute, stirring constantly. Remove from heat. Skim foam if necessary. Ladle hot soft spread into hot jars, leaving ¼-inch headspace. Adjust new lids and bands onto jars. Process in a boiling-water canner for the full length of time indicated in the original recipe.

Low or No-Sugar Needed Pectin

Measure the unset soft spread to be re-cooked. Re-cook only one quart (4 cups) at one time. For each quart of unset soft spread, measure 4 teaspoons low or no-sugar needed pectin and ¼ cup water. Bring pectin and water to a boil in a saucepot, stirring constantly to prevent scorching. Add the unset soft spread, stirring to blend evenly. Boil hard for 30 seconds, stirring constantly. Remove from heat. Skim foam if necessary. Ladle hot soft spread into hot jars, leaving ¼-inch headspace. Adjust new lids and bands onto jars. Process in a boiling-water canner for the full length of time indicated in the original recipe.

Without Added Pectin

Boil the unset soft spread to the temperature indicated in the original recipe or to the gelling point if a temperature is not given. (see page 29). Ladle hot soft spread into hot jars, leaving ¼-inch headspace. Adjust new lids and bands onto jars. Process in a boiling-water canner for the full length of time indicated in the original recipe.

Identifying And Disposing
Of Spoiled Foods

Examine each jar carefully before using it to ensure a vacuum seal is present. Do not use any product that shows signs of spoilage or the lid is unsealed. Spoilage produces gases that cause the lids to swell and/or break the seal. Products sealed with lids that do not require a can opener to pry them off must not be used. Also, visually examine jars for other signs of spoilage which might be present. Indications that the food has spoiled include:

- Broken Seals
- Mold
- Gassiness
- Cloudiness
- Spurting Liquid
- Seepage
- Yeast Growth
- Fermentation
- Slime
- Disagreeable Odors

Home canned food that shows signs of spoilage must be discarded in a manner that no human or animal will come in contact with the product. Jars that are suspected of containing spoiled low-acid or tomato products must be handled carefully. Spoiled vegetables, meats, poultry, seafoods and tomato products must be detoxified to prevent any possible contamination from botulin that could be present. To detoxify the product, jar, lid and band, place all items into a deep saucepot. It is not necessary to remove the contents from the jar. Carefully cover all items with 1 to 2 inches of water. Cover the saucepot. Bring the water to a boil and boil 30 minutes, being careful not to splash water or food product outside the saucepot. Allow the contents of the saucepot to cool. Discard all contents of the saucepot.

A solution of chlorine bleach and water, 1 part chlorine bleach to 5 parts water, can be used to clean surfaces that come in contact with suspect product. Allow the cleaning solution to stand for 5 minutes before rinsing. Dispose of dishcloths and sponges used in the detoxifying process.

glossary
of food preservation terms

Altitude — The vertical elevation (distance) of a location above sea level.

Antioxidant — An agent, such as lemon juice, ascorbic acid or a blend of ascorbic and citric acids, that inhibits oxidation and controls discoloration of light color fruits and vegetables.

Ascorbic Acid — White, crystalline Vitamin C found in some fruits and vegetables. A commercially-available product used to control discoloration of light color fruits and vegetables.

Bacteria — Microorganisms, some of which are harmful, found in the soil, water and air around us. Some bacteria thrive in conditions common in low-acid canned food and produce toxins that must be destroyed by heating to 240°F for a specified time. For this reason, low-acid foods must be processed in a steam-pressure canner.

Band — *See Metal Band.*

Blanch — To loosen the skin of fruits and vegetables by dipping in boiling water. Also, to dip vegetables in boiling water or steam to slow the action of enzymes.

Boil — Water or food heated to 212°F at sea level. Boiling water, when referring to the boiling-water canner, means a rolling boil for the entire processing time.

Boiling-Water Canner — A kettle large enough to completely immerse and fully surround canning jars and two-piece caps with water. The boiling-water canner is used for processing high-acid foods.

Botulism — A poisoning caused by a toxin produced by the spores of *Clostridium botulinum*. The spores are usually present in dust, wind and soil clinging to raw food. The spores can grow in any tightly sealed jar of low-acid food that has not been processed correctly. The spores belong to a species of bacteria which cannot grow in the presence of air, and they do not normally thrive in high-acid foods. Using the correct processing temperature and time to preserve low-acid foods will destroy toxin-producing spores.

Cap — Two-piece vacuum closure for sealing home canning jars. The set consists of a metal band and a flat metal lid. The lid has a flanged edge and sealing compound.

Case Harden — When dehydrating food, the formation of a hard shell on the outside of produce that traps moisture inside and causes deterioration.

Citric Acid — An acid derived from citrus fruits, such as lemons and limes, used with ascorbic acid as an antioxidant to control discoloration of fruits.

Cool Place — Term used when referring to a storage place for home canned foods. The ideal temperature is 50° to 70°F.

Dehydration *(or drying)* — The process of removing water from food.

Dry Pack — When freezing food, to pack without added liquid or sugar.

Enzyme — A protein that functions as a catalyst in organisms. In food, enzymes start the process of decomposition, changing the flavor, texture and color. Enzyme action slows down in frozen food, increases quickly at temperatures between 85° and 120°F and stops at temperatures above 140°F. The preservation methods for canning and freezing neutralize the action of enzymes.

Exhausting — *See Venting.*

Fermentation — Caused by yeasts which have not been destroyed during processing of canned food. With the exception of some pickles, fermented canned food should not be used.

Flash Freezing —Accelerated method of freezing foods often done at home by placing individual items on a baking sheet for quicker freezing before storing food in freezer bags, plastic freezer boxes, can-or-freeze jars or vacuum packages.

Freezer Burn — Dehydration of improperly packed foods for freezing which leads to loss of flavor, texture and color.

Headspace — An area left unfilled between the top of the food in a home canning jar or freezer container and the rim of the jar or freezer container.

High-Acid Food — Foods which normally contain enough natural acid to result in a pH of 4.6 or less and foods which may contain very little natural acid but have a sufficient amount of vinegar or lemon juice added to them to be treated as high-acid foods. High-acid foods may be safely processed in a boiling-water canner at 212°F *(see page 5 for Altitude Chart).*

Home Canning — Preserving fresh or prepared foods in glass home canning jars that seal with two-piece vacuum caps using a heat process to destroy microorganisms that cause spoilage.

Hot Pack — Filling jars with precooked, hot food prior to processing. Preferred method when using firm food. This method permits a tighter pack, reduces floating and requires fewer jars.

Jar — A home canning jar, sometimes called a Mason jar, designed to withstand repeated use and heat processing in the boiling-water and pressure canners.

Lid — The flat metal disc with sealing compound. Used in combination with a metal band for vacuum sealing home canning jars.

Low-Acid Food — Foods which contain little natural acid and have a pH greater than 4.6. Bacteria thrive in low-acid foods. They can only be destroyed by heating to 240°F (at or below 1,000 feet above sea level) for a specified time in a steam-pressure canner.

Metal Band — A threaded screw band used with a flat metal vacuum sealing lid to form a two-piece metal cap.

Microorganism — A living plant or animal of microscopic size, such as molds, yeasts and bacteria, which can cause spoilage in canned or frozen food.

Mold — Microscopic fungi that grow as silken threads and appear as fuzz on food. Molds thrive on acids and can produce mycotoxins. They are easily destroyed at processing temperatures between 140° and 190°F.

Overnight — A time period of 8 to 12 hours.

Pectin — A complex colloidal substance found in ripe fruits, such as apples and citrus fruit. Pectin is available commercially in powdered and liquid form. Pectin, in the correct balance with fruit, sugar and acid, assists in forming the gel structure in jellies and other soft spreads.

pH — *Potential Of Hydrogen* — A measuring system in chemistry for determining the acidity or alkalinity of a solution. In canning, foods are separated into high-acid and low-acid. Different heat processing methods must be used for each.

Pickling — Preserving food, especially cucumbers, in a solution of brine or vinegar, often with spices added. Pickled foods must be processed in a boiling-water canner.

Pressure Canner — A heavy kettle with a lid which can be locked in place to make a steam-tight fit. The lid is fitted with a safety valve, a vent and a pressure gauge. The pressure canner is used for processing low-acid foods. Steam created under 10 pounds pressure at or below sea level reaches 240°F which is hot enough to destroy harmful bacteria that thrive in low-acid food (*see page 5 for Altitude Chart*).

Pretreatment — Blanching or treating produce with an antioxidant to set color, slow enzyme action or destroy bacteria.

Processing — Sterilizing jars and the food they contain in a pressure or boiling-water canner to destroy harmful molds, yeasts, bacteria and enzymes.

Produce Protector — An ascorbic acid and dextrose blend used to inhibit oxidation and control discoloration of light color fruits and vegetables.

Raw Pack — Filling jars with raw, unheated food prior to processing.

Rehydration (*or reconstitution*) — Restoring water (liquid) to dried food.

Simmer — To cook food gently just below the boiling point (between 180° and 200°F). Bubbles will rise gently from the bottom of the pot and slightly disturb the surface of the food.

Syrup — A mixture of water (or juice) and sugar used to add liquid to canned or frozen food.

Two-Piece Cap — Two-piece vacuum closure for sealing home canning jars. The set consists of a threaded metal band and a flat metal lid with a flanged edge and sealing compound.

Vacuum Packaging — A method to remove air from a container and seal the container to prevent air from reentering without heat processing. Perishable foods must be refrigerated or frozen. This is not a substitute for home canning.

Vacuum Seal — The absence of normal atmospheric (air) pressure in jars which are airtight. When a jar is closed at room temperature, the atmospheric pressure is the same inside and outside the jar. When the jar is heated, the air and food inside expand, forcing air out and decreasing the inside pressure. As the jar cools and the contents shrink, a partial vacuum forms. The sealing compound found on the underside of home canning lids prevents the air from reentering.

Venting — Forcing air to escape from a jar by applying heat. Or, permitting air to escape from a pressure canner. Also called exhausting.

Yeast — Microscopic fungi grown from spores that cause fermentation in foods. Yeasts are inactive in foods that are frozen and are easily destroyed by processing at a temperature of 212°F.

index